CONFLICT RESOLUTION IN UGANDA

Peace Research Monograph Number 16 from the
International Peace Research Institute, Oslo (PRIO)

CONFLICT RESOLUTION IN UGANDA

Edited by

KUMAR RUPESINGHE

INTERNATIONAL PEACE RESEARCH INSTITUTE
Oslo

in association with

JAMES CURREY
London

OHIO UNIVERSITY PRESS
Athens

International Peace Research Institute, Oslo
Fuglehauggata 11
N-0260 Oslo 2

in association with

James Currey Ltd
54b Thornhill Square, Islington
London N1 1BE

Ohio University Press
Scott Quadrangle
Athens, Ohio 45701, USA

Available in Uganda from

Uganda Bookshop
P.O. Box 7145
Kampala

First published 1989

British Library Cataloguing in Publication Data
Conflict Resolution in Uganda
1. Uganda - Politics. Violence
I. Rupesinghe, Kumar
322.4'2

ISBN 0-85255-334-X
ISBN 0-85255-333-1 (Pbk)

Library of Congress Cataloguing in Publication Data
Conflict Resolution in Uganda
edited by Kumar Rupesinghe
p. cm.

Papers from the International Conference on Internal Conflict in Uganda, held Sept. 21-25 1987, at Makerere University, Kampala, and sponsored by International Alert, London, the Makerere Institute of Social Research and the International Peace Research Institute, Oslo.

Includes index.

ISBN 0-8214-0929-8 (Ohio Univ. Press). --ISBN 0-8214-0930-1 (Ohio Univ. Press : pbk)

1. Uganda--Politics and government--Congresses. 2. Uganda--Economic Policy Congresses. 3. Uganda--Foreign relations--Congresses. I. Rupesinghe, Kumar. II. International Conference on Internal Conflict in Uganda (1987 Makerere University) III. International Alert (Organization) IV. Makarere Institute of Social Research. V. International Peace Research Institute, Oslo.

JQ2951.A2U33 1989
987.6'104--dc19 89-30799
CIP

Typeset at
the International Peace Research Institute, Oslo
and printed in Great Britain by
Villiers Publication, London N6

Contents

Contributors

Kumar Rupesinghe, Senior Research Fellow, International Peace Research Institute, Oslo (PRIO).

Samwiri Lwanga-Lunyiigo, Senior Lecturer, Department of History, Makerere University, Kampala.

A.G. Gingyera-Pinycwa, Professor, Department of Political Science, Makerere University, Kampala.

Yoramu Barongo, Associate Professor, Department of Political Science, Makerere University, Kampala.

Abraham Kiapi, Professor, Faculty of Law, Makerere University, Kampala.

Dan Mudoola, Associate Professor in Political Science and Director of Makerere Institute of Social Research, Makerere University, Kampala.

Edward Khiddu-Makubuya, Associate Professor, Faculty of Law, Makerere University, Kampala and Advocate of the High Court of Uganda.

Ijuka Kabumba, Senior Lecturer, Uganda Institute of Public Administration, Kampala.

Ruth Mukama, Senior Lecturer and Head of Department of Languages, Makerere University, Kampala.

Firimooni R. Banugire, Professor, Department of Economics, Makerere University, Kampala.

Apolo Nsibambi, Professor, Department of Political Science, Makerere University, Kampala.

Akiki Bomera Mujaju, Professor and Dean of Faculty of Social Science, Makerere University, Kampala.

Oliver Furley, Head of Department of Politics and History, Coventry Polytechnical School, Coventry.

Acknowledgements

This book is a collection of essays meant as a modest contribution to the discussion on the resolution of internal conflicts which are endemic in so many parts of the world. The book represents an effort primarily by Ugandan scholars to comment freely on issues in Uganda.

Editing this book has not been an easy task, particularly since it was to select from 36 papers which were presented at the "International Conference on Internal Conflict in Uganda", held in September 1987. The overriding concern in the selection was the relevance of the papers to the issue and the constraints of space.

I would like to thank Professor Dan Mudoola, Director of the Makerere Institute of Social Research, Makerere University, for his untiring co-operation in the production of this manuscript. His able assistant, Abbey Nalwanga-Sebina was particularly helpful in co-ordinating the revisions between Kampala and Oslo.

The advice of Peter Anyang Nyongo and Oliver Furley, both with experience and scholarly knowledge of the country, facilitated the selection of papers for this volume. Oliver Furley also provided editorial assistance throughout the publication process.

At the International Peace Research Institute, Oslo (PRIO), I am grateful to Arild Angelsen who looked after the technical planning and editing of the manuscript, and Susan Høivik for language editing. A special thanks also to my other colleagues at PRIO for reading the manuscript and for their comments, in particular Kethesh Loganathan.

I would also take this opportunity of thanking Martin Ennals of International Alert for his comments and co-operation.

Once again, I would like to thank all the authors who have been so enthusiastic and helpful in responding to my pleas to get the manuscript ready as soon as possible. It has indeed been a pleasure to work with them, and if there have been any errors or omissions it is not to them but to me that blame should be appropriated.

Finally, I would like to thank the Norwegian Ministry of Development Co-operation, International Alert and the United Nations University in Tokyo for financial support.

Kumar Rupesinghe

Foreword

The conference in Kampala in September 1987, organized by International Alert, the Makerere Institute for Social Research and the International Peace Research Institute, Oslo, was an exciting and innovative venture. With the active encouragement of President Museveni and with the participation of some of his ministers, people of widely varying views and backgrounds debated the internal conflicts which have divided Uganda and Ugandans throughout the period since Independence. There is not a family in the country that has not suffered its own tragedy.

In the light of the misfortune that Uganda and her people have suffered, and the bitter memories that it evokes, the result of the conference was a surprising consensus. The series of recommendations addressed itself to all parties involved in the conflict. The message of peace and reconstruction of the country was carried to all levels of Ugandan polity and society.

A selection of papers presented at the conference has now been edited into a book publication. I am particularly pleased by this because my duties in South Africa prevented my own participation at Makerere University and in the discussions. I am also happy that through this publication the international community would have a better understanding of the nature of the conflict and the possible resolutions.

In South Africa we are acutely aware of the meaning of conflict. We are still living through it, which makes us acutely aware of the harsh realities yet to come before the conflicts of Uganda can be resolved.

No solutions are easy or painless. But the methods which are advocated by International Alert and the other sponsors in the case of Uganda must be welcomed by anyone who prizes peace, equality and human rights.

Archbishop Desmond Tutu

Preface

This book is the product of an international seminar that was held from 21 to 25 September 1987, at Makerere University in Kampala. The seminar itself was the result of initiatives taken by International Alert, London, in collaboration with the Makerere Institute of Social Research, Kampala and the International Peace Research Institute, Oslo (PRIO).

The Conference was divided into several working groups:

1. International and regional implications of internal conflict.

2. Economic policies to sustain democracy and growth in Uganda.

3. The role of political and legal institutions.

4. The role of the international community and NGOs in resolving the conflict.

A total of 36 papers were presented at the Conference. The conclusions arrived at by each working group were placed before the whole conference in plenary sessions. The general report of the rapporteur (Oliver Furley) was based on the workings of the Conference as a whole, and these proposals were widely discussed before they were adopted. The recommendations and the summary of the plenary sessions are given in Appendix 1.

This volume, which is a compilation of 12 papers presented to the seminar and further developed by the authors since then, did not spring out of the splendid isolation of an ivory tower. The Conference was unique in that it was held in Uganda itself, in an atmosphere of free and open discussions - a concrete manifestation of a period of transition, away from the cycle of violence and terror that had confronted the Ugandan people. As the Norwegian Minister of Development Co-operation posited at the opening session of the Conference, "Who would - only a couple of years ago - have thought it possible that a conference dealing with human rights and internal conflicts and with international participation would take place in this capital?"

The period of transition in which the seminar was being held generated an atmosphere of great hope and expectation - but not complacency. Understandably, the present is always infected with memories of the past. During the week of the Conference, some 260 registered participants from about 20 countries deliberated on the nature of the conflict in Uganda, and its resolution. The main concern of the participants, the overwhelming majority being Ugandans representing a cross-section of the Makerere academic community, non-governmental organizations, donor agencies, religious bodies and politicians, was to discuss how the endemic cycle of violence in Uganda could be broken and not be allowed to reproduce itself in the future.

The tone of the deliberations that characterized the Conference, captured in this volume, was voiced at the outset by Uganda's President Yoweri K. Museveni, in opening the seminar:

> In order for the conflict to be effectively resolved, apart from adopting a democratic style of government which accommodates everybody who has got any legitimate political interest, we must try to expand the base of the economy so that it is able to satisfy the interests of different social groups and therefore maintain harmony.

President Museveni reflected, in many ways, the frame of mind of the organizers as well as that of the participants: namely, that deliberations should not concentrate entirely on searching for the causes of the conflict. Instead, it became clear that the thrust of the deliberations at the Conference would be directed towards articulating a common endeavour to create political structures and institutions and a viable, broad-based economy which, together, could provide the basis for long-lasting peace that goes beyond a mere cessation of hostilities, to one firmly grounded in social justice and equality. As the Conference concluded:

> However, the peace that Uganda ultimately deserves has to be established on principles of social justice and equality (positive peace) and not injustice and inequities (negative peace). Inequities and unjust peace are inherently temporary and unlikely to endure. The architects of peace in Uganda are therefore encouraged to bear this in mind.

That the Conference itself was symbolic of new expectations for peace and reconciliation was expressed in an editorial of Weekly Topic on 7 October, 1987:

> Our country has been unstable politically for more than two decades. On this there can be no disagreement. What has proved more difficult is to agree on the policies to bring stability to our land. There is a wide diversity of political views held within our borders and as many of these interests

as possible need to be accommodated if we are to have meaningful peace. That consensus seems to have been reached last week at the seminar on internal conflicts at Makerere University. At this seminar, the present conflict in the North and the East was analyzed and discussed at great length. These discussions resulted in several recommendations. The major recommendation was that internal conflict cannot be truly resolved by only a military solution. To build a nation of such diversity we need to concentrate on political, social and economic solutions.

The recommendations themselves were modest and practical, but contained the seeds for a future development strategy which is now being explored. The theme which recurred in all of the working groups was that of extended democracy, reflected in a decentralization of decision-making as far as possible to those who would be most affected by each decision.

A mission is planned to visit Uganda and report back to a wider donor conference on the projects identified for assistance in the geographical areas of conflict. This approach to conflict resolution, through development strategies and decentralized decision-making, is one that found favour in Makerere and which would justify more intensive research.

There is no instant peace formula. What does exist is a framework within which those directly affected by conflict can have their say in development issues. This is a considerable advance on the military dictatorship of the past in Uganda and elsewhere.

Martin Ennals
Secretary General
International Alert

Kumar Rupesinghe

Internal Conflicts and their Resolution: The Case of Uganda

1. Internal Conflict and Ethnic Conflicts in Perspective

1.1. Some Problems of Conceptualization

Uganda, in a way, has come to represent the worst forms of aberrations associated with internal conflicts. It has had more than its toll of natural and man-made disasters. This introductory essay, in an attempt to introduce the book and the scholarly contributions, will try to focus on some conceptual issues which may be relevant to the discussions on internal conflicts, both in the case of Uganda and in general.

The case of Uganda as a study of an internal conflict is not exceptional; neither is it unique. In fact, many of the elements-tyranny, violation of human rights, genocide, state terrorism, civil war - that contribute to its specificity are also endemic in many societies and incipient in most others. The issues involved in such internal conflicts are primarily questions of political power. They manifest themselves in ethnic, minority or secessionist claims or demands for autonomy or issues of ethnicity mixed with questions of religion. These conflicts are themselves the consequences of nation building, particularly in post colonial state formations.

There is no general theory of internal conflicts applicable to all situations. There are difficulties in conceptualizing an internal conflict, particularly as every conflict has its own historical setting, interacting with external factors in a particular configuration. We are here dealing with a situation where the past not only has a bearing on the present, but where it is also difficult to distinguish between external and internal root causes.

Harry Ekstein suggests some of the features which are characteristic of deeply divided societies. A characteristic feature in such conflicts is the use of legitimate and illegitimate use of violence.[1]

1. They all involve the use of violence to achieve goals which also may be achieved without violence.

2. They all indicate a breakdown of some dimensions of legitimate political order, as well as the existence of collective frustration and aggressive tendencies in a population.

3. They all presuppose certain capabilities for violence for those inciting the internal war and certain incapacities for preventing violence among those on whom internal war is made.

4. All tend to scar societies deeply and to prevent the formation of consensus for an indefinite period.

Yet another common tendency in the discussion on group conflicts or collective conflicts is to lump all such conflicts as "ethnic conflicts". The mass media tend to relay news of episodic events, bloody violence, local wars, collective struggles, and struggles for self-determination - terming them "ethnic conflicts". Such events are portrayed as riots, communal riots, terrorist attacks, without any adequate picture of the contextual situation. The desire to present episodic news means that "ethnic conflicts" have no history - they come and go, claiming the attention of the news media for a brief moment.

There is today a vast and growing literature on ethnicity and it is not the purpose of this introduction to go into this issue. What is obvious and which needs repeating however is that all internal conflicts cannot be merely ethnic in character. Ethnic conflicts, class conflicts, caste and group conflicts, occupational conflicts and regional antagonisms are all part of a multi-dimensional and complex reality. All forms of identity exist-ranging from class, ethnic, religious, tribal, occupational to regional and linguistic groups. Ethnicity is, therefore, a dynamic concept which may have an ethnic character as well as a class character; class and ethnic conflicts may be waged simultaneously. It is for this reason that some have defined ethnic conflicts as "protracted social conflicts", characterized by such enduring features as economic and technological underdevelopment and unintegrated political systems. This problem is succinctly identified by John Burton:

> The conflicts which are of global concern involve deep issues of ethnic and cultural identity, of recognition and of participation that are usually denied to ethnic minorities, in addition to issues of security and other values that are not negotiable.[2]

Thus, behind ethnic conflicts are often structural issues transcending immediate grievances. The pervasiveness of these conflicts are a challenge to the modern nation state.

1.2. The Role of the State

Contrary to theories which define the state, particularly in Third World formations, as an arbitrator or a neutral actor, it is important to bear in mind that the state is neither an arbitrator nor neutral: it is itself a focal point of competition, an actor in the conflict.

With political independence, the ruling classes in many parts of the Third World inhabiting the political space of the state were - for a time at least - secularist and modernist in their approach to state formation. The elites promised rapid modernization and industrialization along with increased political participation. The state was defined as strongly interventionist, particularly in the management and direction of economic activities.

In this connection, we must note that the post colonial secular vision with its liberal values was sometimes in conflict with sub-nationalist claims within the inherited boundaries of the post colonial state. It was also at odds with the growing perception of failed promises among the oppressed who increasingly resorted to seeking self-validation in religion and ethnicity. It is precisely here, in this business of nation building and state formation, that ethnicity assumes particular salience.

In the process of post-colonial state formations, the weakness and fragility of political structures allowed for the "ethnicization" of the state. The concept of ethnicity or religion became increasingly useful for political legitimation and domination. Anti-imperialist or anti-colonialist ideologies were replaced by hegemonic assertions, providing ideological impetus towards authoritarian rule. What evolved was a type of state formation strongly bound by patron-client loyalties which became all-pervasive, with some groups included and others excluded.

The above process has been characterized as the formation of a "defective state". The defective state clearly reflects the particularistic, personalized social structures from which it arose. The apparatus of these states is interwoven through thick, intricate networks of patron-client relationships. It is these networks individual citizens depend on through a chain of patronage in order to exercise their claims upon the state. The state is unable to reform itself, to transform itself in accordance with the changing requirements of its citizenry. Individuals tend to be recruited into the state primarily on the basis of ethnic, political and personal loyalties.[3] State formation evolved by increasing the power of the centre at the expense of the periphery. And it is precisely in the mediation of relations between hegemonic elites and heterogenous ethnic communities, that ethnic conflict has risen to prominence. This in turn underscores the declining capacity of existing institutions to manage conflicts. It is inevitable in this process that as hegemonic elites become more self-assertive, a sense of territorial, linguistic or religious fundamentalism provides a new basis for mobilization and action.

The above mode of mobilization contain elements which, ironically, create the conditions for depoliticization - a deliberate, state-directed social demobilization. Nelson Kasfir[4], among others, has highlighted this powerful trend in many Third World countries. Ethnicity and state building, and the relationship between them, have been vital to this depolitization process. The function of ethnicity in depolitization is two-sided. On the one hand are the increasing ethnic claims of communal groups on the states which have recently expanded. On the other hand, it is ethnicity which often provides for mobilization based on narrow, parochial and sectarian interests.

The state is potentially a vehicle for mobilization. Pre-modern and modern states alike have had the capacity for mobilization of resources, allegiances, manpower and revenues, but have differed in the persistence and effectiveness of their mobilizing efforts. Thus ethnic groups, which also have impressive mobilizing capacities, are often in direct competition with states.

Another tendency which has become institutionalized is the way in which the state has interpreted ethnic or minority claims. Over the years, suspicion and intolerance have increased to a point where minority grievances are met with increased police and military repression. Ethnic claims are often interpreted as security threats or as threats to the very existence of the state itself. To make matters worse, the state has often itself been party to the conflict, or has been partisan or has escalated the conflict by imposing authoritarian stratagems. Frequently, the police and military are the exacerbators, not the resolvers of conflict in multi-ethnic societies. State regimes that feel insecure because of the ethnic diversity of their constituencies often bolster up state security by so changing the ethnic composition of their coercive armies. As a result, inter-ethnic distrust turns into the alienation of weaker groups from the political system itself. At the same time, such deliberate recruitment and promotion policies often encourage favoured ethnic groups to think of the state as their own special protective agency and thus to resist any demands by weaker groups for a greater role.[5]

The role of the state and its relationship to the periphery thus is central to an understanding of ethnic conflicts. The structure of dispersed ethnic systems encourages inter-ethnic co-operation while the structure of centralized ethnic systems impede it. They involve the whole state. Whether ethnic politics is localized or central will depend on the ethnic balance of power. This reflects not only demographic conditions but also differences between different ethnic groups, resource bases, economic power and the relationship between ethnic stratification and the state. Another factor which has a bearing on the relationship between the state and the periphery is whether the ethnic group enjoys a contiguous resource base and whether ethnic stratification has a cross-border or regional dimension.[6]

In many comparative studies of internal conflicts and their escalation, state violence has served to exacerbate cleavages. The violation of human rights, be it extra-judicial killings or torture, has produced a vicious cycle of violence and terror. State violence brought with it a sense of insecurity: this tended to act as a strong force of mobilization which too often took extra-parliamentary or militant forms. The misbehaviour of state actors, often ethnic armies, served to provoke criminal behaviour on all sides. This became a never-ending spiral of violence with civilians, on both sides, as the main casualties. The case of Uganda is then merely a case in point.[7]

1.3. State Terrorism

Basing his information from Amnesty International and the International Commission of Jurists, Guest cites that "at least two million people have been summarily executed around the world in the last 15 years for their opposition to governments."[8]

In early 1980, Wolpin suggested that institutional repression or more extreme violent forms characterized 91 of 105 developing countries.[9] The absolute majority of the population in developing countries exist under regimes characterized by torture, execution, disappearances and brutal prison treatment of those suspected of opposing the government.

Powell's analysis of 40 democracies revealed a "significant relationship between ethnic fragmentation and death by political violence".[10] His examination of individual riots suggests that police are likely to use deadly force in crushing ethnically based riots.

The more obvious forms of state violence can be considered under four classifications, according to von der Mehden:[11]

1. attacks upon power contenders,
2. efforts to instil unity or maintain order,
3. quelling those expressing opposition to the regime where such individuals or groups are not of immediate danger to those in power and do not employ violent tactics, and
4. elimination of persons or groups considered "undesirable".

But, whatever may be the specific form that state terrorism assumes, it is designed to defend the interests of those controlling the state. It inevitably destroys the morality of the society. Some have maintained that the more a country develops its repressive capabilities, the less it develops its political capabilities in setting up communication and bargaining networks between government and society.[12]

Within the context of state terrorism, we are also discussing regimes of terror applied to societies. Organized terror has played a central role in the social and political life of many peoples. In the terror process, no one can be secure, for the category of transgression has in reality been abolished: anyone may become a victim, no matter what action he chooses.

The violent process is itself a part of terror, which may be a means of destruction, an instrument of punishment or a method of control. It may shift from war to terrorism, to punishment and back.

In an explicit study of terror and resistance, Walter[13] challenges prevailing assumptions about the relationship between violence and authority because there are systems of terror supported by authority consent and tradition. Terror is not confined to anomalous circumstances or exotic systems. It is potential in ordinary institutions as well as in unusual situations; reigns of terror are not properly understood if conceived of exclusively as ephemeral states of crisis produced by adventitious events or as alien forms of control. In discussing civil terror, Walter suggests that we are dealing with two processes, one dependent on the other: "the process of violence in the service of terror and the process of terror in the service of power."[14] State terrorism therefore has to be understood within the context of a specific form of terror which are applied in destabilizing the opposition.

1.4. Problems of Transition, Democratization and Civilian Rule

Rarely, if ever, do discussions on militarization take up the special problems associated with demilitarization after a despotic or tyrannical regime has been overthrown. Yet this research and practical task is very much on the agenda, precisely because we are now experiencing a complex process of demilitarization and a gradual transition to democracy. Even where foreign armies have been involved and have tried to play a role in conflict resolution, (e.g. Afghanistan, Angola, Namibia, Kampuchea and Sri Lanka) the possibilities of a complete withdrawal have also prompted a discussion on the role of domestic forces in conflict resolution, where the problem is seen essentially as one of peace-building, not peace-keeping.

What is more pertinent to many countries is demilitarization through a popular democratic process where military regimes have been overthrown and where serious efforts are made to effect the transition to democracy and civilian rule. Attempts at demilitarization are now being undertaken in some countries in Latin America - Argentina being a notable example. As to whether such transitions are successful and sustainable, of course, remains to be seen.

The literature on civil-military relations abounds with examinations of why and how individual coups occurred. According to Welch, few if any academic generalizations exist for military disengagement from politics, for the simple reason that most instances appear to arise from ad hoc combinations of circumstances, and it is often difficult to determine when disengagement can be deemed "successful".[15] In surveying the conclusions of a host of writings on this problem in Africa, Welch suggests at least some conditions for the successful removal of armed forces from politics. Such removal is likely to succeed if voluntary rather than coerced. "Long term disengagement rests fundamentally on military willingness to reduce the scope of their political involvement. In this case a trusted military leader plays a key role, being both symbol and agent for recivilianization."[16]

In the case of Uganda the military has played a key role in politics over the past two decades. With the revocation of the Constitution, Obote resorted to the military; eventually it was a military coup that propelled Idi Amin to power. In turn, it was mainly an external force, in the absence of internal mechanisms, which led to the overthrow of Idi Amin and the re-installation of Obote which constituted an externally imposed re-democratization markedly different from the internally generated restoration of electoral politics. And it was also an overwhelmingly internal popular guerilla intervention which was to help to overthrow Obote and substitute Museveni into power. The question of transition therefore is important in the discussion, only insofar as the current regime under President Museveni has openly advocated respect for human rights in general, and a willingness to consider ways and means of restoring civilian rule.

Martin Doornbos in discussing some of the pertinent factors leading to the transition in Uganda, suggests that one could consider a historic transition in two major aspects:

> One, for the first time in post-colonial Africa a popularly based guerilla movement has demonstrated the practical possibility of overthrowing one of the notorious and illegitimate military regimes that had become so characteristic for the continent. Second, for the first time in post-colonial Uganda, the power balance shifted in favour of the South, that is a mainly southern recruited armed force came to provide the basis of government power. Together, these two transitions are likely to have a major impact on the future trajectory of the Ugandan state and politics, potentially giving it a significant different direction as well as greater stability.[17]

This transition period will no doubt give rise to many discourses, some silent and others more articulate, as to the direction of the democratic process. What is important to bear in mind, however, is that in the long term there are a range of policies which are bound to determine the direction of the transition. The search for accommodation and coalition-building towards the forging of a consensus, is only a short term solution - a solution that is necessary, but not sufficient. Further, political will is by itself not enough, since even the best leaders can be swayed by powerful organized forces in society. Eventually, political institutions and structures will have to be developed to ensure a sense of participation, security and protection for all citizens. The question is how to develop political institutions so as to reduce ethnic tensions and conflicts. We are thus speaking about the need for a coherent and a cohesive political programme.[18]

It is therefore encouraging that almost all the writers in this volume have cited the long term search for a political solution and the institutional framework for conflict resolution as the critical issue facing the regime in today's Uganda. To suggest political structures and institutions however is a starting point for the institutionalization of conflict but it the task of comparative research to find ways of evolving these institutions after decades of destruction and war.

1.5. Problems of Economic Transformation

Protracted social conflicts within the African region, as in the case of other Third World societies, must be viewed within the common trajectory of the transition to capitalism. The uneven development of capitalism in the periphery also implies the exclusion of some peoples and groups. There is still a vast subsistence sector, an informal sector, but most important, there are different social formations which co-exist within the same society. Such social formations are pre-capitalist in origin, and are often unique in that they have a shared language, shared symbols, and often a shared economic life. The existence of such pre-capitalist social formations has meant that strategies of nation-building and, particularly, state building with its thrust towards centralization, assimilation and integration, have sometimes come into strong and divisive conflict.

Another aspect of relevance in studying the transition to capitalism and internal conflicts is the role of merchant capital, which is often still the hegemonic form of capitalism. Merchants may be traders, acting as link-persons in buying and selling, or petty artisans who sell their produce in the market. Often some ethnic groups will have a preponderance of merchants compared to others. Most ethnic riots and pogroms occur in urban settings - in towns and in cities where there is inter-ethnic competition in trade, business and commerce.

In the Ugandan case, the above scenario is particularly relevant. For any political system to be responsive to the needs of pluralism and participatory democracy, it must have an economic base that is itself decentralized, self-sustaining and equitable. It is in this context that one should also continuously review the IMF "structural adjustment" programme currently being implemented in Uganda. The experiences of other peripheral social formations experimenting with the IMF/World Bank "liberalization" policy package have not been encouraging. On the contrary: "disindustrialization" and the undermining of the domestic manufacturing sector catering to the home market are some of the consequences of the policies advocated by these international financial institutions. It is clear therefore that any structural adjustment needs to address the internal dichotomy that exists between state capital and merchant capital, the related problem of absentee landlordism and the nature of relations between agriculture and industry. Consolidation of the national economy through appropriate agrarian reforms and rural industrialization is a matter of national priority that neither the politicians nor the policy-makers can afford to ignore.[19]

2. On the Contributions to this Volume

The debate on the process and direction which Uganda should take has already begun, as illustrated by the discussions raised in this book. They show that the key issue really concerns social transformation. The problems identified by the authors pertain to democracy, security, national unity and the economy: all of which are inter-related and require the management of various processes simultaneously.

Samwiri Lwanga-Lunyiigo in his chapter on **"The Colonial Roots of Internal Conflict"** traces the historical roots and the structural causes of the reproduction of violence in Uganda today. Colonialism failed to create the necessary political institutions and structures for the transition to independence. Colonial policy finds its classic form in the formation of the army, which had evolved on the concept of the "martial tribes": in Uganda recruitment was primarily from the North. Even after Independence, it was not possible to build a true multi-ethnic national army, since "this key institution of the post-colonial period was built on the British foundations of remoteness and hostility to people in the centre of the country".

Lwanga-Lunyiigo argues that the administrative boundaries enacted were to reproduce ethnicity where policies provided for the institutionalization of parochial tribally-oriented local government. This constitutional division made the unity of Uganda extremely difficult to achieve, and was to be a potential cause of conflict in the post-Independence decade. British policies had both favoured and aided the continuation of tribal loyalties while blocking the development of supra-tribal links and the participation of Ugandans in centralizing or nationalizing institutions. The colonial economy was built on a division of labour between the "productive South" and the "unproductive North". The North was neglected, its labour becoming a reservoir for the South.

These structural deficiencies were compounded by the lack of a language policy, with English as the common language of the elite. This article demonstrates how some of the structural causes of the internal conflict were to reproduce themselves in structural violence during the transition period.

"Is there a Northern Question?" asks A.G. Gingyera-Pinycwa, a question highly relevant to the internal conflict in Uganda. He attributes the creation of the so-called "Northern Question" to colonial policy. This was characterized by a system of indirect rule, where some parts of the country came to acquire more privilege than others. Furthermore, through the colonial economic division of labour not only was the region neglected: it was converted into a reservoir of cheap labour to the South. Gingyera-Pinycwa also draws attention to the propensity for ethnic categorization, a past-time of the colonial powers, which stereotyped ethnic groups in a rank order of stratification.

Structural imbalances were compounded in the persons of Idi Amin and Apollo Milton Obote, both from the North and both deeply involved in exacerbating conflict through the recruitment of ethnic armies based on their homelands. The repressive instruments of state power - the army and security personnel - were used as instruments of terror on different national and ethnic communities. However, it would be a mistake to present this merely as a Northern domination of the State; Gingyera-Pinycwa points to inter-group conflicts within the North, and reprisal and revenge mass killings between the armies and peoples of the North.

The essay demolishes the myth of a monolithic entity called the "North" posing a threat to the "South", the main issue being the political will to integrate the North into the nation-building process. However, problems in the North could turn into a "Northern Question" if the issues are not dealt with sensitively, particularly in the use of language in stereotyping Northerners and by correcting the misbehaviour of the army among civilians.

Yoramu Barongo has entitled his contribution **"Ethnic Pluralism and Political Centralization: The Basis of Political Conflict in Uganda"**) The mediation between political power and ethnic and regional sub-groups is a classic problem confronting many countries in the Third World. State building has to balance between economic integration of the nation, while recognizing ethnic pluralism and the search for identity. Barongo argues against the view that the internal conflict in Uganda is an expression of ethnic or tribal conflict. He maintains that the violent conflicts bedeviling Uganda since 1966 are basically political in origin.

Barongo traces the rupture of the balance between ethnic pluralism and centralism to the termination of the Independence Constitution which attempted to accommodate political pluralism in the country. He traces the violent conflicts which emerged as a result of the monopolization of power by the centre at the expense of the power of regional and local institutions. The emergence of a highly centralized state narrowed the areas of participation and political power, resulting in intense political struggle within the central government. "Political conflicts and violence in Uganda have tended to acquire ethnic dimensions because of the excessive centralization of power which has led the struggle to control the centre to be very intense indeed among the elite members of ethnic groups. In this struggle, political and military elites have tended to mobilize and use their ethnic bases and resources, such as military manpower, in order to struggle effectively to control political power at the centre."

In comparing the experience of Nigeria, he draws attention to the ways in which Nigeria has moved towards greater expansion of political pluralism, through increased decentralization of power and diversification of centres of political participation. The purpose in comparing the Nigerian experience is, however, to focus on the importance of the principle of political decentralization in managing group conflicts, particularly of the ethnic kind. For Uganda, he advocates a strong central government in harmony with a strong system of local government. "It is a strong system of local government that can provide the much desired opportunities for ethnic groups to manage the affairs of vital interest to them."

In the various approaches to conflict resolution in multi-ethnic societies, the Constitution plays a critical role in mediation between claims made upon the State. This is the subject of Abraham Kiapi in his **"The Constitution as a Mediator in Internal Conflict"**. The making of the constitution, the checks and balances on the executive, the role of political parties, the relationship between centre and periphery, the protection of nationalities, and the protection of the individual are some of the many complex matters which a constitution is to solve. The constitution must also find means, particularly in multi-ethnic societies, to provide for inter-ethnic co-operation as well as institutional means to prevent grievances. The constitution can be a mediator of internal conflicts only if the political authorities respect it and abide by its provisions.

Professor Kiapi examines the various constitutional alternatives within the specificity of Uganda. After posing a choice between a unitary constitution, a federal constitution, and a unitary state with substantial regional autonomy to the regions, he recommends a unitary constitution with substantial devolution of power to the districts. Given the historical experience and potential conflicts in the distribution of powers between parliamentary and cabinet forms of government, Prof. Kiapi suggests a Presidential executive form of government with checks and balances provided by the judiciary and the legislature. The legislature should be bicameral so the voice of every district and minority opinion would be equally represented. Bearing in mind the unfortunate experiences of electoral malpractice and rigging, he suggests that the constitution should set up an independent electoral commission with representatives of all political parties. He rejects the various arguments normally adduced for a one-party system: i.e. that nation-building requires the combined efforts of all available manpower; that traditional African cultural attitudes and communal practices favour decisions by consensus; that a multi-party system is a artificial luxury in the struggle against underdevelopment; or that national unity in a multi-ethnic setting can be forged only by a single party. It is his argument that the tragedies of the past had been due to the arbitrariness of the rulers, where no respect was shown to a multi-ethnic plurality. In this context he argues for the multi-party system as a guarantee for the diversity and plurality of Uganda. All citizens should participate in making the new constitution through a constituent assembly; a constitutional commission, after due consultation with people, should submit a draft constitution to the constituent assembly.

The role of the military in politics and in conflict escalation has been widely discussed in the literature on domestic conflict. The experience from Uganda is explored by Dan Mudoola in his **"Communal Conflict in the Military and its Political Consequences"**. The role of the military is particularly important in the context of its deployment in a multi-ethnic society such as Uganda. In various social formations, it is common that in the search for hegemony over a fragile state institution, leaders will resort to military means trying to resolve what are typically political problems. Frequently in terms of political mobilizations, recruitment is based on "ethnic" criteria. These armies are then deployed against other competing ethnic groups, which often leads to gross violations of human rights. In such circumstances, the civilian population often become innocent victims. When it concerns other ethnic groups, the ideology of the army is one of conquest rather than resolution. Misbehaviour of such armies eventually help to militarize the entire society as well as encourage thinking in terms of military solutions. The state is then merely an instrument for aggrandizement, with the army a means of terror against all parties. Therefore, the demilitarization of thinking and the withdrawal of the army from politics is a critical issue in countries where attempts are made to restore a democratic process. The need to establish and strengthen institutions and political centres, and to civilianize the political process are main challenges during the transition period to democracy.

Mudoola's major argument is that the interventionist role of the army has been the result of the failure of successive Ugandan political leadership to work out widely accepted institutionalized peaceful means of resolving conflicts. He argues that the Ugandan military after Independence was built, expanded and equipped in response to internal political and military crises, which eventually led to its pronounced activist role. He traces the evolution of the military into politics since Independence, and argues that when the Constitution was undermined and the military brought into politics, it was a matter of time before all other contending sources of power would be undermined. Milton Obote, in his attempts to resolve a typically constitutional crisis, was operating outside the established constitutional rules of the game. He had undermined civilian institutions, and had not sought to resolve the crisis within the Parliament or through his own political party, the Uganda People's Congress (UPC). The introduction of a new constitution by extra-legal means created a political institutional void. The attempt to create an alternative power centre within the UPC was a failure. Attempts at checking the military by establishing and strengthening the General Service Unit and the Special Force - essentially para-military intelligence agencies - served to create more tensions within the security apparatus.

According to Mudoola, Amin simply pushed to a logical conclusion trends already set by Obote - trends which increasingly rendered powerless any political institutions for resolving conflict. The political problem posed by Mudoola, particularly during the post Obote regimes, is that the military has been a liberating instrument which is not only a critical factor in the power game, but also an institution which must be domesticated. Mudoola sees a number of implications arising out of the NRM victory likely to have a strong bearing on civilian-military relations and the building of political institutions. Several myths regarding the special role of some groups - or the "martial tribes" thesis - have been undermined. Today, there is an opportunity for the army to become a true national multi-ethnic army. The NRM victory has wrested the monopoly on the use of force away from some ethnic groups and created the preconditions for viable political institutions.

Edward Khiddu-Makubuya takes up an issue rarely discussed and theorized in the literature on internal conflicts: the role of paramilitarism in conflict escalation. In **"Paramilitarism and Human Rights"**, he suggests that paramilitarism is not peculiar to Uganda: the problem is universal, but it has performed a special role in the historical configuration of Uganda.

The major problem of paramilitarism is its lack of accountability. Paramilitary institutions reside within the twilight of illegality, with powers and operational codes unknown to the public-their powers are unlimited and not subject to controls. The operational methods of paramilitarism are irregular, where torture, extra-judicial killing, kidnapping and blackmailing are methods used with impunity.

It is difficult to distinguish between the requirements of state security and the politics of survival of incumbents in power. In some cases, they act as instruments of state terrorism and political terror. The growth of these agencies acts to undermine the role of law and order. Recruitment is not public, but frequently drawn from criminal and lumpen elements in society. In the case of multi-ethnic societies, recruitment is drawn from the ethnic groups near the current President. In tracing the evolution of paramilitarism in Uganda, Khiddu-Makubuya shows how it has played a significant role in the massive violations of human rights, inhumanity and brutality. He focuses on the evolution of three paramilitary institutions - the General Service Department, the State Research Bureau (SBR) and the National Security Agency (NASA). He records how these agencies were used as instruments of terror against all political opposition, and how recruitment was based on ethnic criteria. "We must emphasize that Uganda's paramilitary agencies have not only been principal instrumentalities of violations of human rights in Uganda: they have also served to perpetuate regimes in power. Selective ethnic composition has tended to exacerbate sectarian conflicts within Ugandan society. They have thus undermined the development of national democratic institutions and the emergence of rules of fair play in Ugandan public life."

Khiddu-Makubuya calls for a collective review of policy on paramilitarism as an urgent national matter. The Commission of

Inquiry into Violations of Human Rights, appointed by the NRM government to inquire into the atrocities committed during the period 1962 to January 1986, will also have as its mandate the task of finding possible ways of preventing the recurrence of the reproduction of violence through paramilitary institutions. The NRM government has also enacted the Security Organizations Statute of 1987, where a notable feature is the accountability of paramilitary operatives. Khiddu-Makubuya recognizes this as a necessary step in the right direction. However, a good deal more will have to be done at the intellectual and practical technical level to guarantee security to the people of Uganda.

The complex interaction between state and civil society, state institutions and economic organization, state personnel and those outside the state sector, would seem more pronounced in deeply divided societies. A problem confronting the state in the Third World is the existence of a multiplicity of ethnic groups or nations. Often nation-building is associated with the centralization of power, which comes into conflict with claims of various ethnic groups for autonomy and greater identity. In such societies, classes are still in the process of formation; there are no distinct classes but different groups, from intellectuals, the educated and salaried middle classes, to military factions, bureaucratic groups or political parties who perform the role of patrons in a complex web of patron - client networks. The state is an instrument for patronage, resource allocation and ideological control.

The most universal gift of colonialism was the concept of state and bureaucracy; those in control of this apparatus after Independence thus emerged as the ruling class. In a limited but interesting sample survey of the public service in Uganda, Ijuka Kabumba discusses the pervasive role of **"Ethnic Conflicts within the Public Service"**. Where there is intense ethnic competition, the state and bureaucracy become a mirror of conflicts outside. These conflicts are pronounced at the top of the administrative hierarchy and are often related to political alignments. Politics and administration are very much inter-linked, even if top appointments are made within the public service. There is an overt policy of excluding some groups from the decision-making process, and typically there is often negative stereotyping of other groups within the system. The present system in Uganda tends to emphasize differences rather than similarities. Inter-ethnic conflicts cannot be eliminated from the system; what is necessary is to minimize such conflicts. Here Kabumba provides proposals for administrative reforms and training of an administrative cadre. However, to a large extent, the administrative system depends on the political system and the relationship and inter-linkages between them.

Ruth Mukama in her contribution "**The Linguistic Dimension of Ethnic Conflict**" explores a subject which is both pervasive [another word. Also used in the above paragraph] and complex in a multi-lingual society like Uganda. Her major premise is that the vacillation surrounding the language question on the part of the Ugandan government is an epitome of the seething ethnic discord confronting the nation. Selecting a relevant road to a viable linguistic solution for the future becomes both a dilemma and a challenge. So far, Ugandan governments have remained caught in the dilemma and unable to take up the challenge. Mukama argues that many governments in multi-lingual states resort to vacillation when, amid other formidable national problems, they fear to aggravate emotive sensibilities by making a definite ruling on language choice. In a situation with 26 ethnic groups demanding language representation, a policy has to be formulated which takes into account the question of national and local identity without flouting or ignoring the importance of regional and international co-operation. Since most Ugandans live in rural areas, effective means must be developed for the centre to communicate its policies, and means must also be found for inter-ethnic communication.

Mukama explores several alternative solutions to the language question. She recommends that English, an international language, and Kiswahili, a regional language, should be declared as official languages. The schools should teach the language of the area, say Luganda or Luo, and then both English and Kiswahili. She notes that language policy is primarily a question of political will, particularly the willingness to implement the decision down the line. She also proposes the founding of a National Communication Centre to establish well-organized means of reaching the rural masses and involving them in national affairs and activities.

Firimooni R. Banugire raises in his essay "**Uneven and Unbalanced Development: Development Strategies and Conflict**" questions concerning the relationship between uneven regional development, unbalanced development strategies and the cause of social conflicts in Uganda. He sees the development potential of Uganda and its natural resource base as fairly evenly distributed, whereas there are marked regional differences in the level of development. Such uneven regional development is largely explained by the development strategies pursued during the Colonial period and reproduced after Independence. The emphasis on export cash crops spurred intra-rural migration and led to the neglect of traditional food crops. Even though the disparity between the richest areas in the South and the poorest areas in the North has been highly significant, the crisis cannot be explained merely by a centre-periphery theory, as it was the North who controlled the instruments of state power until recently.

Banugire draws attention to a characteristic feature of the economy since around 1975: the deterioration of wages and real income and the extensive reliance on magendo ("unofficial" or "black market") activities as a survival strategy. The extent of magendo activities is such that the poorest wage earners of the formal sector cannot meet more than 2% of their needs from their official wages. Even the privileged group of professional wage earners in the civil service and in the teaching profession can meet only 5% of their needs. The crisis in the economy is encapsulated as follows: "Uganda's is essentially a regressive economy. Upward social mobility has been reduced: middle class professionals and civil servants have fallen into the poverty trap while the lower-income groups have been thrown out of formal employment into informal unproductive magendo activities. This social retrogression has taken place without any adjustments in formal payment systems, so that these activities have become dominant survival mechanisms. Such survival mechanisms cannot be relied upon to promote economic recovery and reconstruction; indeed most of them are inconsistent with social transformation. This inconsistency lies at the core of the institutional and political traps which are propelling Uganda's economy towards regression and stagnation."

Banugire calls for fundamental political reforms, without which a progressive economy cannot be realized. He argues that a precondition to restore the economy is to build institutions and institutional mechanisms for popular participation. Institutional reforms include an effective national planning commission, reforms in the co-operative movement, a system of decentralized regional development as well as a progressive social service delivery system .

In his essay **"The Land Question and Conflict"**, Apolo Nsibambi discusses a most fundamental and complex problem which has been a source of conflict in the transition period in Uganda. The land question (or as some may pose it: the agrarian question) naturally represents ideological positions as to the future land policy of Uganda. There are bound to be political cleavages based on notions of collective ownership to individual ownership of land, but also rules governing tenancy, eviction and land consolidation. Nsibambi locates the debate within the current discussion of the land question. He is not ambiguous - neither with regard to his own position which is to call for a clear land policy, nor to the development of viable political institutions to mediate between the different parties in land disputes. He does argue, and here he takes up a clear political position, that the process of reforming land tenure must take place within a clear ideological framework. In the case of Uganda, his argument is that such a policy must be based on recognition of private ownership of land.

In a book devoted to internal conflicts and its resolution it is important to focus on external factors which can contribute to the escalation of internal conflicts. This is what Akiki Bomera Mujaju does in his chapter on **"Internal Conflict and its International Context"**. Internal conflicts are a product of the country's own history, and in most African countries the result of the colonial heritage. There remains also the inheritance of fragile institutions never allowed the time and the space to mature.

Mujaju discusses the international and regional context which fuels and helps to escalate internal conflicts. A major condition for conflicts to take a violent form are the weak and fragile political systems in many countries. Frequently, leaders pursue zero sum approaches to conflict resolution, with an attitude which does not recognize diversity and the need for pluralism. Given the internal fragility of political systems, there is an increasing potential that armed conflicts will take the form of civil wars. "Because our political systems are initially incoherent and because aspects of their internal form are projections of the external environment, they are easily manipulated from outside." A major characteristic of such systems is that power is strongly concentrated at the centre. There are no checks and balances among various institutions of the state, since institutional autonomy is viewed with suspicion. Nor are there strong structures mediating between the centre and the periphery. External interventions can escalate and fuel conflicts into violent ones precisely because of the lack of internal mechanisms for conflict resolution. Mujaju points especially to the serious escalation of conflicts through the sale of lethal arms to conflicting groups within a country. He sees a trend leading to increased potential for armed conflict which may take the form of either civil wars, with jockeying for power, particularly among ethnic groups, or military coups, used as a means of transferring power, and regional clashes between sovereign states resulting from irredentist claims.

In order to demonstrate more concretely the interconnections between the external and the internal, Mujaju cites various instances from contemporary history: Mozambique, Nigeria,

Ethiopia, the Sudan, Angola and Zaire. In each of the cases there is or has been a strong regional or super power involvement in the conflict. The presence of cross-border affiliations fuels conflicts and refugees become pawns in the power-brokering of states.

While reiterating the need to develop institutions capable of sustaining a multi-ethnic society, Mujaju draws attention to the need within the African continent to strengthen conflict resolution. He suggests that the OAU should develop a cumulative experience and capacity to resolve and mediate over potential conflicts. Furthermore, he recommends a stronger OAU secretariat, with capacity for early warnings, and able to mobilize the rich traditions of mediation and resolution within the African culture. Distinguished leaders and statesmen could be deployed to mediate over potential conflicts. More work has also to be done with regard to the increased flow of arms and efforts to restrict it, particularly the flow of arms to the Third World.

Oliver Furley, in his essay on **"Britain and Uganda from Amin to Museveni: Blind Eye Diplomacy"**, examines the special relationship and contradictory policies pursued by Britain towards successive Ugandan regimes. A complex range of interests has governed British policy. Obviously, continuing traditional trading interests and protecting them from new competitors has been dominant concern. In addition comes the fact that Uganda had a distinct preference to be within a broadly Western alignment, as well as the general goodwill in Britain towards what has been regarded as the "Pearl of Africa".

Furley also sheds light on the role of certain British firms who continued supplying the Amin regime, especially his army and secret service, with vital equipment and morale-boosting luxuries. The most notorious form this took was the so-called "whisky run" where twice-weekly flights were loaded with luxury goods from British suppliers. There were also British firms who had been supplying vital equipment to the secret service. British military training teams attempted to instill regular methods and discipline into small groups of officers, who were in turn to diffuse this training amongst their own units. This was a failure, given the huge size of Amin's army and the fact that so many troops were irregulars.

3. Conclusion

Institutional approaches to conflict resolution or conflict management have been the subject matter of a variety of disciplines, including peace research.[20] A growing body of literature exists on social conflicts and their management, and various institutions have been established to manage social conflicts. Further, theoretical advances have been made in the role of third parties in conflict resolution, as well as improving bargaining and negotiating strategies. New forms of conflict resolution mechanisms have been suggested, from problem-solving approaches to professional facilitators in conflict resolution. However, most of these theoretical advances have been tried out within stable democracies, where there has long existed an evolving tradition in managing conflicts.

The challenge for those who argue for an institutional approach to conflict resolution is to see how many of these institutional mechanisms and third party interventions can be developed particularly in deeply divided societies. We need to study the question of competence building, in particular the development of local institutions and mechanisms for conflict resolution.

During the period of decolonization, Third World elites were frequently so involved in nation-building that they may have ignored or neglected to develop legal and other institutional means to sustain multi - ethnic societies. More comparative studies are necessary on how constitutions and law can create the framework for political competition, compromise and accommodation. Law can, in the long term, affect the framework in which these forces will operate and can reinforce or weaken the claims of particular groups in society. There is no universal prescription for making laws; the type of legislation and institutional mechanisms will depend on the political leaders and their willingness to give serious consideration to institutions which can accommodate ethnic bargaining or minority claims.

Resolving a conflict requires a change of world views. It requires an active learning and unlearning process of purposeful transformation. Unfortunately, in societies such as Uganda, polarized by antagonistic and rigid social stratification and full of memories of the recent past, a mixture of imagination and pragmatism will be necessary for reconciliation and reconstruction. This will have to include a national debate on the nature of the political system (one-party versus multi-party, executive presidential system versus the Westminster model etc.). Any experimentation on the institutional approach to conflict resolution will have no meaning if the political system as such, irrespective of the particular modality it takes, is not responsive to pluralism and participatory democracy. An absolute precondition for all this is, of course, a cessation of armed hostilities on all sides so as to create a climate conducive for confidence-building and good-will on all sides to the conflict.

At present the government of Uganda has passed legislature on the development of Resistance Committees as a grass root movement for development and mobilization. These committees go up to five levels of representation, and the highest level will be the National Assembly. The Resistance Committees were born during the guerilla struggle and now the attempt is to see that these organs become truly representative of the whole country . It is not clear as to the future direction of this new organization. Will this body be a representative of the state, government or the creation of a new political party? There are still many unresolved problems, and one of them will be the relationship of political parties to the Resistance Committees. The government has argued for a period of transition in which to resolve these issues and through public debate evolve structures which can best suit the conditions of Uganda. These issues are being discussed in Uganda today. The future of the constitution will be debated and proposals put forward in a constituent assembly. The relationship of the state, government, party and the people is always a contentious issue. The present volume draws attention to the importance of pluralism and multi party democracy. The multi-party structures does not have a favourable historical record and the challenge for Uganda is precisely how to reconcile a strong tradition of political democracy with new political institutions.

In conclusion, it must be noted that it would be pretentious for anyone to claim to have the last word on internal conflict and its resolution. In Uganda, as well as in other societies, what we are witnessing is an on-going process which cannot be captured or "frozen" in a given volume or a conference. What this volume can contribute towards is the opening-up of space and a forum for the national discourse on the transition towards national reconciliation, peace and social progress. In the final analysis the burden of creating the internal conditions for national reconciliation and the restoration of peace lies with the Ugandan people, their leaders and the institutions that they create.

Notes

1. Wai, D.: "Sources of Communal Conflicts and Secessionist Politics in Africa", in Ethnic and Racial Studies, vol. 1, no.3, 1978.
2. Ekstein, H.: "On the Causes of Internal War", in Nordlinger E. (ed.): Politics and Society. Englewood Cliffs, N.J.: Prentice Hall, 1970.
3. Burton, J.W.: "International Conflict Resolution Priorities", in Forum, Peace Institute Reporter, June 1987, p. 5. See also Azer, E.E.: "Protracted International Conflicts, Ten Propositions", in Azer, E.E. and J. Burton (eds.): International Conflict Resolution.: Theory and Practice. Sussex & Boulder: Lynne Rienner Publishers, 1986, pp. 28-40.
4. Heiberg, M.: The Defective State and Its Implications for Development: The Case of Italy. Oslo: International Peace Research Institute, Oslo. Working Paper no. 8, 1983.
5. Kasfir, N.: The Shrinking Political Arena: Ethnicity and Participation in African Politics. Berkeley: University of California Press, 1976.
6. Enloe, C.: "Police and Military in the Resolution of Ethnic Conflict", in The Annals of the American Academy of Political and Social Science, September 1977.
7. For a useful discussion on ethnic stratification and cross-border affiliations, see Rotschild, J.: Ethnopolitics: A Conceptual Framework. New York: Columbia University Press, 1981, chapter 3.
8. For a discussion on some interesting case studies, see Rupesinghe, K. (ed): Ethnic Conflicts and Human Rights. Bulletin of Peace Proposals, vol. 18, no. 4, 1987. Also published by the United Nations University, Tokyo, 1988.
9. Guest, I.: "Report to UN Panel Cites 2 Million Executions", in International Herald Tribune, 17 February 1983, p. 3.
10. Wolpin, M: State Terrorism and Repression in the Third World: Parameters and Prospects. Oslo: International Peace Research Institute, Oslo. Report no. 10, 1983.
11. Powell, G. Bingham jr.: Contemporary Democracies: Participation, Stability and Violence. Cambridge, Mass.: Harvard University Press, 1982.
12. Mehden, S. von der: Comparative Political Violence. Englewood Cliffs, N.J.: Prentice Hall, 1973.
13. Sloan, J.: "State Terrorism and Enforcement terrorism in Latin America", in Stohl, M. & G. Lopez (eds.): The State as Terrorist. London: Aldwych Press Ltd., 1984.
14. Walter, E.: Terror and Resistance: A Study of Political Violence. London: Oxford University Press, 1969.
15. Ibid., page 26.
16. Welch, C.: "Military Disengagement from Politics? Incentives and Obstacles", Baynham, S. (ed.): Military Power and Politics in Black Africa. London and Sydney: Croom Helm, 1986.
17. Ibid., page 68.
18. Doornbors, M.: "The Uganda Crisis and the National Question", in Holger, B.H. and M. Twaddle (eds.): Uganda Now. London: James Curry Publishers, 1988.
19. For a useful discussion see Mamdani, M.: "Uganda in Transition: Two Years of the NRA/NRM", in Third World Quarterly, vol. 10, no 3., July 1988.
20. As Mamdani, op.cit., correctly observed, "the need of the hour, therefore, is not for the adjustment of these structures to changes in the international economy; it is for structural (institutional) change."
21. Rupesinghe, K.: Theories of Conflict Resolution and Their Applicability to Protracted Ethnic Conflicts. Oslo: International Peace Research Institute, Oslo. Report no. 1, April 1988. Also in Bulletin of Peace Proposals, vol. 18, no. 4, 1986.

Samwiri Lwanga-Lunyiigo

The Colonial Roots of Internal Conflict

1. Introductory Remarks

By and large, independent Uganda has been characterized by violence and a ruthless, dictatorial leadership; until recently, the pervasive atmosphere has been one of despondency and hopelessness amongst the majority of her people. Viable political institutions have not developed, there is no basic consensus and the country is hopelessly divided. Independence has become a traumatic and debilitating experience indeed.

The purpose of this paper is to establish the role of colonialism in the post-colonial agony of Uganda. Colonialism, we hope to demonstrate, failed miserably through omission or commission to lay the foundations for the building of a nation out of the Protectorate. The manner in which protection was effected, the nature of the administration established and the colonial economy imposed - all were basic elements of the recipe for the chaos of the post-colonial period.

2. The Conquest

Both the sword and the Bible, those familiar twins of imperialism, were effectively wielded against the pre-colonial leadership and people of what emerged as the Uganda Protectorate at the beginning of this century. Bible and sword became weapons of division. The Bible plunged one part of Uganda, Buganda, into a civil war in the 1880s which left her divided and weak. It destroyed her monarchy in the process, leaving her an easy prey for incorporation into the British Empire by Captain Lugard and his motley crew in the 1890s. The divisions introduced by the Bible soon embraced what became the Protectorate; and these divisions still plague independent Uganda and influence her negative politics. These divisions are a solid legacy of colonialism.

Between 1890 and 1920, imperialism wielded the sword in earnest to secure and pacify her colonial possession, Uganda.

Those three decades were decades of violence, with a premium on the establishment of law and order, and the virtual purpose of government to police the populace. Violence or the threat of violence was widely used to put down the natives during the colonial period. Imperialism was intolerant of opposition, relying more on the sword than on dialogue. This is the legacy of violence that imperialism bequeathed to a whole generation of leadership in post-colonial Uganda.

When Uganda acquired her final geographical shape in the early 1920s, she embraced a people from three linguistic groups, namely Sudanic, Nilotic and Bantu, from two distinct major African language families - Nilo-Saharan and Congo-Kordofian.[1] There was very little or no linguistic or cultural affinity amongst these people. Indeed, it should have been obvious to those who brought them together into one central protectorate administration that a lot of work would have to be done to mould them into nationals of one country. This work was not done, however - because British imperialism thrived on division. For a long time, the idea of creating a future nation-state was hardly contemplated at all.

The British conquered Uganda through the use of force and fraud, and these two methods created wounds within the body-politic of Uganda that Independence has not yet healed. In establishing colonial rule, the British used Africans to fight for them, Africans who then stayed under one administration with the conquered people and became citizens of the same country. Nubians and Baganda played a prominent role in the conquest of Uganda, and a bitterness transcending generations was created which forms part of the tale of our more recent agonies.

Nubians were used by Baker, Emin Pasha and Gordon to man forts in Acholi from the early 1870s to around 1890. Pain notes that the behaviour of these Nubian forces left a bitter folk memory among the Acholi.[2] On the eve of his sojourn in Uganda, in 1890, Captain Lugard assembled 70 Nubian askaris. Lugard further sought the services of the remnants of Emin Pasha's troops under the command of Selim Bey stranded on the Zaire side of the Semliki River. In October 1891, Selim Bey crossed the Semliki River into Toro with around 2,000 Nubian soldiers and another 13,000 followers, women and children. This Nubian contingent was further consolidated in 1894 when another 10,000 men and families under another Nubian commander, Fadhl-el-Maula, were ferried into Bunyoro across Lake Albert. It is these Nubians who helped defeat Bunyoro and Buganda in the 1890s and assisted in the many "pacification" campaigns that the British carried out in Uganda and elsewhere up to the outbreak of World War I. They formed the core of the Uganda Rifles, established in 1895. Thus we see an essentially alien force had formed the core of the colonial army in Uganda. Commenting on the Nubian visitation H.H. Johnston, Uganda Commissioner (1899-1900), tellingly observed:

> themselves ex-slaves, they had all the cruelty and unscrupulousness of the Arab slave-traders, whose names, principles and religion they had inherited.

Apollo Kaggwa and Semei Kakungulu, rival chiefs in Buganda, were used extensively in the conquest of Uganda. Thus the incorrect impression was created that Buganda per se was responsible for the conquest, and that Uganda as a nation participated in the grand designs of British imperialism in Uganda. If Buganda had participated as a nation, then why was Mwanga a rebel? Why was he hunted like a wild beast by Kakungulu?

Between December 1893 when Colonel Colvile declared war on Bunyoro and 1895 when conventional warfare came to an end there, Kaggwa had deployed around 20,000 men to fight the Banyoro. In 1897, when Mwanga started the struggle for the self-determination of Buganda in Buddu, Kaggwa again mobilized a large army to fight Buganda nationalists. Mwanga rendezvoused with a Bunyoro general, Ireta, in May 1898, then crossed the Nile in July 1898 to join Kabalega in Lango, where both were captured by Kakungulu on 9 April 1899. Kakungulu, thereafter encouraged by Johnston, the British Commissioner, embarked on the conquest of eastern Uganda in the mistaken understanding that the British would allow him to establish a kingdom and a dynasty of his own as king of the Bakadi.[4] The depredations of the Baganda mercenaries in Bunyoro and eastern Uganda left a bitterness that has still not disappeared. Through their use of the Baganda to conquer Uganda, the British managed to establish a lasting hatred between the Baganda and much of the rest of Uganda - weak premises on which to build a nation. With this all-embracing deployment of the Baganda by the British, a colonial myth was woven into the historiography of Uganda: namely that the Baganda had a long tradition of martial dominance over their neighbours.[5] Deepening this bitterness, when the Banyoro were conquered, the British annexed all Bunyoro territory south of the River Kafu to Buganda as a reward for the support Kaggwa and his men had given to the British. This Bunyoro territory was incorporated into the Kingdom of Buganda, when for the first time Buganda's boundaries were defined both on the ground and on paper in the 1900 Uganda (Buganda) Agreement.[6] The territory excised from Bunyoro was estimated to have comprised around one quarter of pre-colonial Bunyoro territory; it included the heartland of precolonial Bunyoro-Mubende where the earlier royal burial grounds were located. Colonialism created the problem of Bunyoro irridenta, a problem which the British tried to side-step by thrusting it upon Uganda leaders - leaders who had not created this problem at all - to solve on their departure.

Kaggwa's and Kakungulu's men were sent by the British, once conquest had been accomplished, as agents of their imperialism in western and eastern Uganda. They were deployed as administrators whom Kabwegyere refers to as "tutor mechanics"[7] to peddle the so-called Kiganda model of administration in other parts of the Protectorate. Missionaries used Baganda agents to peddle their catechism as well. Truly, the Baganda had come into their own as the "Japanese of Africa",[8] an accolade that scarcely endeared them to their neighbours. Buganda became the favourite child of imperialism and aroused the envy of the other children. This partly explains the many skulls that now litter the Luwero Triangle.

Where force was not used to conquer, fraud was. Fraudulent agreements were concluded between the British and Buganda, Toro and Nkore at the beginning of this century, providing for the acceptance of British protection and loyalty to the British Crown and establishing a local constitution. A Privy Council judgement (Sobhuza II vs. Miller, 1926) established that agreements with Native Rulers can never bind the British Crown.[9] Ibingira observes that agreements lacked the force of law and bound the British Crown at its pleasure.[10] Initially the Native (agreement) rulers did not know that the agreements they concluded did not have the force of law, but even when they found out they continued the charade. They, indeed, turned these agreements into fortresses against nationalism. To this theme we shall return later. Suffice it to note that the British had created a major divide in Uganda between the agreement and non-agreement areas, a divide which soured political development in Uganda.

3. The Army

Having used force and fraud to establish the Protectorate, the British proceeded to use the same means to maintain themselves in power. They established a force of internal coercion whose loyalty to them had to be unquestioning. The Uganda Rifles Ordinance (1895) specifically included a clause (clause 58) empowering the Uganda Rifles to take action against any local group(s) in the Protectorate which engaged in active opposition to the administration.

The formation of a loyal force was vital to the founders of the Uganda Protectorate. According to Lugard, the founding father of the colony, the Nubians constituted the best material for soldiery in Africa.[11] By the beginning of World War I, the British had made up their minds as to whom they wanted to man their colonial armies in Africa. They had evolved the "martial tribes" thesis, according to which the Central African "races" were seen as possessing military qualities in direct proportion to the amount of influence left by foreign invaders.[12] In the Uganda context, "the Nilotic and Sudanic tribes of northern Uganda show signs of the effects of former Asiatic invasions to which they owe their war-like characteristics".[13]

Omara-Otunnu argues convincingly that the factors governing the deployment of colonial troops were that a soldier should be of a different "race" from the people of the area in which he was to be deployed, that he should be geographically distant from the people into which he was deployed and that he should be of a different religious faith from the local population. The British tried as much as possible to look for soldiers who fulfilled most of the above criteria. As a matter of policy, colonial armies in Africa were recruited from "remote" tribes detached and even hostile to tribes central to the colonies.[14] In Ghana, for example, 60% of the colonial army at the time of Independence had to be recruited from the northern nationalities. In Nigeria, the Hausa dominated the colonial army; and in Sierra Leone, it was the northern Karankos, the Mandingos, the Fula and the Limbe.[15] These tribes were also largely Moslem, the religion preferred in the African colonial forces. In Uganda, the Nubians were ranked first in the order of preference, because they were an entirely alien mercenary element who did not have any sentimental attachment to Uganda and could be trusted to be brutal without any reserve or compunction. They were also Moslems, which ensured that they remained safe from the virus of Westernization, a virus cultivated through the agency of Christianity.

Towards the end of the 19th century (1897), the Nubians messed themselves up through the "Sudanese Mutiny", a mutiny which became the most serious threat to the establishment of colonial rule in Uganda the British had faced yet. The Baganda and the Indians were called in to rescue the Union Jack.[16] Thereafter, Nubians never quite regained their ground within the colonial army, and it was not until the overthrow of the first Obote regime in 1971 that they were to recover their dominant position within the armed forces. By 1914 the Acholi had gained the ascendancy. As Omara-Otunnu observes: "the largest contingent (of soldiers) was recruited from the north, especially from the people of Acholi and by 1914 Acholi had become the main recruiting ground for the K.A.R. (King's African Rifles), a pattern which continued well into the post-colonial period".[17] Omara-Otunnu argues that it was not the martial race concept that guided the British into recruiting Acholi: the Acholi were the ones who offered least resistance to the establishment of British rule. He further notes:

> The Acholi were preferred to the Baganda because of their political disposition. Having been exposed to British rule for longer, the Baganda were familiar with the British and were more assertive of their interaction with them. Whereas the Baganda were perceived by British military officers to be arrogant and insubordinate, it was hoped that the Acholi would be more amenable to the authority of the British. <u>The Acholi were also preferred because they had very loosely organized and territorially small political and military units. So large-scale military mobilization under a single political leadership was impossible</u>.[18] (emphasis added)

However, it is not true that the Acholi offered the least resistance to the establishment of colonial rule. Between 1911 and 1912, the Lamogi people of Acholi rebelled against the British. Considerable resources were deployed by the British to put down this rebellion, and many lives were lost amongst the Lamogi.[19] What recommended them, and northerners in general, to the British was their remoteness from the centre of the country, their relative lack of the trappings of western civilization and their rather simple political and military organizational backgrounds. Around these factors was woven the myth of the "martial races" of the north, a myth which prospered throughout the colonial period and up until January 1986 when the remnants of the King's African Rifles were at last driven from power in

Kampala. So powerful was this myth that northerners believed themselves to be the only ones divinely ordained to bear arms in Uganda, while the rest believed themselves incapable of bearing them.

In colonial times, the army remained largely invisible. Since Independence in 1962, and especially after the 1964 mutiny of the Uganda Army, it has become very visible and a key institution in the political life of the country. Soldiers have maintained that visibility and importance up to today. However, this institution was neither national nor nationalist, nor - given the above background - could it have been expected to have been so. Considerable internal conflict, leading to virtual genocide in some parts of Uganda in the more recent past, arose over the fact that this key institution of the post-colonial period was built on the British foundations of remoteness and hostility to people in the centre of the country. Colonialism built up the army as an instrument of coercion, as a pacifying army, not as a peoples' force to ensure defence against external aggression. Until recently, the army in Uganda remained an instrument of internal coercion. It could not be truly national because some Ugandans were not thought or meant to have the precious "martial qualities" which the British had attributed to Ugandans of northern origin.

This concept beautifully fitted Obote and Amin: both were northerners who clearly appreciated the political advantages of having armies where they had a close linguistic and cultural link.

So confident was Obote about this linkage that in the campaigns leading to the general election of December 1980 he could ask his rivals, the leaders of other political parties who happened to come from the south and west of the country, where their armies were; and if they did not have them, he asked, how did they hope to take power. To Obote, with his ethnic army in place, the ballot was irrelevant. For some 20 years of Uganda's independence, the hegemony of the north was made possible by the faithful pursuit of colonial policies in recruiting and deploying the army, and by actually retaining as military leaders K.A.R. veterans of the colonial era, veterans with little or no education at all.[20] It is no coincidence that all the defeated armies and factions of armies, from the Amin coup d'etat of 1971 to the debacle of the Okellos in January 1986, have retired to the north and beyond into the southern Sudan and north-eastern Zaire to take refuge amongst their relatives; nor is it any coincidence that armed opposition to the National Resistance Movement government is from the north. This is one of the most bitter legacies of colonialism.

4. The Administration

From the triumph of conquest, the British moved on to the next logical stage requisite to the consolidation of power: administration. A dual system was devised, with native authorities and central administration. In the domain of native administration, the boundaries of the native authorities were delineated, wherever possible, along ethnic lines. Thus, except for the districts of West Nile, Bugisu, Bukedi, Toro and Kigezi where the ethnic units were not considered viable enough for each to form a district, native authorities coincided with ethnic boundaries. This ethnic delineation of administrative boundaries did not change even after Independence.

Accompanying this was the indirect rule system of administration. Cohen observes that this policy developed as a result of local initiative without being laid down from London, and that it was not until the 1930s that the Colonial Office began to encourage the pursuit of such a policy.[21] That great historian of British Africa, M. Perham, found merit in indirect rule because it broke the shock of western annexation, was economical, kept the peace and induced a sympathetic inquiring attitude in colonial officials towards African society.[22] Indirect rule held centre stage in the field of administration and politics in Uganda until the late 1940s, when in a despatch to the colonies, Colonial Secretary Creech-Jones in 1947 enunciated a new policy on local government aimed at converting the system of indirect rule into a democratic, efficient and modern system of local government. This despatch led to the enactment of the Local Government Ordinance in 1949, which gave legal and corporate powers and responsibilities to the district councils and introduced the elective principle within the local administrations. The ordinance, however, did not apply to Buganda. Analyzing the ordinance, Burke concludes that "as the administrative districts (including kingdoms) generally coincided with tribal residence, the 1949 ordinance in effect provided for the institutionalization of parochial tribally oriented local governments".[23]

Within the domains of native administrations, Buganda was governed by the Uganda Agreement of 1900 and the rest of Uganda by the Native Authority Ordinance of 1919 - a constitutional arrangement which emphasized the division between

Buganda and the rest of the country. As Ibingira observes, Buganda was legally just another province of Uganda and the agreement, as noted earlier, bound the British Crown only at its pleasure; yet agreements with African rulers were for political reasons strictly adhered to by the British rulers, who departed from them only in rare cases when it seemed in the best interest of peace, good government or imperial authority to do so.[24]

Many historians of Buganda emphasize the importance of the agreement in creating a distance between Buganda and the rest of the country. Morris argues: "the kingdom of Buganda stood in a completely different position from the rest of the country. In Buganda there existed what may conveniently, if not accurately, be termed a native state, whose relationship with the Protectorate Government was defined in considerable detail by the terms of the Agreement of 1900".[25] In a book published in 1987 Omara-Otunnu asserts: "the agreement ensured for them (the Baganda) a privileged status vis-a-vis the rest of Uganda, thereby regularizing and fostering inequalities between Buganda and the other provinces of the country".[26] So whether or not Buganda's agreement really gave it a special and privileged position in Uganda, that is what both the Baganda and non-Baganda believed, and the British encouraged this belief. This constitutional division made the unity of Uganda extremely difficult to achieve and was to be a potential cause of conflict in independent Uganda. Indirect rule operated within the framework of this Uganda Agreement and the Native Authority Ordinance.

Perhaps Pratt's definition of indirect rule is as good as any: by "indirect rule" is meant the appointment of tribal chiefs as agents of local rule - the use in local government of those men whom the people were accustomed to obey.[27] In Uganda, despite claims to the contrary, classical indirect rule as was practiced by Lugard in northern Nigeria could not be applied to the whole of Uganda; "indirect rule" as imposed wholesale on the atomistic societies of the east and north of Uganda, where the search for the traditional authorities proved an uphill task.

Buganda had a highly centralized and hierarchical system of traditional administration. Although the monarchy had become seriously emasculated by 1900, the rest of the traditional administration still held. It was a system much admired by the British, so the "Kiganda model" of administration was exported to the rest of Uganda, accompanied by experts from Buganda, the agents who imposed it wherever the British established a civilian administration. This imposition of the "Kiganda model" went against the grain of classical indirect rule where the native traditional authorities were to be the agents of indirect rule. Failure to find the indigenous chief, or in some cases where these were available, to use them, and the consequent imposition of Buganda agents, caused much bitterness and trouble. In Bunyoro, for example, the imposition of the Kiganda model and agents led to the Nyangire Revolt in 1907, a revolt that Uzoigwe dubs a passive revolt against British overrule.[28] There were many such revolts in the east and west, revolts which forced the British to withdraw the agents from most of Uganda by 1930. The anger of the people was directed not so much against the British as against the Baganda, and this agency system further sharpened the cleavage between the Baganda and the non-Baganda. The British were adept at diverting people's anger against themselves, but in the process they also removed the possibility for the development of a genuine national consciousness amongst the people of Uganda. Instead, their system of administration served to create enemies amongst the people of Uganda.

In some areas where the native authorities were not coterminous with ethnic groupings, secessionist movements developed, as was the case in Toro. So serious were the Bamba and Bakonzo grievances that in March 1962 they formed the Rwenzururu Movement. Isaaya Mukirane, their leader, asked for a separate district for the Bamba and Bakonjo, complaining that 70 years of being ruled as slaves by an alien and arrogant people should be ended.[29] In June 1962, Mukirane established the kingdom of Rwenzururu, comprising the counties of Bwamba, Bunyangabu, and Busongora, and declared Rwenzururu an independent state. The Rwenzururu Movement maintained its momentum in and around the Rwenzori Mountains until the second ruler of the Mukirane dynasty, Charles Iremangoma, came down the mountain in 1983 and handed over his kingdom to the Uganda Government.[30] Even after the handover, however, sentiments of Rwenzururu nationalism still linger today. For a good 20 years, the Rwenzururu Movement tied down considerable resources in attempts to suppress it. Lives and property were lost, and the real cost of that conflict has not yet been worked out. Even in the divide and rule game the British were not purists. The Bamba and Bakonzo wanted a district of their own since they had been badly treated by their Batoro overlords, imposed on them by the British. The British argued that a Bamba and Bakonzo district would not be economically viable; yet throughout the colonial period around 70% of the revenues of Toro originated in the countries of Bwamba, Bunyangabu and Busongora. At times the British simply paid lip service to indirect rule in situations where the policy could have worked well. A state of neither unity nor disunity was sometimes fostered by British imperialism, to the great suffering of its subjects.

Throughout the colonial period, "government" meant local administration to most people. The protectorate administration at Entebbe remained remote and the people largely uninvolved in it. The protectorate administration was mostly a white man's affair. It remained mysterious and was deliberately mystified by the colonial administration. True, the people from time to time did see the District Commissioner on baraza,[31] but that was the limit to which protectorate administration stretched itself in most cases. The daily and basic concerns of ordinary people were taken care of by the local or native administrations. Very few looked beyond their local administrations to the other local administrations or to the protectorate administration, and those who did were viewed as trouble makers by the protectorate administration.

5. The Economy

Colonies were basically looked upon as sources of raw materials needed to feed the industries of their owners and as markets for their manufactures. The colonial economies were, therefore, geared to this basic function, not to the development of the economies and people of the colonies. The little development that did take place was incidental to the basic functions of colonial economies, and any infrastructure was designed to facilitate the movements of raw materials from the colonies. The social infrastructure was largely developed by non-governmental organizations, mainly missionaries. Cohen tells us that, "there was more emphasis put on the protection of African society than on helping Africans to develop, and this opinion pervaded the colonial office".[32] The cornerstone of Gladstone's finance principles was self-sufficiency; and this policy guided the colonial administrations for most of the colonial period. Grants-in-aid were given grudgingly by the British Treasury and then only in cases of extreme difficulty. Deficit financing was not allowed at all.

Uganda was considered self-sufficient in 1915, and grants-in-aid from the British Treasury were stopped. This policy was modified somewhat at the beginning of World War II, when through the Colonial Development and Welfare Acts, British money was made available through the Colonial Development

Corporation for social and economical development. However, the amounts were small and they had come late.

In 1903 colonialism found a raw material that Uganda could produce - cotton. Cotton and plantation rubber, cocoa and later coffee divided the country into "productive" and "non-productive" zones, zones of production and labour recruitment respectively. This division was to have dangerous political and social ramifications.

Cotton was first introduced into Buganda and then into the Eastern province because of easier communication - water and rail transport being available. European planters also established their plantations there mainly for ease of communications. These, therefore, in British colonial officialdom became the "productive" zones, while the rest of the county, the north and the west, became the "non-productive" zones by the early 1920s. There was a deliberate policy of holding back agricultural development of the "non-productive" zones. In 1925 the Director of Agriculture, who was either not yet aware of this policy or had overlooked it, started encouraging cotton production in West Nile: he was curtly warned by the Chief Secretary that "the policy of government is at present to refrain from actively stimulating the production of cotton or other economic crops in outlying districts on which it is dependent for a supply of labour for carrying out of essential services in the central producing districts".[33] The policy had the effect of keeping the "non-productive" zones underdeveloped, because most able-bodied men migrated to the "productive" zones to labour in the cotton fields and on the rubber, coffee and cocoa plantations. It also inculcated inferiority and superiority complexes amongst Ugandans along the "non-productive"/"productive" zones axis. The Ormsby-Gore Commission warned:

> When among such people as the Baganda and Basoga, labourers were introduced who came from tribes considered inferior and who worked under conditions which the Baganda and the Basoga could not themselves accept, the latter tended to feel that unskilled manual labour was a form of employment suitable only for inferior tribes. There was even a danger that the question might in time become one of "caste".[34]

So colonial economic policy had helped bring about a polarization amongst Ugandans, inadvertently encouraging development in the "productive" zones while preventing development in the "non-productive" zones. Unfortunately, these colonial economic structures are still with us: very little effort has been made since Independence to take development to the "non-productive" zones, especially in the north. The enthusiasm with which the destruction of property was undertaken in the Luwero Triangle was a logical conclusion to colonial economic policies: the two zones were evening up the score.

Since there were no raw materials to extract from the "non-productive" zones, there was also no need to develop infrastructure. This meant total neglect of these zones. This economic zoning of the country is perhaps the most terrible legacy of British imperialism, leading inevitably to conflict in the absence of vigorous economic plans for the "non-productive" zones after Independence.

6. The Lingua Franca

Ugandans had no common language; indeed, they still have no common language in which to communicate with one another. How, then, can a people who cannot communicate with each other really become united?

In the inter-war period there were attempts by the colonial government to introduce Kiswahili in the school curriculum, and between 1930 and 1943 the teaching of Kiswahili was enforced in primary levels 3 and 4 outside Buganda; but after that the policy was to subordinate vernaculars (and that apparently included Kiswahili) to English. At a conference on language education policy in 1945 it was decided that, "the development of a lingua franca has very little connection with immediate expediency, being essentially concerned with enduring values and hence with a penetration which, however gradual, shall steadily become co-extensive with the country".[35] On these criteria, neither Kiswahili nor Luganda nor any other "vernacular" had admissible claims. Therefore the policy became to encourage English, and Kiswahili was abandoned. Furthermore, Kiswahili was seen by the influential Christian leadership as the language of Islam, so they discouraged it. To the Baganda conservatives, Kiswahili was the language of prostitutes and thieves. Kiswahili was maintained in the colonial army, however, and after Independence the language acquired notoriety as the language of violence.

Despite a colonial language policy intent on promoting English, throughout the colonial period English was taught only from the upper primary classes onwards. Thus, by the time most Ugandans ended their formal education (primary 6) they normally had had only two years of English. This meant they never really learnt the language enough to become able to communicate effectively. So, unlike the situation in Tanzania and Kenya, Ugandans cannot yet communicate to each other across the board because of what happened to Kiswahili in 1945. This serious impediment to unity is again a legacy of colonial bungling.

7. Decolonization

During the inter-war period, British colonial policy makers began to think about the future of their colonies. They envisaged the possibility of self-government within the British Commonwealth or their colonies - but at some remote future not yet on the horizon, as they believed they had almost unlimited time in which to work on the political development of the natives. Indeed, where self-government was mentioned at all it was casually presented as the end product of indirect rule. Even when the British began to envisage self-government in the remote future, they continued to regard Uganda merely as an administrative unit, never in terms of a nation.

No encouragement was given to peoples' participation in, or the creation of, national institutions. For example, in 1922 there was a suggestion that an African Central Assembly should be formed to provide all the natives of Uganda with a single political forum, but this suggestion was vetoed at a meeting proposed for the leaders of Buganda, Bunyoro, Busoga and Toro. When both the Legislative and Executive Councils were established by Order-in-Council in 1920, the Legislative Council became a planters' and merchants' forum for championing European and Asian political and economic interests. Africans did not gain access to the Legislative Council until 1944, or to the Executive Council until the early 1950s.[36]

Representative institutions were opposed by imperialism: the basis of the colonial state was autocracy. How could a legacy of autocracy be translated into democracy overnight once independence was granted? It was feared that representative institutions might divert the attention of educated Africans away from their tribal institutions, thus bringing these de-tribalised Africans into prominence. Imperialism also made the false claim that educated Africans were unrepresentative and, more importantly, that they would be less amenable to official guidance than native administration chiefs. British policies, both directly and indirectly, favoured and aided the continuation of tribal loyalities, while blocking the development of supra-tribal links and the participation of Africans in centralizing or nationalizing institutions.

Natives like Kulubya were the favourite children of imperialism because they went along beautifully with their masters when it came to preventing Uganda from becoming a nation. Asked why he was opposed to representation in the Legislative Council, Kulubya answered: "If we get a representative in the Legislative Council, it is quite possible that with one or to representatives that he will be outvoted ... by the majority and when he has been outvoted in that way it will be difficult for us to open the questions because we have our representative there"[37] (emphasis added). Clearly, Kulubya was thinking in the narrow terms of Buganda; the we and the outvoting was within the Buganda context. These "representatives" were not conceived to pursue the interests of Uganda, but those of Buganda. Such thinking led directly to the rejection of direct elections in Buganda, to the advocacy of electoral college status for the Lukiiko in the 1962 elections, to the formation of Kabaka Yekka to act as a power-broker in the National Assembly, and ultimately to the desecration of Mutesa II's Kingdom in 1966.[38]

The nature and shape of self-governing Uganda exercised the minds of colonial policy makers during the inter-war period and more specifically after World War II. The format was perceived in terms of a loose federation of independent native states, in an assembly of native authority delegates to stand alongside the Legislative Council which would eventually have powers and a status equal to it; in terms of regional councils of native authority and urban representatives to which eventually wide delegation of power would be given; and also in terms of a Central Assembly whose members would be drawn from the native authorities.[39] At this juncture, metropolitan institutions were deemed unsuitable for such politically "primitive" colonies as Uganda. And yet, at Independence we were bequeathed the Westminster model!

As noted earlier, Colonial Secretary Creech-Jones issued a new local government policy in a despatch to the governors in 1947. This policy was intended to offer the possibility of building a foundation of local democracy on which one hoped to base the structure of parliamentary government. In Uganda, this despatch was translated into the Local Government Ordinance of 1949. This ordinance did not apply to Buganda at all, and was rejected in several other places as well.[40] So the new policy did not prove the democratizing agent it had been conceived as; it was superceded by the District Councils (District Administrations) Ordinance of 1955 where the district councils emerged as the local authorities in charge of a variety of local services and with increased access to finance to take on such services.[41] The new-style local administrations spawned local notables each representing his own, largely ethnically homogeneous district, in the Legislative Council. Many of them peddled anti-colonialist slogans, but they were by no means nationalists with any Uganda-wide consciousness or appeal. They represented the narrow interests of their districts, not those of Uganda as a whole. Obote, for example, who became Prime Minister of Uganda in April 1962, could, as late as 1960, accept the chairmanship of the Lango District Council!

This is the kind of politician that the colonial policies of indirect role and parochialism had helped to create. Once the anti-colonialist rhetoric was over, would this brand of politicians be able to forge a nation? Or would they use the central government bequeathed by imperialism to advance parochial interests, as they were accustomed to during the colonial period? It is notable that only an insignificant number of politicians stood <u>outside</u> their tribal areas of origin for elections either before or after Independence.[42]

In the 1950s the British pursued a contradictory policy in Uganda. Cohen tells us that the policy was on the one hand to build up central institutions, namely the executive and the legislative, and on the other to build up the political and social institutions of each part of the country. In Buganda this meant giving the Lukiiko an elected majority and the Buganda Government a ministerial system of its own; in the rest of the country, it meant an increased elected element in the district councils. How could both central and local institutions be strengthened concurrently? Was not imperialism setting the two on a collision course? In the pursuit of this policy, the Buganda Agreement of 1955 created virtually a state within a state - a situation for which Uganda has since had to pay in considerable blood.[43] Burke's remarks on the development of local government in the 1950s are instructive:

> Local government in Uganda had developed in the shadow of the Buganda Agreement. The quasi-sovereign status of this large kingdom encouraged the smaller and less powerful monarchies to acquire a similar status. The prestige, ceremony and special privileges surrounding the kingdom governments in turn, colored the development of local government throughout the remainder of the country. Not only were British administrators accustomed to thinking in terms of special agree-

> ments, prior consultation, hereditary deference, but the leaders of the newly emergent non-monarchical districts were quick to emulate the kingdoms and to demand similar prerogatives for themselves. Thus in contrast to Kenya and Tanganyika local government in Uganda evolved in a quasi-federal milieu.[44]

In the first year of Uganda's independence (1962-63), most of the non-monarchical districts appointed their district constitutional heads, vying with each other to invent impressive titles for their constitutional heads.[45] Each district became a mini-state with its constitutional non-hereditary monarch. This was the "quasi-federal" milieu: yet Uganda was not a federal state. The 1962 Independence Constitution was a composite one, with elements of unitarism, federalism and semi-federalism. Clearly it was not a suitable basis for successfully forging a peaceful and united nation. The contradictory policies referred to earlier, pursued by the great reformer Sir Andrew Cohen, were, unintended by him, to lead to the constitutional crises of the 1960s, crises moderated by the sword. If Sir Andrew had been less timid, he would have seized the opportunity offered in 1953 by the deportation of Ssekabaka Mutesa II to impose a unitary system on Uganda across the board, and indeed he was inclined towards unitarism. Instead, Cohen and his less able successors at Entebbe allowed constitutional development to drift helplessly without any real guidance or policy. In order to muddle through the constitutional jungle of the 1950s and early 1960s prior to independence, the British appointed commission after constitutional commission, so as to buy time - time to jettison the colony and set it adrift after a decent period of constitutional development confusion.[46] The real problem was that the British neither dared to agree nor dared to disagree with Buganda. They simply continued to muddle through these constitutional problems - and thus the constitution bequeathed to Uganda at Independence was a real disaster.

It is true that Africans were brought into the Legislative Council at a reasonable pace in the 1950s; it is true that Cohen promised direct elections by 1961 and appointed the first African ministers to his Executive Council in 1955. It is also true that in 1958 some members of the Legislative Council were directly elected by the people, for the first time in the history of Uganda. However, Karamoja, Bugisu, Ankole and Buganda were not part of this exercise - and these represent a considerable part of the country. In the 1961 general elections, the Mengo establishment manouvered Buganda into almost completely boycotting the poll.[47] Uganda had very little experience in operating a parliamentary democratic system and most of Uganda's leaders joined the Legislative Council for the first time in 1961, just on the eve of Independence. Somehow, with no more preparation than this, the British expected our leaders, without any experience behind them, to operate the Westminster model successfully! Moreover, colonial regulations had prevented civil servants from participation in politics so that, in the main, politics had attracted people who were unemployed or unemployable. As Professor Ingo von Munch observes, "politicians without a profession are a great misfortune".[48] That was Uganda's misfortune at Independence. In addition, political practices imported without suitable modification from the metropolis were simply imposed on the colonies.

During the colonial period, very little effort was made to train Africans for responsibilities in the civil service. Although some three ministers were appointed by Cohen in 1955, there were very few senior African civil servants. For example, the first Assistant District Commissioners were not appointed until 1958, and there was no African permanent secretary until after Independence. Pratt had this to say on the matter: "There were still no Africans in the provincial administration in responsible positions. In 1951, for example, only five Africans had senior posts in the Protectorate departments. There was therefore, in these crucial year no serious effort made to build the institutions and to train the men for the self-government that would come far sooner than Entebbe dared admit."[49] It is clear that the British had intended to retain residual responsibilities in Uganda. This proved a misreading of post-colonial nationalism.

8. Conclusion

Uganda has been independent for almost a quarter of a century now, so we cannot indefinitely continue to harangue the imperialists for the chaos obtaining in our country. If the will is there, we can begin to build viable political economic and social institutions, but in this effort there will not be much to learn from our former colonial masters. The Westminster model is not easy to replicate. Nor will it be easy to replicate the economic revolutions that turned the British into an industrialized society. Instead, we shall have to establish our own paths to political, social and economic development. Above all, we shall have to remember that we as Ugandans have <u>one</u> destiny, and that we shall rise or sink together.

Notes

1. For a detailed survey of the linguistic complexity of Uganda, see Ladefoged, P., R. Blick & C. Cripper: Language in Uganda. Nairobi: Oxford University Press, 1971, Part I.
2. Pain, D.R.: "Acholi and Nubians: Economic Forces and Military Employment", pp. 23-36, in Dodge, C.P. & P.D. Wiebe (eds.): Beyond Crisis: Development Issues in Uganda. Kampala: Makerere Institute of Social Research, Makerere University & African Studies Association, 1987.
3. Johnston, H.H.: The Uganda Protectorate, vol. II. London: Hutchninson & Co., 1902, pp. 237-238.
4. Roberts, A.: "The Sub-imperialism of the Baganda", in Journal of African History, vol. III, no. 3, 1962, pp. 435-450.
5. Powesland, P.G.: Economic Policy and Labour. Kampala: EAISR, East African Studies no. 10. 1957, p. 25.
6. For a comprehensive study of the agreement, see Wild, J.V.: The Story of the Uganda Agreement. Nairobi: The Eagle Press, 1950.
7. Kabwegyere, T.B.: The Politics of State Formation: The Nature and Effects of Colonialism in Uganda. Nairobi: East African Literature Bureau, 1974, p. 175.
8. Johnston, op.cit., p. 301.
9. Quoted in Ibingira, G.S.K.: The Forging of an African Nation. New York/-Kampala: Viking and Uganda Publishing House, 1973, p. 13.
10. Ibid., pp. 14-15.
11. Quoted in Pain, op.cit., p. 25.
12. Moyse-Bartlett, H.: The King's African Rifles. Aldershot: Gale & Polden, 1956, p. 139.
13. Ibid.
14. Gutteridge, W.F.: "Military and Police Forces in Colonial Africa", in Gann, L.H. and P. Duignan: Colonialism in Africa. 1870-1960, vol. 2. New York: Cambridge University Press, p. 287.
15. Ibid., p. 288.
16. For a detailed study of the mutiny, see Wild, J.V.: The Sudanese Mutiny. Nairobi: The Eagle Press, 1950.
17. Omara-Otunnu, A.: Politics and the Military in Uganda. London: Macmillan, 1987, p. 43.
18. Ibid.
19. Adimola, A.B.: "The Lamogi Rebellion 1911-12", in Uganda Journal, vol. 18, no. 2, 1954.
20. All the army commanders that Uganda had between Independence and January 1986 - Opolot, Amin and Tito Okello - were K.A.R. veterans who had joined it in the 1940s.
21. Cohen, A.: British Policy in Changing Africa. London: Routledge & Kegan Paul, 1959, p. 25.
22. Perham, M.: The Colonial Reckonings. New York: Alfred A. Knopf, 1962, p. 68.
23. Burke, F.G.: Local Government and Politics in Uganda. Syracuse: Syracuse University Press, 1964, p. 39.
24. Ibingira, op.cit., pp. 18-19.
25. Morris, H.P. and M. Read: Indirect Rule and the Search for Justice. London: Oxford University Press, 1964, p. 27.
26. Omara-Otunnu, op.cit., p. 37.
27. Pratt, R.C.: "The Politics of Indirect Rule, 1900-1955", in Low, D.A. and R.C. Pratt: Buganda and British overrule, 1900-1955. London: Oxford University Press, 1960, p. 163.
28. Uzoigwe, G.N.: "The Kyanyangire, 1907: Passive revolt against British overrule", in Ogot, B.A. (ed.): War and Society in Africa. London: Frank Cass, 1972, pp. 179-214.

29. Burke, op.cit., p. 233.
30. For a more detailed study of the movements see Syahuka, M.: "The Origin and Development of the Rwenzururu, 1900-1962", in Mawazo, vol. 5, no. 2, December 1983, pp. 60-75.
31. Baraza were open air meetings called by colonial administrators to listen to people's grievances and problems.
32. Cohen, op.cit., pp. 18-19.
33. Entebbe Secretariat Archives: SMP 8297 (o.s.), paragraphs 68-84.
34. Report of the East African Royal Commission, cmnd 2387, 1925, p. 73.
35. Kabwegyere, op.cit., p. 217.
36. The first Africans to be appointed to the Executive Council in 1952 were Mukasa and Kulubya, and to the Legislative Council in 1945, Kawalya-Kaggwa, Zirabamuzaale and Nyangabyaki.
37. Report of the Joint Select Committee on Closer Union, vol. II, 1931, p. 577.
38. Obote unilaterally abrogated the 1962 Independence Constitution and replaced it with his own constitution, in which he made himself executive president and removed the federal status of Buganda and the semi-federal status of the western kingdoms, thus making Uganda a unitary state.
39. These views are advanced in Pratt, op.cit., p. 278.
40. Busoga and Bunyoro did not welcome this ordinance.
41. For a more detailed account of the Legislation see Wallis, C.A.G.: Report of an Inquiry into African Government in the Protectorate of Uganda. Entebbe: Government Printer, 1953.
42. J. Kakonge stood in the East Mengo constituency of Buganda and not in his native Bunyoro. He was returned in the general elections of 1961 simply because that constituency was dominated by the Lugazi Sugar estates where the dominant voters were workers not of local origin. Daudi Ochieng was to go to the National Assembly in 1962 as a Kabaka Yekka member for, although he was not a Muganda, he was a great friend of Ssekabaka Mutesa II.
43. Between 1964 and 1983, starting with the Nakulabye incident in which police opened fire and killed innocent people at a night club, through the large-scale killings of Baganda carried out following the 1966 constitutional changes to the Luwero Triangle Genocide of the 1980s, the bloodshed in Buganda seemed almost endless.
44. Burke, op.cit., p. 230.
45. The Langi got a "Won-Nyaci"; the Sebei, the "Kingoo", the Bakiga, the "Rutakirwa", the Bukedi District, the "Benkulu", and so on.
46. The following reports were produced:
(i) Reports of the Constitutional Committee. Entebbe: Government Printer, 1961.
(ii) Report of the Uganda Relationship Commission. Entebbe: Government Printer, 1961.
(iii) Report of the Constitutional Conference. HMSO: Command Paper, no. 1523, 1961.
47. Only 3% of the potential voters in Buganda were registered for the 1961 general election.
48. Quoted in The German Tribune, no. 275, 31 May 1987.
49. Pratt, op.cit., p. 284.

A.G. Ginywera-Pinchwa

Is there a "Northern Question"?

1. Introduction

The prevalence of internal conflicts within human societies has long been recognized by social theorists as an inevitable consequence of the co-existence of large numbers of human beings in a situation limited not only spatially in the geographical sense, but also in terms of the resources people require for their sustenance and survival.[1] These two limitations, together with the human and social diversity normally found in a society, create a naturally fertile ground for internal conflicts. Obviously then, a chapter like this one can hardly do justice to the plethora of internal conflicts that may exist in any given society - most of which will, in any case, tend to lend themselves to handling through peaceful, constitutional, or other less sensational methods of settlement, leaving normally only a few to be tackled through such force and violence as have "helped" Uganda to "win" for herself notoriety as a country riddled with problems of internal conflicts. It is, thus, only the latter type on which we focus in this chapter.

Conflicts of this kind assume in young or newly independent countries, like those of Africa, a degree of significance rarely possible in the older states of the world. For, as Clifford Geertz has argued,[2] in states of this kind politics tend to be characterized by intensive and furious inter-group rivalries which assume at times a life or death intensity. Groups based on party affiliations or on tribe, nationality, ethnicity, region, religion etc. fend for their particular interests in the new political situation created by independence and by the departure of the colonial rulers who used to serve as umpires, to keep the peace among such groups as they had brought together into a single colony. In the process, rules of the political game as prescribed e.g. in the independence constitutions - rules which spell out how and when to replace people in power, or to extend their tenure, or to dish out the meagre resources available to the various groups - are prone to be violated, with force or violent conflict remaining as the only means available to remedy group grievances.[3] In the case of Africa, we need not look far to identify states whose recent political histories conform to this classic statement on internal conflict - Rwanda, Burundi, Kenya, the Sudan, Nigeria, Zimbabwe, Chad - all have been going through the experience Geertz prophesied back in 1963.

2. A Brief Survey of Uganda's Violent Internal Conflicts

All the same, Ugandans, compared with other fellow Africans, would seem to have had more than their due share of violent internal conflicts. Indeed, as we meet at this seminar to discuss the problem of internal conflict in Uganda, a real and bloody war is raging in the North and North-East of the country between soldiers of the National Resistance Army and the so-called "Rebels" - a collective term for several groups of armed combatants, such as the Uganda Peoples' Army (UPA), the so-called Force Obote Back Again (FOBA) movement, the Holy Spirit Movement of Alice Lakwena, and others.

Whatever the war may be all about, and despite all the secrecy surrounding such internal conflicts, some highly disturbing consequences of the fighting have managed to filter through to the rest of Uganda and the rest of the world. Take, for example, the staggering "Kill Counts" as they come through the news media. The essence of war may indeed be violence. But when the violence is against one's own people, one cannot help being shaken by the staggering "Kill Counts" that have been reaching our ears. Yet even these are only a partial picture of what may be happening to human life in that apparently far-away corner of Uganda. Such counts do not, for example, include civilian non-combatants and their property - both, in a situation like this, like the grass on which two elephants are fighting. With human beings and their personal property, various social and economic institutions and other infrastructure catering for the general public also tend to go - things like schools, hospitals, ginneries etc., are either closed or destroyed outright in the course of fighting.[4]

This particular case of internal conflict has been presented first in this brief survey of violent internal conflicts in Uganda only because of its current topicality. Otherwise, pride of place should have gone to the older and better known tragedy of the "Luwero Triangle" which, for five full years until January 1986, darkened the political horizon of this country. Like the above war, and indeed like all "Guerilla versus Government" conflicts the world over, it was shrouded in secrecy, with neither the guerillas nor the Government sufficiently generous with public information about their encounters or progress.[5] Fortunately, with the coming to power of the National Resistance Movement/Army, that veil of secrecy has now been rolled back, and relatively much is now known about that tragedy. I myself had, in June 1986, the welcome opportunity, as a member of a Commission of Inquiry into the Local Government, of touring virtually the whole of Uganda, except for Acholi and Lango where the war with the Rebels was already escalating in violence.

Thanks to that opportunity, I traversed almost the whole of the "Triangle". While the human skulls heaped along some roads within the Triangle told their ghastly story, the blown-down or roofless structures along roads once booming with prosperity, told in their own grim way of the sorry toll that the war in the Triangle took of the inhabitants and their property. The deeply gullied roads and the unduly overgrown wild grass and bushes along them also in their own equally grim way bore witness to what the war in the Luwero Triangle must have meant.[6]

Both the war in the Luwero Triangle and the war in the North and North-East of Uganda have been singled out here because they are the most recent. Otherwise, they are only two stories in a long drawn-out saga of tragic violent and destructive internal conflicts that have bedevilled the political history of this country since political independence a quarter of a century ago. Numerous other examples are available for mention. These would include: the Rwenzururu Movement which, like a volcano, has been emitting violent conflict on and off since 1961; the seemingly eternal conflicts in and revolving around Karamoja; the whole "Buganda Question" with the many facets it has presented for internal conflict, particularly between 1961 and 1966. In all of these instances, various groups with diverse membership criteria as tribe, nationality, region, religion, ideology, "defenders of national integrity", etc. as those in power tend to claim, have come to use violence and force in the pursuit of their claims. The result has been killings and other damaging violence and destruction.

Quite obviously, the people of Uganda still have a lot to tell to each other as to why we have had to go through so many violent internal conflicts. Many have answers, but harbour them within their breasts. Now they should speak so as to understand their predicaments and be better able to overcome or to circumvent them. This is why this publication on internal conflict is a welcome development on behalf of a people, like ours, who do not talk to each other about their problems even when there is so much suffering and anger.

Now, if all the people of Uganda still have a lot of exchange of ideas to do to understand their predicament and the problem of violent internal conflict, why pick on the "North" in particular? Is this not to re-affirm the opinion that Northerners have been responsible for the lack of progress, as well as for the damages and suffering that this country has had to suffer?[7]

Let me offer the following assurances before we go any farther. First, it always takes at least two individuals or groups to have a conflict. Thus, any attitude on the part of any group in this country bordering on the notion "We are holier than they are" would clearly not be useful in the understanding of our internal conflicts. Secondly, here is my preliminary answer that I intend to elaborate upon in the rest of this paper: the issue as to whether or not there is a "Northern Question" is a matter both complex and delicate, necessitating very careful diagnosis of the problem and identification of remedies, and considerable tact and level-headedness in judgement. Let us now proceed to examine the issue more closely, beginning with this question: What do we exactly mean by the term "North" in the context of Uganda?

3. The "North" before Independence

Before Independence, the term "North" carried a distinctly political meaning. It referred specifically to the Northern Province, one of the four large administrative units above the district level, into which the British organized the country they had created at the turn of the century and had named Uganda. As such it referred collectively to the districts of Karamoja, Lango, Acholi, West Nile and its sub-district of Madi.

Prior to this, the peoples of the area had lived in different tribes or segments of tribes of various cultures and political set-ups. Culturally and economically each had its own forms of sustaining activities; and like other people on the globe, each of these tribes had its own cultural pride, too.[8] Trade, diplomatic relations and also warfare among them did take place, particularly between the neighbouring Lango and Acholi; the Acholi and Alur; the Acholi and Madi; and the Lugbara, Kebu, Lendu on the one hand, and the Alur on the other.

Significantly, in this period prior to the advent of British rule, inter-tribal exchanges and communication extended well into the South, covering a large portion of what is today referred to as Southern Uganda in contradiction to Northern Uganda. Mention must, in particular, be made of the political relationship that existed across the Nile between the Kingdom of Bunyoro-Kitara and other "kingly" houses in Northern Uganda.[9] Nor must we forget the political asylum and ready hospitality that the two major Southern Kings, Mwanga of Buganda and Kabalega of Bunyoro, received in the North when they fled from their pursuers, the British, who were bent on despoiling their kingdoms in order to create their own political regime at the end of the last century.[10] It is thus difficult to avoid the conclusion that there was a time, not in the far distant past, when the peoples of the North and those of the South could look at each other as individuals or groups to be accepted, rejected on the strength of their own humanity or friendship without such eye blinkers as we encounter later here. These were prejudices to be introduced during the years of British rule. Before that, people in this part of Africa now covered by modern Uganda could have hardly thought of the "North" or "Northerners" as constituting any particular question in inter-group relationships - as the question here before us might seem to imply.

But this generally happy state of affairs underwent considerable changes in the course of British rule. This author does not believe too much in assigning to the imperialists the blame for all Africa's woes. Nevertheless the hard facts of history sometimes make this unavoidable, and the best that can be done under the circumstance is to promise even-handedness in meting out blame in our treatment as to the causes that underlie the socalled "Northern Question". Further, another paper in this publication of the colonial roots of internal conflict goes into much greater detail on the matter than is possible here.[11] Suffice it here to say that the British made at least three contributions toward the creation of a "Northern Question", in the sense in which the term "Question" is applied to such problematical geographical areas as the Sudan, Palestine, etc.

First, through the system of indirect rule which they administered in discriminatory or different "doses" to different parts of the country, some parts of the country came to acquire more privilege than others. Here the North had quite easily the least privileged position. Secondly, through Britain's development and labour policies, the North became not only an under-exploited region, but indeed a reservoir of cheap and generally mean and contemptible labour to the South.[12] In some cases, Karamoja in particular, and West Nile and Madi, there was even outright under-government[13] - the inability of a government to fulfil roles expected of it and to respond effectively to the demands imposed upon it by its environment and people. In short, in the course of the sixty years or so that it lasted, British colonial policy, whether deliberately or not, was busy differentiating or setting apart the North from the rest of the country.

Another contribution toward differentiation between the North and the South came through the spate of scholarship in the field of Social Anthropology that swept through the country, particularly after World War II. This development served to categorize the peoples of the country into various ethnic/racial/-linguistic groups. Terms like the Bantu, the Nilotics, the Nilo-Hamites, the Sudanics, and all that, began to crop up in school classrooms, so that a child who was a "Nilotic" was now made to learn in his Primary 3 or 4 that he was; while another child in another class was similarly now made to know that he was from the "Bantu" group. All this was, in itself, not bad education. If the best study of man is himself, thence the desirability of making education to help us to know the various forms and positions we occupy in the cosmos.

One negative effect was, however, to emerge out of all this educational awakening in regard to the ethnic/linguistic/racial categories to which Ugandans belonged. Some people simply took it too seriously. "Categories" eventually came to assume too much significance, especially among the educated classes who have been the main "vector factors" for the dissemination of divisionism or sectarianism in this country today. However, more of that later on. Here let us stress that another important line of division between the North and the South had been drawn by using these categories, with the South being generally taken to be predominantly "Bantu" and the North generally taken as predominantly "Nilotic".

Nor was the matter allowed to end there. On the basis of political organization, social anthropologists had pumped into these categories notions of cultural superiority and inferiority. Those with large state organizations were seen as culturally superior, and those without them were culturally inferior. Here again the Bantu and the Nilotics diverged, as the Bantu were said to have large state organizations while the Nilotics and others were found wanting. Thus here was yet another important line of differentiation between the North and the South.

These lines of differentiation would all seem to put the North at a clear disadvantage as an underprivileged back-yard of Uganda inhabited by people whose cultures, at least politically, were generally presented as inferior. And yet these "disadvantaged" peoples did not articulate their deprivation and neglect in the form of a "Northern Question", as might easily have been the case for a people so much neglected and undergoverned as they were supposed to be, or as their neighbours and fellow ethnics in the Sudan have been attempting since Sudanese independence in 1956.

To be sure, at the beginning of the modern nationalist phase in Uganda in the early 1950's, Northerners felt quite uncertain and suspicious about the prospect of an independent Uganda, which some of them assumed, would be dominated by the Baganda. But then two developments intervened; and the manner they were handled for many years disarmed many Northerners of any fears that they might have had about their position in an independent Uganda.

The first was the new and stridently combative form that the Buganda Question assumed on the eve of Independence, with the founding of the Kabaka Yekka (King Only) or KY Party in 1961, and its strong determination to maintain the "political status quo" in relation to the position of the Kingdom of Buganda in an independent Uganda. The second development was the emergence of two nationalist leaders determined to uphold the unity and "national" integrity of Uganda: the late Benedicto Kiwanuka and Milton Obote, with their respective parties the Democratic Party (DP) and the Uganda Peoples' Congress (UPC) firmly behind them.

The first of these developments completely commanded much of the country's political attention and concern on the eve of Independence, overshadowing such lukewarm restlessness on the part of the Northerners as could have become hot enough to give rise to a major "Northern Question". Secondly, whatever the result of the triangular battle for national power between the KY, DP and UPC, as long as it did not lead to the complete or single-handed ascendancy of the KY Buganda party, it could not have exacerbated Northern fears about Buganda domination in the nation, as the North regarded both Kiwanuka of the DP and Obote of the UPC as genuine nationalists who would not disregard the interests of the North.

Obote and his UPC finally won the courtship of the KY and hence of official Buganda. The country thus proceeded to Independence without much ado or fear by the North about its position in an independent Uganda. Thus, even at this crucial stage there was still no significant "Northern Question" to worry about.

4. Independence and Political Dominance of the North

Not only did Obote and his UPC/KY alliance come to power at the centre: he held on to it for eight solid years without any break between the years for popular elections. Then another Northern man, Idi Amin, overthrew him and again held on to power for another eight solid years. When Amin finally had to make his exit from the centre, three Baganda leaders - Yusufu Lule, Godfrey Binaisa, and Paul Muwanga - had short spells of power at the centre, only to give way again to Obote. Nor was Obote's second regime really so short, as it lasted nearly five years from December 1980 to July 1985. Thus, between them, these two Northern leaders ruled Uganda for more than 20 years out of the first 25 years of Uganda's independence. Further, it must be remembered that Tito Okello and Bazillio Okello, two other Northerners, also came in after having expelled Obote from power in July 1985 to round off this story of almost uninterrupted Northern rule. Indeed, Uganda's first quarter century of independence has been the quarter century of Northern political dominance. But dominance also entails some unique problems of social and political relations among groups, as we must realize if we are to appreciate the place of the North in internal conflicts in Uganda today.

Generally, in Africa today, to have a president from a given sector of a country always results in other people taking it for granted that particular sector is as a whole dominant in the political system, even if the President attempts to spread out his appointments to higher offices of state as well as development projects throughout the country. Nor is it generally taken into account that the vast masses of the people from the President's home area will generally neither come near him nor acquire, during his tenure of office, anything extra to improve their hard lot in life. Should large numbers of the security forces also happen to hail from the president's particular sector of the country, then the verdict as to the dominance of that sector is deemed verified beyond any reasonable doubt. Again, the lot of the ordinary masses in the sector where such a president and his fellow tribesmen in the armed forces come from is not considered important: the particular sector of the country as a whole will be seen as in political ascendancy in the country.

Now, political dominance, as thus conceived, has consequences relevant to our analysis here, both for the so-called dominant group as well as for those other sectors of society who consider them to be dominant. Here, let us learn from the "Buganda Question" referred to briefly. In a large measure, that question concerned the politically dominant position of Buganda and how to secure it in the newly emerging independent Uganda. Two important consequences emerged. The first was the feeling of "specialness" or "apartness" felt in and about Buganda. The Relationships Commission of 1961, for example, articulated this correctly when it stated:

> The problem of Buganda overshadows all other problems in Uganda.[14]

How then was Buganda to relate to the rest of independent Uganda? There was also a second consequence. The reaction from outside to Buganda's political dominance was one of suspicion, fear, and even hatred in some quarters, resulting in political parties being formed in other parts of the country to face up to the challenge or "Question of Buganda".

And yet Buganda's so-called political dominance was a carefully circumscribed and restricted dominance that held sway only over Buganda and over affairs touching closely on Buganda. It was never as extensive in geographical area or in scope of responsibility as the political dominance that Obote, Amin and the two Okellos with their security forces appeared to enjoy throughout the country after Independence. If the far more limited political dominance Buganda enjoyed could have the two serious consequences observed above, what guarantees were there that these consequences would not manifest themselves in the relatively long period of Northern dominance?

The answer is: there were no guarantees. In fact the North came to be singled out as a special region enjoying an undue share of the national cake, particularly as presented by the numbers of men and officers in the security forces. Even concerning the civil service and in parastatal bodies, notwithstanding Obote's general disposition to spread out his appointments across the nation, murmurs could be heard, especially during the second regime. As for Amin, although he set off initially with a broad-based cabinet of highly educated men, he soon began to disband and to replace them mainly by Nubians/Moslems and other people - his main criterion being that the candidate be either a Nubian/Moslem or from West Nile. This, too, was noted and murmured about; and although Amin's arena for recruiting fellow Nubians or Moslems extended over the whole country, and even beyond sometimes, it went down in some people's minds as over-patronization of the North.

As we have noted in the case of Buganda, the second consequence of "regional specialness" is resentment, in the form of an urge to unity on the part of those who feel excluded. The North did not escape becoming the object of such resentment. While it started off unobtrusively around 1964 among Parliamentarians and within the UPC, resentment gathered considerable momentum, thanks to the unwitting contributions of both the Obote and Amin Government in keeping it alive. People in power suffer from a peculiar disadvantage in the context of internal conflict: through the multifarious executive decisions they must take, they easily run the risk of alienating many people.

This is the risk to which both Obote and Amin succumbed during their long tenure of power. A number of their decisions impinged upon Buganda and the Baganda, or had to be executed within the area of Buganda. Thus, Buganda's resentment became the pivot around which the move for unity against the North by non-Northerners came to revolve.

It was in this context that the "North" came to loom large, especially in the minds of some young intellectuals from the South, as a distinct problem or "Question" to be reckoned with head-on. This can best be showed by turning now to the period after Amin's exit from power. As will be recalled, the fall of Idi Amin was followed by a spell of freedom of the press and expression, eventually culminating in the general elections of 1980.

While those elections have since been shrouded in controversy, the campaign was conducted most vigorously and frankly on the campus of Makerere University. The leaders of all four contending political parties - the UPC, the DP, the UPM, and the CP- were welcomed and given a forum to address the University Community, always hosted by the University authorities as a matter of courtesy and decorum. Apart from such highly formal occasions, various members of the University community took up the cudgels on behalf of their respective parties in such informal fora as the Senior Staff Club, the Senior Staff Common Room, etc., to argue and further the causes of their parties in the campaign. It was on occasions like these that one frequently heard among non-Northerners the blunt assertion which went more or less like this:

> We are tired of Northerners - they have had enough of a chance to prove themselves, but have failed.

Indeed, even before the election campaign, this opinion had sufficiently formed in the minds of many Ugandans, particularly those then in exile who were about thinking about the future of their country.

The North and its place in the country - or more precisely, in the leadership of the country - had thus become a major question to be resolved. And this was a resolution to which neither the general elections, whether free and fair or rigged, or the displacement of Obote by the two Okello's - Tito and Bazillio - held the key. Since Independence, the North had become a problem in the eyes of many people, and the only way seemed to smash that problem, to make room for others in the national political scheme of things. If this interpretation is correct, as I contend it is, going to the bush was inevitable. Its consequence we now know, of course. However, in case one requires specificity: thanks to that war, what had increasingly become to some Ugandans a "Northern Question" during the 20 or so years of independence-namely continued Northern political dominance - was arrested, giving rise to a new political situation. How the North is fitting itself into this new situation is our next step in this analysis.

5. Recent Changes in the Political Character of the North

We have already seen how the North had been organized by the British into a single political unit. In appreciating the continued potential of the North as a political "Question" to the rest of Uganda as well as for devising suitable politics towards the North, we must understand the nature of the transformation that the traditional North has undergone as a political entity.

First, the large unit that the British had set up as Northern Province was very badly shaken up by the abolition of the structure that held it together politically, the post of the Provincial Commissioner for all the three provinces, outside Buganda, which carried these posts. True, other provincial officers who bore the responsibility for professional and technical duties in the province were left in place, but these could not bring the kind of political coordination that the existence, status, and prestige of the Provincial Commissioner had made possible.[15]

Accordingly, while both Obote and Amin were able to cash in politically on the support of Northern soldiers, in the absence of the central political institution of a Provincial Commissioner, centrifugal forces were also at work setting apart the various districts and peoples of the region. Eventually these forces were to propel them to wreak as much havoc on their own peoples of the North as they did on people elsewhere in the country. This is the pattern within which the military coup d'etat of Idi Amin in 1971 and the consequent wanton massacres of Acholi and Langi soldiers must be understood. In this regard, it has not been sufficiently appreciated that even before extending his murderous wrath all over the rest of the country, Amin had seen to it that even his own fellow West Nilers like Col. V. Ocima; Mr. Martin Okello, a former Member of Parliament; Mr. Martin Rubanga, a former Secretary for Defence, all of whom belonged to the Alur tribe, were massacred.

Eventually Amin's own time to go came in 1979; and with that a "re-action" against his home and his people in West Nile was launched by the Acholi and Langi, his fellow Northerners whom he had so ruthlessly misused, but who now had the better of him. The Tanzanian soldiers who overran his home town and area of Arua did almost everything humanely possible to preserve the area, perhaps for fear of being described by the outside world as ruthless revanchists. But the Acholi and Langi had no qualms on that score. Extensive destruction of life and property was therefore carried out, leaving much of Arua the eye-sore it is today in terms of destroyed building structures and many others in the process of construction which may remain uncompleted for years to come, because their owners were killed in this ruthless exercise of revenge.

Finally, as is well known, these two brotherly tribes themselves fell apart in 1985, with their quarrel culminating in the overthrow of the Obote II regime in 1985. The havoc and damage wreaked by Acholi soldiers upon Lira and the surrounding areas of their erstwhile ally, the Langi, again defy description and will remain for long a matter of great shame.

All in all, then, that is the new political picture of the North that emerges. Against this background of violent internal conflicts within even the North itself, it is difficult to put forward the North as a single political entity currently in any position to represent a serious "Question" to the rest of Uganda. In fact, just like the Italy of the 19th Century which von Metternich described before its unification as a mere "geographical expression", the North as a political entity could today also be described as a mere "geographical expression", lacking any internal political cohesion.

We still must reckon with one point on this sub-theme before leaving it altogether. Old beliefs or myths do die hard, and tend to hang around to help some people to sustain their collective moral or interests. It was, in fact, in this context that the late Hans J. Morgenthau made the following brilliant observation which I find highly apt in this connection:

> All nations live by myths. That is, they paint a picture of the past that satisfies their needs but does violence to the historic record. Some myths are beneficial. They are those that strengthen a nation's confidence in having been, and being able to do what the tasks of the moment demand of it...
>
> Other myths are pernicious. They draw from a distorted reality lessons for the understanding of the past and the charting of future action which please collective emotions, but lead judgement and action astray. They are a special curse which the past casts upon the future, a curse with which the dead threaten the living.[16]

The idea of the "North" of Uganda as a single monolithic political entity posing a question at the moment to the rest of Uganda would, in my view, be one such myth. But, to go along with Morgenthau, it would also be a dangerous myth as far as the national integrity of this country concerned, however suitable it may be for serving the sectarian interests of some people.

Not only is the North a mere geographical expression as this is written. It is in the terms of its boundaries a unit that is highly permeable politically. Therefore, people who mean well, whether they be from the East, Buganda or West, can penetrate it easily and do there such good national work as sowing the seeds of political unity and harmony, thereby promoting a speedy assimilation of the North into the rest of Uganda. The understanding between the NRM/NRA under Museveni and the UNRF under Moses Ali provides an example of such desirable penetration of the North. Similarly, extension of the recruitment ground of the NRA into Nebbi, Arua, and Madi districts and now even into Gulu, Kitgum and Apac districts provides yet another example of this kind of bona fide penetration. So are the efforts to spread the NRM ideology as embodied in the Ten Point Programme, and the innovation the Government intends to introduce in local government. Were it not for the current war in the North and North-East, these bona fide penetrations now being attempted mainly in West Nile would be possible in the rest of the North, too: hence the urgency of ending that war.

But just as "bona-fide" people are free to penetrate the North, so are those who are not politically well-meaning. These can do such evil things as sowing the seeds of disunity and discord, promoting in the process the alienation of the North from the rest of Uganda. This group is so important in the context of the theme in this book, that it deserves a word or two more to itself.

Any successful revolutionary change tends to bring to the fore in positions of leadership ideological zealots, fanatically committed not only to the ideology of the movement that brought about the change, but also to its discipline and code of behaviour. On its part, the National Resistance Movement now in power had a good supply of such people, particularly in the forefront of its leadership - the commanders and cadres, as they have been called. Indeed, a great part of their success in the "Luwero Triangle" and elsewhere was the fruit of the contribution of people of this type. But it would be remiss of us not to draw attention to certain lapses from the original code of commitment and behaviour now beginning to be noticed by the masses, particularly the masses in the North, in the ranks of those once so careful about their behaviour in the public eye.

Indeed, I find myself writing these paragraphs precisely on the day when the President himself has been reported to express concern about the behaviour of soldiers along these lines when he recently addressed a meeting of the Defence Council.[17] The behaviour of soldiers and other people from outside the North without good political will, behaviour that could sow the seeds of disunity and discord, and hence alienate the North from the rest of the country, includes the following: the wanton and careless application of insulting stereotypes that keep drumming into the ears of Northerners the highly questionable presumption that they are "primitive and backward", that they are "idiots" or "Banyanya" etc. NRM/NRA personnel addicted to such facile phraseologies are definitely not suitable apostles of conciliation or friendship to the North. Fortunately, the NRM/NRA has a large team to choose from; it should, therefore, not be a problem to replace such missionaries of alienation with others who can serve as missionaries of national conciliation and assimilation. Traditional cultures in Uganda are diverse, often very complex and highly sophisticated in their own unique ways. Moreover, cultures are sensitive aspects of group life: can any country really afford to have them tinkered with lightly by any Tom, Dick, and Harry, merely because they happen to wear military uniforms?

The other important matter of concern that could give rise to alienation in the North would be the behaviour and discipline of Government soldiers among civilians dwelling in largely rural communities. These civilians, by the very nature of the community within which they live, can be victimized, violated, or deprived of their possessions with almost complete impunity, since the state agencies which should act as "countervailing" forces against such wandering armed personnel are either not available or too distant from the rural setting. But, following on what the issue of the New Vision to which we referred in note 17 above has reported about the President's concern with indiscipline among soldiers, this particular issue seems now to be in good and proper hands.

So much, then, for the ease and generally encouraging prospects with which the one-time politically solid North may now be politically penetrated. But if we leave the story at this point, it would fail to convey the fullness of the point we wish to convey in this section. Let us proceed now to fill in that missing portion.

We have said that from the political perspective, the North is now not a political monolith, if it ever was; and is therefore now easily available for penetration by political forces and influences from the rest of Uganda. However - and this is the missing link we now wish to put in place - the penetration of peoples, whether in the narrower sense of political penetration, or in the much wider sense of cultural penetration, is never sound if it is only a one-way affair. When such penetration goes but one way, it can give rise to unnecessary and serious complications in inter-group relations. In the global context, the African states and the rest of the Third World nations are now complaining about precisely such complications - the problem of dependency in its multiple forms - political, cultural, economic, etc. Penetration must, therefore, always be a two-way affair, such that the other group from "outside" can come in while the group "inside" can also have ease of access to the "outside" group.

Concretely, the peoples of the North must also have free and unquestionable penetration into the rest of the country. For them this is a more crucial point, because the South, particularly the Kampala-Jinja area, is a metropolitan area, enjoying such facilities, amenities, and opportunities as have tended to draw rural people the world over to such metropolitan complexes. The educational, social and health institutions of this area, the employment opportunities, and so on, available here must be available to all other Ugandans outside this area, on the basis of equal opportunities and terms. The salient point here is that metropolitan areas are metropolitan areas, and that unless we want to go the way of Apartheid South Africa, they must be managed on the basis of an open door policy for all citizens of the countries in which they are situated.

In the course of preparing this Chapter, I personally had the opportunity of discussing the topic with a number of Northern friends living in Kampala. The point we have just been discussing was one of the greatest concern to them. Many feared that there was an apparently deliberate plot to dislodge or exclude Northerners from positions they held in Government and parastatal bodies, merely because they were from the North, so that they could be replaced by Southerners.[19] Others reported that some irresponsible people from the South had begun to urge them to go back and develop their places in the North instead of "wasting" time in the South which is already "developed". Still others reported rumours of such bizarre plans as to "localize" all education below the tertiary level, such that instead of being able to attend such prestigious and well established secondary schools in and around Kampala as Budo, Kisubi, Namagunga or Gayaza, one's child, irrespective of his or her merit, would have to attend the local so-called "Third World" school [20] near one's village in Pakwach in Nebbi District or in Nabilatuk in Moroto District in the North!

Disintegrative approaches of this kind quite obviously have little to do with the modern times in which Ugandans are not only now living, but into which they would like to advance more vigorously and more deeply. In terms of the North, if policies of this type by some misfortune should come to prevail, those who really desire to see one integrated Uganda will have missed a heaven-sent opportunity for the North to be fully assimilated into the rest of Uganda. Is it necessary to add to this what should be obvious, namely that the adoption of such policies would push us inexorably to what I presume no one wishes Uganda to have: a serious "Northern Question" at par more or less with such other contemporary issues as the "Southern Sudan Question", the "Palestinian Question", the "Black Question" in Apartheid South Africa, and so on?

Let us, however, end this sub-section on a far happier note. Towards that end, we submit that with the new development in the political position of the North and with some measure of good political will particularly within the country's political leadership, the North is now politically ripe for assimilation rather than alienation from this nation. Significant in this regard is that even the rebels fighting in the North - if the report of Atwoma Tiberio Okeny's Goodwill Mission is a fair summary of their position - would seem to be seeking for exactly this, in as far as the relation of the North to the rest of the country is concerned, as may be seen from the following extract from the Report of the Mission:

> The leaders of UPDM/A informed our mission that they are fighting for their survival and for the preservation of fundamental human rights in Uganda; for the integrity and independence of Uganda; for democracy, freedom and the establishment of an independent national army; for the introduction of a populist constitution; for peace and prosperity for all the people of Uganda.[21]

6. Conclusion: Is there a Northern Question?

As we said above, the answer to this question is complex. Although the North could once have assumed a posture in the politics of the country that might have made its place in Ugandan politics highly problematical, it did not assume such a posture. We are referring here to the period on the eve of Independence, when, with its many disadvantages - political, economical and educational - the North might have dragged its foot in the march towards independence or asked for special treatment to enable it to catch up with the others, or to have imbalances corrected, as Southern Sudanese have been clamouring for since the independence of the Sudan in 1956.

But it was a Northerner who took up the chief executive position in the country, and with the assistance of largely Northern security personnel, stayed long in power. He was followed subsequently by another Northerner, who again with the assistance of largely Northern/Nubian personnel also stayed long in power. Further when the latter eventually did fall from power, the very same first Northerner who had taken power of Independence returned to power, remaining for some five years, again with the support of largely Northern security personnel. This long period of over twenty years covered by these two Northerners was, unfortunately, the period in which internal conflicts became endemic in the country in the manner Clifford Geertz had postulated for the new states of Africa and Asia. These two Northerners, and security men who were predominantly

Northern, were thus deeply involved in executive decision-making relating to the many internal conflicts of their times and in their application and enforcement.

We here also postulated that in African politics people generally tend to think that when a leader comes from one section, then that leader and all the people from his section will benefit. In the same way, we now need to add their misdeeds tend to be also attributed to all the people from the section from which the leader comes. Both Obote and Amin and their people of the North must have come to be viewed in this way by people in the rest of the country - how else could one explain such sentiments as those commonly articulated during the electoral campaign of 1980 as: "We are tired of Northerners"?

Thus we may now submit as our second point that it could only by such reasoning that associates people from the sector from which a leader comes with the advantages and the misdeeds of that leader that one might say, in the context of the internal conflicts endemic in the years of Northern dominance, that there has been a "Northern Question" with the North and Northerners as the source of problems.

At this point we must sternly appraise the validity of this popular habit in African politics of associating the ordinary masses with such advantages enjoyed by their "sons" who are privileged to attain state power, as well as their misdeeds. This "rule-of-thumb" association is unfortunate and grossly unfair to the masses. We know only too well that the masses from such tribes/nationalities or regions continue generally in a world of their own, wallowing in their poverty as they have long done, without being rescued from such poverty by their "lucky" sons who happened to have reached the pinnacle of power in the state. That being the case, the ordinary masses of the North should not be so easily implicated in the bickerings, quarrels, killings, and extensive destruction that have tragically accompanied our internal conflicts, as some careless people might be led to do.

The Northern masses have continued to till their land, to tend their animals, and generally to attend to such of their chores as are required to eke out an unenviable existence in a context of unbearable poverty - all that without ever taking an axe or panga to harm any non-Northerner, because of politics. What is even more, such of these ordinary Northerners as did come to the South lived among Southern fellow countrymen so amicably that those of them in the rural areas of the South, particularly in Buganda, absorbed the cultures of the South absolutely. Indeed, some of them are now not only speaking Luganda fluently and without any strange accent, but have also given such typically Kiganda names as "Musisi", "Musoke", "Mukasa" to their children.

We need to make this distinction between the leaders and the masses, because as we pointed out at the end of Section 2, the issue we are dealing with is also a delicate one. In the course of these conflicts many Ugandans have lost their dear ones and possessions. It is, thus, not fair to associate the broad and innocent masses with the sufferings that the various conflicts have wreaked upon Ugandans.[22]

All the above had to do mainly with the Obote-Amin years in Ugandan politics. Let us now take our last step and advance into the present. Is there a "Northern Question" threatening us in this period? Our treatment has been very emphatic on this point. With the North now so badly disintegrated politically, we must conclude that in as far as such a question is associated with Northern dominance in national politics, there exists no peculiarly Northern Question of a political kind. Thus we maintain that with tact and political goodwill on the part of all, particularly that of our leadership, today's North is ripe for assimilation rather than alienation. But the potential for the North to turn itself into a political "Question" in the sense in which the Southern Sudan, for example, has become a question or a problem hanging over the Sudan, should not be forgotten either. The final section of our treatment explored the circumstances under which such a grim prospect might become a reality, although it is to be hoped that, with enlightened political leadership, all that will remain in the realm of academic speculation.

Finally, let me now point out the obvious: that our analysis here has been done mainly through the political periscope. Should we have employed another equally relevant periscope - namely the socio-economic one - our answer would have been far less re-assuring than it is now. For, when we view the North through the latter periscope, its character as a problem area in the socio-economic transformation of Uganda becomes only too apparent. That, however, is an exercise for another occasion.

Notes

1. The phenomenon of internal conflict caught the attention of Aristotle, who discussed it in his Politics as far back as the 4th century B.C. While in our modern times sociologists, economists, political scientists, etc. - all have made substantial contributions to our understanding of the importance of the phenomenon within social groups. Sille, D.L. (ed.): The International Encyclopedia of the Social Sciences. London: Collier Macmillan Publishers, 1972, Vol.3, contains a good synopsis of their respective contributions.
2. Geertz, C.: "The Integrative Revolution: Primordial Sentiments and Civil Politics in the New States" in Geertz, C.: Old Societies and New Societies: The Quest for Modernity in Asia and Africa. London: The Free Press of Glencoe, 1963.
3. I have personally found Geertz' argument so compelling that I have had to refer to it again and again, although in different contexts, as for example, in my article "Soldiers and Society in Uganda: Some Lessons from the Past", in a forthcoming issue of Mawazo.
4. Apart from what the newspapers and Radio Uganda have been releasing on this war, the author had the opportunity to glance through some of the papers prepared by Mr. Tiberio Okeny and his "Goodwill Mission" to the Rebels in the "war zone" in Northern Uganda - Dec. 1986 - April 1987. He was given to understand that these papers are open documents, hence his taking the liberty to read them and to quote from them here.
5. Actually, Luganda-speakers in and around Kampala must have been relatively much better informed than the rest of us who did not speak Luganda and who, therefore, had to depend on the morsels of news the then English Weekly DP Newspaper Munnansi kindly chose to let us have. The paper, incidentally, folded up its business as soon as the Obote regime was overthrown, something which many Ugandans regret and do not understand.
6. These trips were made between July and December 1986. The vigorous programme of rehabilitating the area that the Government launched had not yet begun to make much of a difference.
7. See Section 4 where the slogan "We are tired of Northerners" that is discussed there appears to imply this opinion.
8. The theme of cultural pride will be picked up again for treatment in a subsequent section of this paper.
9. According to Aidan Southall, for example, a number of Alur Chiefs either claim their descent from the kings of Bunyoro or had to come for confirmation of their title after accession to chiefship - see Southall, A.: Alur Society: A Study in Processes and Types of Domination. Cambridge: W. Heffer & Sons Ltd., 1953, pp. 218-219.
10. Ingham, K.: The Making of Modern Uganda. London: George Allen & Unwin Ltd., 1958.
11. See the paper by Lwanga-Lunyiigo, S.: "The Colonial Roots of Internal Conflict in Uganda."
12. There is perhaps no better way to impress upon readers the importance of this labour "reservoir" than by explaining that in the case of West Nile the whole of that complex that now comprises the military barracks at Pakwach was fully occupied twice a week by indentured workers from upper West Nile who then took the "SS Robert Coryndon" to come by water and subsequently by train to Jinja to work on the Kakira and Lugazi Sugar Estates. But many other Northerners from West Nile itself, Acholi and Lango found their own other way to cheap labour in the South. The category of "mean and contemptible" labour must include for this period both the Police and the King's African Rifles (K.A.R.) about which Southerners, particularly Baganda, were none too keen at this stage, even if one takes into account that official Government policy started off initially by not encouraging them, as Ian Grahamme correctly confirms in his book: Amin and Uganda. London: Granada, 1980, p. 27.

13. The theme of "undergovernment" as opposed to misgovernment or even dictatorship about which we speak so often has been fascinating me recently; and I do hope that my continued reflections over it will one day yield at least one paper in which I relate it to some of the contemporary political ills in Uganda.
14. Uganda Protectorate: Report of the Uganda Relationships Commission. Entebbe: Government Printer 1961, p. 28.
15. Ibid, Chapter 19, Para. 448.
16. Hans J. Morgenthau, in his "Foreword" to Tang Tsou's monumental study of the political pathology behind what the latter aptly titled: America's Failure in China, 1941-50. Chicago: The University of Chicago Press, 1963, p. VII. Morgenthau's own examples of pernicious myths were the idea that Algeria was an integral part of France, and the idea that "America lost China" in 1949 when Mao-Tse-Tung and his communists swept into power, although China never "belonged" to the United States.
17. The New Vision, 18 Sept.,1987, p. 1.
18. Incidentally this is one of the developments about which most Northerners I have talked to have expressed grave concern and anger. Thus, the sooner action is taken to advise NRM/NRA personnel about the harm to North-South relationship this careless verbal assault on the cultural status of the peoples of the North is doing, the better for the nation.
19. In the report that Mr. Atwoma Tiberio Okeny's "Goodwill Mission" to the Rebels submitted to the Government on its return that we mentioned earlier in the chapter, "The discriminatory dismissal of serving men and officer in the Uganda Police and Prison forces and other officials from public institutions" is presented as one of the "Immediate causes" for the UPDM/A involvement in the war in the North. The report is included as appendix 2 in this book.
20. This is how some people in and around Kampala contemptuously refer to the many secondary schools that mushroomed in the Obote II regime in almost every constituency in the country.
21. From the report of the "Goodwill Mission".
22. I have dealt with the role of Northern soldiers with whose misdeeds the ordinary masses of the North should, again, not be associated, in another paper: "Soldiers and Society in Uganda: Some Lessons from the Past", in a forthcoming issue of Mawazo.

Yoramu Barongo

Ethnic Pluralism and Political Centralization: The Basis of Political Conflict

1. Introduction

Ugandan society is characterized by two inherently contradictory and conflictual social and political formations. On the one hand, ethnic pluralism with its multiple centres of interests, identities, loyalties, patterns of action and power, features as a basic structure of society. On the other, political centralization, which is basically incompatible with the process of political pluralism, is the dominant form of the country's political organization.

We propose to argue and demonstrate here that the phenomenon of excessive centralization of power in a multi-ethnic political context is an important factor in explaining the incidence of political conflict and violence of the kinds that have characterized political life in Uganda since Independence. In a political arrangement like that of Uganda, there is only one major centre of political power. And this means two things that tend to create forces of political conflict. First, the base for political activity and decision-making is narrowed to a uni-focal political arena, allowing the participation of only a small section of political elites. Secondly, in the absence of effective lower levels of participation, the struggle to gain access to political power at the centre gives rise to acute political competition. The exclusion of some sections of society from political decision-making and the struggle of the elite members of ethnic groups to control the centre, heighten and intensify political conflict. Many observers, particularly those of foreign (western) origins, have seen this struggle, which in recent years has assumed violent dimensions, as an expression of ethnic or "tribal" conflict and hostility. Contrary to such views, the analysis in this presentation attempts to show that the violent conflicts that have bedevilled Uganda since 1966 are basically political in origin, cause and effect. My contention is that the struggle for participation and control of political power at the centre is a major cause of political conflict in this country.

In the end, decentralization of power and the creation of a strong system of local government are advocated here as means of minimizing political conflict in Uganda. Decentralization means diversifying the centres of power and widening the areas of political participation. This, in effect, leads to the diffusion of conflict among the various centres of power and thus to the attenuation of the impact and effect of conflict on the political process and the political system. Above all, decentralization encourages local autonomy. It provides opportunities to the broad section of the national population to control local decisions that affect their daily lives and their immediate environment. Such popular and widespread participation in political life helps to stabilize the political process at the local and national levels. The Nigerian experience is cited as an example of how the principle of decentralization of power tends to mitigate conflict and ensure political stability and socio-economic progress. But first, let us examine the theoretical aspect of the relation between pluralism and political conflict.

2. Pluralism and Conflict

Basically, "pluralism" refers to a situation in which there exist in society many groups of various sizes which may have different values, interests, ideas and aspirations.[1] Applied to social and political organization, pluralism denotes two tendencies in group relations. On the one hand, depending on the characteristics of the groups involved, pluralism may result in inter-group consensus, harmony and understanding. On the other, the dynamics of pluralistic life may produce conflict situations leading to incompatibilities in social and political relationships among groups. Social scientists have identified three models of pluralism which account for these two tendencies in group relations: <u>social pluralism</u>, <u>cultural pluralism</u> and <u>ethnic pluralism</u>. A brief review of each of those models is necessary in order to clarify the theoretical thrust of the main themes of the paper.

2.1. Social Pluralism

Social pluralism is essentially a model that explains the persistence of democratic stability in a plural society.[2] The pluralist model of democracy sees society as made up of several social groups of various sizes and interests. These groups are independent of each other and the government, and provide a basis for the dispersal of power in society. Groups intervene between the individual and the government; they check each other's power and that of the government, thereby discouraging the monopoly of power by any one group or by the government.

The various groups in such a society are organized around the common interests and needs of their members. Membership is voluntary, and group solidarity rests on civic ties among its members rather than on primordial or sacred particularism. Individuals join groups in order to advance their interests and provide for their needs in a collective manner. Also, an individual may belong to more than one group, thus creating a network of interlocking relationships among the various groups. Common among the groups in such a plural society are the many groups organized to cater for the social, economic, professional and civic interests of their members - such as trade unions, chambers of commerce, medical and bar associations, women's and youth organizations, etc. Such groups provide platforms for the expression of numerous demands and create centres for political participation at group level.

Since the various groups have different interests, needs and demands, the interaction among themselves and the government will inevitably create situations of conflict. However, the intensity of any violent tendencies of group conflict will here be mitigated by the existence of underlying value consensus among group leaders and members. Through the process of negotiation and compromise, individuals and groups can arrive at mutual adjustment and accommodation of the various competing claims. This mechanism enables society to maintain its equilibrium and consensus in the context of continuing conflict. In addition, the overlapping membership of individuals in various groups creates cross-cutting loyalties, thereby providing channels for integrative communication among different groups. On the whole, the theory of social pluralism believes in the importance of social groups as the basis of democratic stability and integration of society.

It should be noted here, however, that pluralist democracy does not promote or guarantee the dispersal and balancing of political power in society. On the contrary, social pluralism actually encourages the acquisition and monopoly of power by a few individuals and groups, providing grounds whereby the interests of the stronger group of individuals can pre-empt and dominate public policy. Pluralist democracy places a high premium on the freedom of interest-group activity and on the principle that public policy should result from the free interplay of the various competing interests. But attempts at balancing the various group interests become problematic in practice, because what emerges as the common or public interest represents no more than the interests of the stronger and better organized groups.

While allowing competition, therefore, pluralist democracy also promotes in reality the interests of organized vested interests and strong pressure groups which disproportionately represent the interests of wealth and those of a minority section of society that controls and dominates the means of production. Pluralist politics does not safeguard the interests of the weaker groups, which, in terms of numbers, may represent the interests of the majority.[3]

There is no doubt that Uganda has a pluralist social structure: but this structure is dominated by a few, well-organized and urban-centred elite and business interests. The power and influence of these groups stand in stark contrast to the powerlessness of the ill-organized groups of the masses of the workers and peasants. Thus, whereas social pluralism is a reality of Uganda's social and political scene, it does not function effectively to provide centres for the popular participation of a wide section of the national population. In terms of the need for mass participation, social pluralism provides no viable alternative to the requirements of diverse centres of power at the various decision-making levels which a decentralized political structure can provide. Hence, conflicts arising out of the struggle for political participation and power continue to persist in the context of social pluralism.

2.2. Cultural Pluralism

In recent years social scientists have developed another model of pluralism - that of <u>cultural pluralism</u>.[4] Unlike the social pluralism model, which finds in the diversity of groups a mechanism for conflict, consensus and stability, the cultural pluralism framework portrays the relation among groups as one of irreconcilable conflict that often leads to political violence and the malintegration of society. In a culturally compartmentalized society, people are divided not so much over concrete social, political or economic interests as over deep-seated cleavages arising out of primordial or sacred ties. Cultural groups exist naturally: they are not voluntary, because membership is reserved for people born into them. Examples of such groups include racial, caste and religious groups. And because membership is exclusive, individuals become highly identified with and attached to their groups. Thus one finds a powerful consensus on values within a group but not between groups. This makes it difficult for the various groups to cooperate and integrate together. Normally, one group will monopolize political power and use its control of the institutions of government to dominate others. Accordingly, political order, stability and social conformity are here maintained by coercion and not by any consensus on values.

The analytical rigour of the cultural pluralist model rests on its assumption that the various groups constituting society exist as separate communities, each with its own distinct cultural values, institutional patterns and political orientations. As was the case when first formulated and applied,[5] the model does reflect the realities of a colonial society where factors of race and culture made it difficult for the various cultural groups to interact and cooperate, and where wealth, power and prestige were distributed along racial lines. Also in contemporary Africa, this model has practical utility in analyzing and understanding the problems of conflict and political violence existing in the racially and culturally heterogeneous white-dominated societies in southern Africa. But in Uganda and the rest of Africa, the cultural pluralism model seems of little value as a viable framework for understanding situations of conflict and group violence today.

2.3. Ethnic Pluralism

Attempts to account for the endemic conflicts that sometimes manifest themselves in traumatic violence in the racially homogeneous but ethnically plural societies of Africa led to the development of the ethnic pluralism model by Leo Kuper and M.G. Smith.[6] This model sees African societies as made up of many ethnic groups of various sizes and influence, distinct from each other on the basis of language, social organization and other socio-cultural characteristics. Each ethnic unit forms a political entity that may constitute a centre of political power and claim the identity and loyalty of its members. But unlike the cultural groups which live side by side but separately, ethnic groups share a certain amount of values deriving from a basically common culture and race as well as common historical and contemporary experiences. This enables people to interact and live together. However, because of differences in interests and the desire to maximize influence in a competitive situation, groups will tend to use the resources available to them to assert themselves in relation to other groups. Using ethnic identity and solidaristic ties as weapons of political bargaining, the elite cadre of the various groups thus engage in constant struggles for the control of state power. And when they gain this control, they use political power to suppress the interests of other groups, ensuring the dominance of members of their own ethnic groups in all sectors of employment and social and political life. Such a state of affairs creates tensions among the "in" and the "out" groups, and leads naturally to political conflict which in turn will often lead to violence.

2.4. Shared Characteristics

Two basic characteristics of the pluralist models discussed above should be noted. First, all three types of pluralism imply the existence of multiple and diverse centres of power and political activity. Recognizing this reality is important in any political arrangement aimed at maintaining a stable political process. In a pluralist democracy, these centres are recognized as independent centres of power, influence and political action. The activities of the various groups are utilized to mitigate conflict and to integrate society. On the other hand, political centralization tends to suppress the activities of independent groups and to destroy these groups as centres of mass political participation.

A second fundamental characteristic is that conflict is the basic feature underlying the process of group relations and interaction. In social pluralism, conflict is mitigated by the underlying consensus on values. In cultural pluralism, conflict is contained through coercion and the political domination which one cultural group maintains over others. With regard to ethnic pluralism, the relation between groups is characterized by competition and rivalry, not hostility and suspicion, as is the case with relations among cultural groups. So, the less frequently ethnic groups are made to compete among themselves for power or resources, the fewer situations will be created for conflicts to develop among them. Ethnic conflicts, particularly those of a violent kind, can therefore be avoided through a political arrangement that allows little competition and rivalry among the groups. Such an arrangement would give relative autonomy to ethnic groups to make decisions affecting the control and utilization of local resources.

It is to this political device of managing conflicts among ethnic groups in Uganda since colonial times that this analysis now turns.

3. Political Accommodation of Ethnic Pluralism: Background

Characteristically, colonial administration in Uganda was based on a system that recognized the multi-ethnic nature of society. Following the 1900 Agreement, the British proceeded to establish a system of administration in which territories or districts demarcated along ethnic lines became the basic political and administrative units.[7] These units, particularly the kingdom areas and more especially Buganda, were given considerable autonomy by the well-known British colonial system of indirect rule. Whereas the British controlled the central government and administration, the power for managing local affairs was retained and exercised by the local political and administrative elites, within the overall colonial policy and under the supervision of the colonial government agents. Thus the kingdom and district political and administrative units provided traditional elites and, later, an increasing number of educated Africans, with a wide range of opportunities for political participation and decision-making.

4. The Local Government System

The 1949 Local Government Ordinance strengthened further the system of local government, as kingdoms and districts became the basic structures through which the country was administered. Increasingly, it became a deliberate policy of the colonial government to encourage educated Africans to work in their respective local government administrations, leaving the central government to British officers.[8] Consequently, local governments became the foci of identity and loyalty for African elites and centres of political participation.

The colonial system of local government, as established in Uganda, had inherent mechanisms of preventing the development of conflicts among ethnic groups. In the first place, the system made sure that there were no major areas of competition and struggle over which ethnic groups could come into contact and conflict. By and large, ethnic groups were politically kept apart from each other. There was no struggle to control the centre and the resources involved, because these were under the exclusive control of the central colonial government. Since a substantial amount of power to make local decisions was decentralized and diffused among local government units, and since these units controlled critical resources such as employment as well as providing opportunities for participation to many traditional and educated elites, ethnic groups had only limited areas of contact where conflicts could develop among them. Dispersing power among local political units ensured that the centre was kept under relatively less pressure of political activity. For the ethnic groups, the centre was not an object for competition and struggle among them - and it is precisely this service that enabled the colonial government to maintain political stability and social harmony in potential situations of explosive ethnic conflict.

5. The 1962 Independence Constitution

The need to control and accommodate conflict arising out of ethnic pluralism was a major factor in determining the structure and provisions of the 1962 Constitution which the British left behind at Independence.[9] The Independence Constitution was indeed an ingenious act of social engineering that reflected an understanding of the complexity of Uganda's social and political forces on the part of the departing British. It sought to continue and strengthen the experiment that had begun early in colonial times of dispersing power among the various ethnic units and broadening areas of mass political participation. The main features of the Constitution aimed specifically at avoiding the possibilities of ethnic tensions and conflicts included granting greater degrees of autonomy to kingdom and, to a lesser degree, district administrations; establishing a strong system of local government; and expanding areas of local political participation and representation in the form of elected councils for each district. Let us look at this important feature of the Constitution in greater detail.

Uganda's Independence Constitution was a unique document that contained both elements of unitarism and federalism. This in itself was a reflection of the country's peculiar social and political structure that needed an intricate arrangement capable of holding the multi-ethnic nation together in relative peace and stability. Required to avoid the problem of ethnic conflict was a political device which the British had tried before with remarkable success: a device, as already mentioned, that provided ethnic groups with sufficient powers to conduct their own affairs and which, therefore, left the centre relatively free from ethnic-based political activity. As long as ethnic groups enjoyed such powers, they could regard the centre as less important as an object of struggle for control. Increasingly, then, a wider section of traditional and modern elites were inclined to seek political participation in local units rather than at the centre. And this device had the effect of maintaining political stability by decongesting the centre of the heat of political struggle and conflict. It is only the nationalist political elites who, unlike the tradition-bound elites, had visions and aspirations that transcended the parochial ethnic concerns, that organized nationalist movements which eventually defeated British colonialism. It is the same nationalist elites who at Independence took over control of the government at the centre.

In full recognition of this need, therefore, the 1962 Constitution decentralized political power, dispersing it among the various local units with varying degrees of autonomy. Buganda, the largest and most prestigious kingdom in the country, was granted full federal status in relation to the centre, while the smaller kingdoms of Bunyoro, Toro, Ankole and the territory of Busoga were each granted federal status of a lesser degree. The remaining ethnic groups which were organized in district political units and which historically did not have hereditary traditional rulers, were to maintain unitary relationships with the central government.

In terms of power, the kingdom of Buganda with its own government and system of administration enjoyed considerable autonomy and controlled a wide range of resources.[10] At the centre of political activity was the institution of the Kabaka (the King) and the Great Lukiiko - the Assembly - constituted by a large number of elected representatives. Administration was organized in ministries, each headed by a political Minister. As a political unit built around the Baganda ethnic group, the Buganda Kingdom government provided a wide range of avenues for highly skilled employment in its system of administration. It also provided broad areas of political participation to a wide section of both traditional and educated Baganda elites. Indeed, many Baganda political elites had built viable political careers in the Buganda political system; they were forced to turn to national politics only after the destruction of the kingdom in 1966.[11] As long as the kingdom government existed as a local political unit, it served to absorb thousands of political and administrative elites and thereby prevent the build-up of conflicts at the centre.

The powers which Buganda enjoyed under the 1962 Constitution, as well as the basic political and administrative institutions which existed in the kingdom, were to be found also in other kingdoms, although of relatively less importance and significance. Thus, each kingdom government had an elected assembly as the centre of political activity and decision-making. It had also comparatively smaller complement of ministerial departments around which the administrative system of the kingdom government was organized. Like the Buganda Government, the other kingdom governments, too, provided opportunities for employment and political participation to large sections of traditional and educated elites, thus relieving pressure that might otherwise have been exerted on the central government by people pursuing these values and goals.

For the non-kingdom unitary districts, the Constitution provided for the devolution of power by the central government to an elected council in each district. Essentially, these districts were directly governed by the centre, but the councils exercised powers and performed functions conferred upon them by law. At Independence, district councils derived their power from, and their functions were defined by, the Local Administration Ordinance of 1962. The functions of these councils were of such magnitude and importance as to necessitate the establishment and maintenance of a system of local administration employing thousands of local traditional and modern elites. As local political and administrative units, therefore, district administrations catered for the needs of employment and political participation, while keeping away from the centre a large section of politically active elites.

Thus we find that the 1962 Constitution embodied important features of political pluralism. The Constitution recognized the political life of ethnic groups by providing for the decentralization and dispersal of power among the political units of the various groups. This principle of constitutional pluralism regulated and controlled ethnic conflicts and stabilized the political process at the national level. As we shall show presently, the abolition of this constitutional provision and safeguard was to signal the entry into national politics of bitter and generally violent ethnic conflict and struggle.

A further legal provision that strengthened the foundations of the politics of political pluralism in Uganda was the Constitutional Heads (Elections) Act No. 66 of 1963.[12] Enacted by the National Assembly barely a year after Independence, the Act indicated the magnitude of the pressure of non-kingdom ethnic groups for more power, recognition and status. The Act provided for the election by District Councils of Constitutional Heads, to occupy the status and perform functions broadly similar to those of the hereditary rulers in the kingdom areas. This Act further expanded the areas of political participation at the local level. Indeed, some notable national political elites did relinquish their positions at the centre to become Constitutional Heads of their districts.[13]

The foregoing analysis has focused on political and institutional arrangements for the control of political conflict and inter-ethnic political violence. As already indicated, these arrangements were to be found in two areas of colonial initiative. The first was the system of local government organized around ethnic groups as political and administrative units. These units were given wide-ranging powers to deal with matters and problems of local concern. The second arrangement was enshrined in the Independence Constitution which decentralized and liberalized the political structure, giving definite constitutional powers to local political units both federal and unitary. As long as these arrangements remained in force, the country enjoyed periods of relative stability, peace and socio-economic development. But this was not to last long, as the proceeding discussion will attempt to show.

6. Trends towards Political Centralization: The Context of Political Conflict in Uganda

For approximately four years, the central government led by Prime Minister Apollo Milton Obote remained relatively stable, strong and free from traumatic conflicts. Its main political challenges and pre-occupations were confined largely to the role of refereeing over conflicts and disputes among local political units, mainly Buganda and Bunyoro.[14] But by and large, the kingdom and district administrations remained inward-looking, apparently content with the powers and functions conferred upon them by the Constitution and other laws under it. As long as the central government refrained from tampering with these powers and functions and was seen as fair in dealing with matters of concern to ethnic groups, local political units remained largely disinterested in politics at the centre. But the moment the central government started encroaching on the powers of the federated states, particularly those of Buganda, and was perceived to be using its powers unfairly to suppress the interests and aspirations of local political entities, then the relationship between the central government and local administrations became increasingly strained.[15] Gradually, these strained relationships between the centre and the local political units, particularly Buganda, forced the local units to enter the central political arena to assert themselves.[16] In the face of such challenges emanating from other centres of power, the central government reacted by attempting to reassert its supremacy over local political units. The increasingly developing conflicts between Buganda and the central government provided opportunity for the central government to accumulate more power by undermining the powers of the local political units. In other words, as time went on, the central government embarked on a consciously calculated process of political centralization which drew more and more local political entities and their most active political elites into the imbroglio of political competition and struggle at the centre.

The process of political centralization passed through three phases representing a period of fundamental political changes in the country's post-independence history. There were (1) the Buganda crisis of 1966 that resulted in the demise of the foundations of political pluralism in Uganda - the 1962 Constitution; (2) the advent of the 1967 Constitution that abolished kingdoms; finally, (3) the imposition of the one-party state in 1969, which signalled the end of the politics of institutional and legal opposition and conferred an authoritarian outlook on the central government.

Coming from Lango district, a non-kingdom area, and guided by the "revolutionary-centralizing" philosophy,[17] Milton Obote was culturally and political inclined to prefer a unitary form of government for the whole country. During the Constitutional Conference in London in September 1961, Obote came out strongly in favour of supreme powers for the central government. But pressures from the kingdoms, particularly Buganda, led to the splitting of state powers between the centre and the federal states. This constitutional encumbrance and the tendencies of Buganda to guard its federal status jealously against the encroachment of the central government prevented Prime Minister Obote from pursuing his vision of political centralization as early as he would have wished. The opportunity for fulfilling this vision was later presented by the events that led to the 1966 crisis, which Obote handled to his advantage with political skills that earned him admiration even among his political opponents.

7. The 1966 Crisis

The 1966 crisis was a culmination of two main political developments. The first was the break-up in 1964 of the ruling alliance between two political parties - Obote's Uganda Peoples Congress (UPC) and Buganda's Kabaka Yekka (KY).[18] This lead to strained political relations between Obote's Central government and the Kabaka's Buganda government based at Mengo. The second development was internal factional conflicts within the UPC which resulted in the arrest and detention of some of Obote's ministers, the suspension of the 1962 Constitution and further deterioration of relations between Buganda and the central government. As these developments have been fully documented elsewhere,[19] only a short outline will be given here.

In what was seen to be an "Unholy Marriage", the UPC led by Milton Obote entered into an alliance with Kabaka Yekka in 1961. The aim was clearly to oust the Democratic Party (DP), led by Ben Kiwanuka, from power[20] at the pre-Independence general elections later scheduled for April 1962. The alliance was seen as "unholy" because of the evidently divergent socio-political outlooks of the two parties. The KY was basically a traditionalist party preoccupied with glorifying and preserving the institution of the Kabakaship and protecting Buganda interests. The UPC on the other hand had leaders with a modern vision of the State-persons who exhibited nationalist outlooks and tendencies in favour of a unitarist government. By and large, the UPC-KY fraternity was seen as a marriage of convenience whose inherent contradictions would sooner or later cause problems for the alliance itself.

The alliance consisted of a series of mutual understandings between the UPC and KY. One of these was that KY would have the exclusive right to field all candidates in Buganda in competition with the DP in the event of a direct election to the National Assembly, while the UPC would field candidates only elsewhere in Uganda. The two parties would then join forces at the national level in Parliament. Details were worked out as to how the two parties were to share power if the allegiance won the elections.

The 1962 Constitution provided for direct elections to the Buganda Lukiiko and gave powers to the Lukiiko to decide whether Buganda's 22 representatives to the National Assembly were to be directly elected by the people, as was to be the case in the rest of the country, or nominated by the Lukiiko. Held early in 1962, elections to the Lukiiko turned out to be a contest between KY and DP which the KY won overwhelmingly. Then during the national elections in April of that year, the Lukiiko decided that Buganda's representatives to Parliament were to be nominated by the Lukiiko. This left the DP without any representatives from Buganda, because those nominated by the Lukiiko to represent Buganda in Parliament were all KY candidates. With UPC winning the majority of seats in the rest of the country,[21] the combined strength of the Lukiiko nominees and the UPC's elected representatives placed the UPC-KY alliance in power.

Uganda, therefore, entered Independence with the UPC-KY delicate political outfit in power. But this was not destined to last long. Incompatibilities between the two parties did not permit them to work harmoniously together, and soon the basic divisions and conflicts between them came into full view. At first Obote had to tolerate many of the problems caused by KY being in government. But when the UPC became increasingly strong and dominant as a result of several cross-overs in Parliament, mainly by DP members, Obote summarily terminated the alliance in August 1964 and removed KY ministers from office. This meant the end of the working relationship between Buganda and the central government and plotted the path of political confrontation between the two. Indeed, this tendency towards the gradual monopolization of power by one group - the UPC - ushered in the beginning of a period of political conflict at the centre.

Yet it was contradictions within the UPC itself, rather than the break-up of the party's alliance with KY, that were to trigger off the 1966 crisis. From its very formation in 1960, the UPC could be said to consist of two factional tendencies: one progressive and socialist-inclined, the other conservative and pro-capitalist. These factions came into open conflict and struggle for the control of the party during the 1964 Annual Delegates Conference of the UPC held in Gulu Town. In the election to the key positions of Secretary-General of the party, the radical socialist-inclined incumbent, John Kakonge, lost to the challenge of Grace Ibingira, who represented the conservative capitalist wing of the party. The accendency of the ambitious Ibingira to the powerful post of party General-Secretary placed him in a position in which he began to aspire to the leadership of the party itself and ultimately of the government, both positions held by Obote at the time. Through scheming, manipulations and forming of strategic alliances, Ibingira and his supporters in the party and government sought to undermine the power and position of the prime minister, with the sole aim of throwing

Obote out of power. In one politically significant incident in February 1966, Ibingira and his group collaborated with DP and KY Members of Parliament to support a motion tabled by a leading KY member, Daudi Ocheng, accusing Prime Minister Obote, three of his close ministers and army chief of staff, Col. Idi Amin, of impropriety in receiving large sums of money. (These were the proceeds from the sale of gold and ivory allegedly derived from the involvement of the Uganda army in the 1964-65 Congolese rebellion.) In particular, the motion called for the immediate suspension of Col. Amin who, apparently referred to in the motion as the leading army officer, was charged together with some members of the government of planning to overthrow the Constitution. Interestingly, before proceeding to undertake an upcountry tour, Obote had summoned the UPC parliamentary group, which formed the majority in Parliament, and decided collectively that Ocheng's motion would not be allowed to be tabled for discussion. But as soon as Obote left Kampala, the motion was not only tabled and discussed but was also adopted by the sitting UPC MPs in conjunction with DP and KY MPs. A lone dissenting vote was registered by John Kakonge.

The political implications of this motion were enormous. A top military officer was to be suspended, a decision certainly destined to cause uneasiness in the leadership and ranks of the army. As was common elsewhere in Africa that year, such action would probably have led to military intervention and the overthrow of Obote. Even more significantly, Obote and his close ministers were to be investigated for gross misdemeanour in receiving and putting to private use unauthorized funds. Such action was calculated to undermine Obote's power and source of legitimacy as the leader of the government.

However, Obote took this challenge with characteristic cool-headedness. He completed his tour as scheduled and upon his return to the capital proceeded to move quickly to deal a decisive blow on those colleagues in government who were plotting against him. On 22 February 1966 and contrary to the provisions of the Constitution, Obote assumed full powers of government, ordering the arrest and detention of five ministers of his government, including Grace Ibingira. It is worth noting for the sake of our interest in inter-ethnic relations and sources of conflict, that all those arrested and detained were southern Bantu politicians. This was followed on 24 February by the suspension of the Constitution itself; this step effectively removed the Kabaka of Buganda, Sir Edward Mutesa, from the office of President and Head of State which he had occupied since 1963 under the terms of the UPC-KY alliance. Then, in April 1966 Obote removed any remaining doubts as to the direction in which he was heading by introducing to the National Assembly, and having that body adopt immediately without debate, the 1966 Interim Republican Constitution which made him President and Head of State.

The most important political outcome of the 1966 crisis, for our purpose, was the abrogation of the Independence Constitution which had been the symbol of political pluralism in the country, and the increasing accumulation of power by the central government. Such tampering with the Constitution, which had been the chief source of the power of the Buganda Kingdom under the Kabaka, and the assumption of extra-constitutional powers by the central government under Obote, could not go unchallenged.

In numerous resolutions, culminating in one in May 1966 calling upon the central government to remove its seat of government from Buganda soil, the Buganda Lukiiko engaged in a bitter political struggle for the survival of the institution of Kabakaship and the Buganda State. In a sharp reaction, the central government interpreted this resolution as an act of rebellion by Buganda and provided Obote with the opportunity to launch an armed attack on the Kabaka's palace under pretext of looking for arms planned for use in the rebellion. After a spirited battle, the Kabaka's forces at the palace capitulated and Sir Edward Mutesa fled into exile, leaving behind the ruins of a kingdom that had played a central role in the historical political development of Uganda.[22]

The defeat and dismemberment of the Kingdom of Buganda marked the end of sub-national centres of power organized around ethnic groups, and ushered in an era of a highly centralized Ugandan state. Henceforth, there was to be one major centre of power - the central government - to which all Ugandan elites would look for political participation and employment. From this time onward, the importance of controlling power at the centre began to dawn on many political elites who had hitherto contented themselves with participation in local politics. The narrowing of areas of participation and political power thus resulted in intense political struggle among political elites for control of the central government. And since the 1966 crisis had dramatized those events as the struggle for power between southern Bantu and northern Nilotics, the struggle for participation and power in Uganda came to be seen and interpreted largely in such ethnic terms.

8. The Republican Constitution and One-party State

After his triumph in 1966, Obote proceeded to make preparations for the complete elimination of the leading centres and symbols of rival power. This was achieved following the adoption of the 1967 Republican Constitution, still in force. A leading provision of that Constitution declared that "The Institution of King or Ruler of a Kingdom or Constitutional Head of a District, by whatever name called, existing before the commencement of this constitution under the law then in force, is hereby abolished."[23]

Not only did this provision abolish the kingdoms which had been Obote's main source of political challenge before the events of 1966, but it also effectively abolished the system of local government established elsewhere in the non-kingdom areas. Hereafter, large sections of elites could no longer look to District Councils for political participation, or to the public services of district administrations for employment. Instead, all now looked to the centre in search of these values. The result was increasing political conflict and tension among the competing members of ethnic groups.

With the Republican Constitution in place and with the reins of power firmly in his hands, Obote then felt sufficiently strong and politically safe to embark on a socialist adventure. For long, he had apparently kept his socialist tendencies under the carpet, for lack of sufficient power, given the power equations within which he had to operate. But now he had this power and therefore, throughout 1968 and 1969, Obote made speeches and released a series of writings[24] spelling out his government's intentions to follow a socialist path of development. His socialist package for Uganda was adopted in December 1969 in Kampala by the delegates conference of the ruling party. And then, as Obote was leaving the conference hall late in the evening at the height of his political triumph, he was shot at by an intending assassin and injured in the mouth. This assassination attempt was naturally blamed on the enemies of the impending socialist revolution in Uganda, which included both internal and external forces. Obote took advantage of this event to strengthen his power and that of his government further by clamping down on opposition parties and declaring a one-party state in Uganda.

The declaration of the ruling UPC as the only legal political party removed completely the remaining elements of political pluralism in the country. Henceforth, political competition was to be confined to within the ruling party. Consequently, the state became highly centralized and authoritarian, while political competition and the struggle for power at the centre became very acute. In order to retain power in the face of serious challenges from other quarters, whether real or imaginary, Obote was increasingly forced to place his most trusted men in key branches of the state apparatus. As it turned out, these happened to be members of his own ethnic group, the Langi, or of an ethnic group closely allied culturally with Obote's, the Acholi.[25] Such a preponderance of people from a few ethnic groups in key centres of power gave the other ethnic groups, which happened to be a majority, a feeling of being politically dominated. This in turn gave further impetus to other groups to struggle to control political power at the centre.

The magnitude of group struggle for power was dramatized violently by the 1971 military coup led by Idi Amin. Among the accusations leveled at Obote by the coup leaders was his favouritism for the Langi and Acholi, particularly in the army and intelligence services. Following the initial success of the coup, Amin and his ethnically determined supporters proceeded to eliminate the Langi and Acholi from the army, and then do precisely what they had accused Obote of doing. Amin established a hegemony that controlled political and military power for eight years, based on a coalition of ethnic groups from Amin's West Nile district and the southern Sudan to which he had close affinity.

After the fall of Idi Amin in 1979 and a two-year interim period of Uganda National Liberation Front (UNLF) administrations, Milton Obote and his UPC party came to power for the second time, following the disputed 1980 general elections. Once again, Obote established a government propped up by the dominance of the Langi and Acholi in the Uganda National Liberation Army (UNLA).[26] In response to this development, and particularly to the widespread belief that the 1980 elections had been rigged in favour of the UPC,[27] Yoweri Museveni organized a resistance movement, the National Resistance Movement (NRM) and a guerrilla army, the National Resistance Army (NRA), both of which came to be dominated by the southern Bantu, most notably the Banyankole and the Baganda. Then in a crude twist of history, trouble developed within the Acholi-Langi alliance in the UNLA, when Obote was accused in early 1985 of his old problem of ethnic favouritism: Acholi officers accused him of favouring Langi over Acholi in appointments to top military positions.[28] In July of that year, Acholi officers under the leadership of General Tito Okello, UNLA Commander, and Northern Brigade Commander Bazilio Okello broke ranks with their traditional Langi allies and overthrew Obote's government in a military coup. The new Head of State, General Tito Okello, proceeded to establish a coalition government in which the Acholis were evidently in dominant positions both in government and the army.[29] But Okello's government was to be shortlived: only six months later, in January 1986, it was removed from power by the force of arms of the NRA. Following the collapse of Okello's government and the disintegration of the UNLA, Yoweri Museveni established a government, currently in power, dominated by the southern Bantu.[30]

Thus, in recent years political conflicts and violence in Uganda have tended to acquire ethnic dimensions because of the excessive centralization of power which has led the struggle to control the centre to be very intense indeed among the elite members of ethnic groups. In this struggle, political and military elites have tended to mobilize and use their ethnic bases and resources, such as military manpower, in order to struggle effectively to control political power at the centre. Hence, we may conclude that the seemingly ethnic conflicts and hostility in Uganda are basically political conflicts, originating from the struggle for popular democracy and political participation. As long as the active political elites are, through the existing political structure, required to participate only in one centre of power at the national level, the struggle for power will continue to reflect itself in such seemingly inter-ethnic conflict and violence. And as long as the old mutual suspicion continues to exist among ethnic groups along the southern-northern divide, the more difficult will it be to achieve the national consensus so vital for political stability.

9. Political Decentralization and Political Stability

Throughout this essay I have argued that political centralization intensifies conflicts among (ethnic) groups, while decentralization of power tends to diffuse such conflicts. Basing my analysis on the colonial system of local government and the provisions of political pluralism in Uganda's Independence Constitution, I have shown how the dispersal of power and responsibility among many local political units in fact worked in favour of political stability by keeping political conflicts among ethnic groups at the lowest level. Further, we have seen how the abolition of political decentralization in 1966 with the subsequent concentration of power at the centre, increased the tempo of political conflict, leading to the development of a culture of violence and endemic political instability.

In the final section of this paper, let us turn to the Nigerian post-Independence experience to take a further, if brief, look at how political decentralization may provide a viable framework for political stability by decongesting the centre of excessive political conflict and undercutting the potentialities of ethnic antagonism.

10. The Nigerian Experience

Nigeria emerged into independence in 1960 with a three-region federal structure.[31] Each region - Northern, Western and Eastern - was organized around a dominant ethnic group: the Hausa/-Fulani in the North, the Yoruba in the West and the Igbo in the East. The federal arrangement provided each constituent unit with a regional government, headed by a Premier, and with a Regional Assembly constituted by elected representatives as the centre of political activity. This arrangement encouraged the development and functioning of regionally-based political parties. Indeed, such parties existed and controlled the governments in their own regions. Thus the Northern Peoples Congress (NPC) led by Sir Ahmadu Bello, the Sardauna of Sokoto, controlled the Northern Regional Government; Chief Obafemi Awolowo's Action Group (AG) was dominant in the Western region; while Dr. Nnamdi Azikiwe led the National Council of Nigerian Citizens (NCNC), a party in government in the Eastern region. By and large, Nigeria's federal government remained a weak outfit run by a weak coalition of the regionally-based political parties, the control of which was an unattractive proposition for many leading politicians.[32] Instead, political parties were preoccupied with being supreme in their own regions. The regions, therefore, rather than the federal centre became areas of intense political participation and activity.

This three-region federal structure, however, served to mask greatly the multi-ethnic nature of Nigerian society. The three main ethnic groups around which the federal structure was organized dominated other important, and in many cases very large, groups within the regions. For example, the Hausa/Fulani in the North were seen to dominate other politically important groups such as the Tiv and the Idoma. Similarly, in the West, the majority Yoruba dominated many local ethnic groups, while in the East the Igbos dominated the equally socially advanced Efiks and Ibibios. This arrangement, therefore, came to cause constant friction and tension between ethnic groups within the regions, in time becoming a basis for demands for further expansion of autonomous power centres - to meet the political aspirations of other important ethnic groups.

Precisely in response to such demands and pressures the Mid-West region, centred around the Benin ethnic groups, was carved out of the Western region in 1963 to become the fourth region of the Nigerian federation. While this action gave political solace to Mid-Western ethnic groups, it also acted to fuel the demands of other "minority" groups elsewhere for "local self-determination". Such demands became so widespread and reached such high degrees of intensity that they were seen by many observers as constituting the greatest threat to the survival of the Nigerian nation as a single political entity. This was the state of affairs when the first military take-over of the federal government occurred in January 1966 under the leadership of an Igbo commander, General Aguiyi Ironsi.

Like many other alarmed Nigerian leaders at the time, General Ironsi mistook the demands for further expansion of centres of power and democratization of the political structure for signs of political disintegration of the Nigerian state. In an attempt to quell what he saw as the sources of disintegration, he proceeded to promulgate a decree that abolished federalism and imposed a unitary form of government in its place throughout the country. This action created more problems than it solved, and demands for the restoration of federalism in its expanded form became intensified. Political calculations should have prompted General Ironsi to back down. But his insistence on centralizing power under one unitary government led to the tragic end of his regime, and his life, in the counter-coup of July 1966.

On assuming power, the new military leaders under the leadership of Lt.Col. Yakubu Gowon immediately recognized realities: that the best way to diffuse political tension and ethnic conflicts was not to narrow areas of participation through the process of political centralization, but rather to expand them further through decentralization and by creating greater numbers of autonomous centres of power. In one of his first few decisions in office, therefore, Lt.Col. Gowon announced the creation of a 12-state federal structure with considerable concessions to the demands of many ethnic groups for greater political decentralization. The civil war that erupted between the former Eastern Region, which styled itself as the Republic of Biafra, and the federal forces prevented immediate implementation of the new federal system. But when this war ended in 1970, Nigerian federalism began to thrive again on the new 12-state structure.

Although the division of the country into 12 states was certainly an improvement on the former 4-region structure, the exercise was not based on sufficiently careful study and thought. It was a haphazard decision, taken to diffuse the serious political situation of the time. Accordingly, in demarcating new state boundaries, no serious consideration was given to grouping ethnic units together on the basis of affinities or compatibilities. Basically, the 12-state structure simply replicated the old colonial provincial structure, so many ethnic groups found themselves either divided across state boundaries or seriously dominated by others. Accordingly, the demands for "more states" continued to be championed by many ethnic groups throughout the country.

Following the coup of July 1975 that toppled the Gowon regime, a high-powered Commission on the Creation of New States was set up to study the problem carefully and recommend how to solve the problem on a more or less permanent basis. Based on the recommendations of the Commission, a 19-state federal structure was then established. This lasted for over ten years until 1987, when two more states were created, bringing the present number of states to 21. Earlier in 1976, Nigerian federalism was also strengthened and perfected by the establishment of an elaborate system of Local Government to provide even greater opportunities for political participation and decision-making at the highly local level.

In marked contrast to many other African countries, therefore, political trends in Nigeria since Independence have been towards greater expansion of political pluralism, through increased decentralization of power and diversification of centres of political participation. Nigerian federalism is constituted by three tiers of government. (1) At the lowest level are the more numerous political and administrative units in the form of Local Governments. These serve the needs of the local elites and smaller ethnic groups for participation and political decision-making. (2) At the intermediate level are the larger centres of power in the form of states with all the complements of the institutions and resources of government. It is at this state level that a greater number of Nigerian political and administrative elites aspire to participate. (3) Finally, then, there is the federal centre whose political and administrative elites represent merely a coalition of political forces and ethnic groups in the federation. Although the federal centre controls enormous national resources and commands supreme power in the land, it is in fact not a major target of political activity for the majority of active political elites. Insofar as the various states control local resources and provide services nearer to the people, it is the states that constitute the main centres for meeting the political and economic aspirations of the majority of the Nigerian people. Indeed, Nigerians within Nigeria are identified or identify themselves primarily on the basis of the states from which they come. It is the state identity that determines what benefits one can get in terms of employment, scholarship or even school admission for one's child. The local state, therefore, is a political unit around which people's hopes, aspirations and sentiments are developing first although, of course, overall at the higher level, the Nigerian nation commands the loyalty and national identity of the people.

In the final analysis, we may conclude that the Nigerian experiment in the atomization of power has, since the Nigerian Civil War, gone a long way towards providing a framework for political harmony and stability in the context of ethnic diversity. What obtains in Nigeria now is not a situation of conflict and hostility among ethnic groups - as had predominantly been the case with the three-region power structure when the participation base was still narrow for many elites - but a situation of healthy competition and rivalry among them. Ethnic groups organized in states compete with each other for the allocation of federal resources; they compete among themselves to achieve increased rates of development in terms of good roads, number of schools, hospitals, number of doctors and other highly qualified personnel. In this sense, political decentralization in Nigeria has not only provided a basis for the control of inter-ethnic conflicts: it has also given impetus to a dynamic process of social and economic progress throughout the country.

11. Conclusion

In citing the Nigerian example here, my intention was certainly not to advocate that country's particular style of governmental organization as the best political device for controlling political violence and inter-ethnic conflicts in Uganda. Rather, the purpose has been to demonstrate, borrowing from that example, the importance of the principle of political decentralization in controlling group conflict, particularly of the ethnic kind. As has been indicated, this principle was first tried in Uganda by the colonial government in the 1950s, and with remarkable success. And before its dissolution in 1962, the same colonial government embodied this very principle in the Independence Constitution. For the first three or four years, the principle of the existence of diverse centres of power was tolerated. This served to ensure political stability for the country during the period. Not until 1966, when this principle was grossly violated and when Obote then embarked relentlessly on the process of political centralization, did there set in the period of acute conflict and violence which has since characterized Uganda's political life.

Now, decentralization of power and unitarism as a system of government are not mutually exclusive. It is perfectly possible to have a strong central government existing side by side and in harmony with a strong system of local government. What is necessary is to broaden areas of political participation and decision-making by creating local political units which still, individually or collectively, cannot successfully challenge and cripple the centre. Such amounts of power and responsibility are then surrendered to them so that they may perform functions and provide services to the local people in a way basically complementary to the functions and services of the centre. It is a strong system of local government that can provide the much desired opportunities for ethnic groups to manage the affairs of vital interest to them. Likewise, it is such a system that can satisfy the needs of the masses of people for popular democracy. And it is the satisfaction of these basic political needs that can minimize the incidence of political conflict and violence in Uganda and ensure the political stability and socio-economic progress of the country.

Notes

1. For a definition and discussion of the concept of pluralism see, among others, Truman, D.: The Governmental Process. New York: Knopf, 1960; Eckstein, H.: Division and Cohesion in Democracy. Princeton: Princeton University Press, 1966; Kuper, L. and M.G. Smith (eds.): Pluralism in Africa. Berkeley and Los Angeles: University of California Press, 1969.
2. The link between political democracy and social pluralism is spelt out in the writings of many theorists of liberal democracy. See, for instance, Kornhauser, W.: The Politics of Mass Society. New York: The Free Press, 1959; Lipset, S.: Political Man. New York: Doubleday, 1960; Almond, G. & S. Verba: The Civic Culture. Princeton: Princeton University Press, 1963; and Duhl, R. (ed.): Political Opposition in Western Democracy. New Haven: Yale University Press, 1966.
3. For another critique of the social pluralist interpretation of democracy see Bachrach, P.: The Theory of Democratic Elitism. Boston: Little, Brown and Company, 1967.
4. The cultural pluralism model owes its inspiration to J.S. Furnival's study of the relations between the cultural and related groups in colonial India and

Burma. See his Colonial Policy and Practice. London: Cambridge University Press, 1948. Those who have applied this model to the study of contemporary societies include Smith, M.G.: The Plural Society in the British West Indies. Berkeley: University of California Press, 1965, and Despress, L.: Cultural Pluralism and Nationalist Politics in British Guiana. Chicago: Rand McNally, 1967.

5. By Furnival, op.cit., to colonial societies.

6. Kuper & Smith, op.cit., especially the Introductory Chapter.

7. For an outline of the history and political developments of colonial Uganda, see Ingham, K.: The Making of Modern Uganda. London: George Allen & Unwin Ltd., 1958, and Apter, D.: The Political Kingdom in Uganda. Princeton: Princeton University Press, 1961.

8. See Apter, op.cit.

9. See Uganda Government: Uganda Constitutional Instruments (The Constitution of Uganda in Force). Entebbe: Government Printers, 1963.

10. See Article 74(1) and Schedule 7 of the 1962 Constitution of Uganda.

11. Prominent among contemporaries who held leading political positions in the Kabaka's Government are the present Minister of Education in the NRM/NRA government, J.S. Mayanja-Nkangi, who held the position of Katikiro (Prime Minister) in the early 1960s and Abubakar Mayanja, current Minister of Information, who at one time served as Minister of Education in the Buganda Government.

12. See the Constitutional Heads (Elections) Act, no 66 of 1963. Entebbe: Government Printer, 1963.

13. For example, Chemonges relinquished his seat in Parliament to become the Constitutional Head of Sebei district with the title of "Kingoo of Sebei".

14. The most politically significant conflict or dispute of the time was the long-standing one between Bunyoro and Buganda over the "lost counties". These were tracts of land that had belonged to the Kingdom of Bunyoro before Britain imposed colonialism on Uganda but which were given to Buganda, first as a punishment to Bunyoro for resisting the colonial invading armies and secondly, as a present to Buganda for assisting the British in defeating the Bunyoro resistance. After successfully dodging responsibility for settling the problem they had created, the departing British left it to the governmently of newly independent Uganda to settle by holding a referendum in the disputed counties after two years of independence. This the central government under Prime Minister Apollo Milton Obote did; two of the counties under dispute were returned to Bunyoro and the dispute was finally solved.

15. The Kabaka's Government resorted to court litigation each time it thought that the central government was acting contrary to the provisions of and powers conferred on it by the Constitution. For a discussion of this see Mazrui, A.: "Violent Constitutionalism in Uganda", in Government and Opposition, vol. 11, no. 4, July-October 1967.

16. It was from the strained relationships between the governments of Buganda and Uganda that the Kabaka and the Buganda Lukiiko became mobilized to play increasingly activist roles in the affairs of the central government. Otherwise, both the Kabaka and the Lukiiko had been interested primarily in Buganda affairs.

17. See introduction in Gingyera-Pinycwa, A.G.: Apollo Milton Obote and his Times. New York, London, Lagos: NOK Publishers, 1978).

18. The Kabaka Yekka (KY) was more of a political movement than a political party. It emerged suddenly in early 1961 and spread rapidly throughout Buganda. As its name suggests (King Only), it was mainly interested in matters related to Buganda, more particularly in preserving the institution of the Kabakaship.

19. See, for instance, Obote, A.M.: "The Footsteps of Uganda's Revolution" in East African Journal, vol. V, no. 10, October 1968, and Gingyera-Pinycwa, op.cit.

20. The Democratic Party led by Benedicto Kiwanuka won the 1961 general elections to the Legislative Council which took Uganda into a period of internal self-government with Kiwanuka as the first Prime Minister.

21. Outside Buganda, the UPC won 38 seats, against 24 seats for the DP.
22. For a full chronicle of the 1966 crisis by an insider and leading participant see Mutesa, Sir Edward: The Desecration of my Kingdom. London: Constable, 1967.
23. See Uganda Government: The Constitution of the Republic of Uganda. Entebbe: Government Printers, 1967, Article 118 (1).
24. The main socialist document authored by Obote was The Common Man's Charter. Kampala: Consolidated Printers, 1969.
25. For instance, Obote's cousin, Akena Adoko, was the head of the powerful and much feared intelligence agency, the General Service Unit; it was generally known that Obote was grooming Lt.Cols. Oyite-Ojok and M. Arach, both from Obote's ethnic group, for top leadership positions in the Uganda army. See Gingyera-Pinycwa, 1978, p. 246.
26. The Army Commander, Gen. Tito Okello, and the Army Chief of Staff, Maj. Gen. Oyite-Ojok were Acholi and Langi respectively.
27. Claims that the 1980 general elections were rigged in favour of the UPC were advanced by the opposition politicians and the Democratic Party. See, for instance, "The rigged 1980 Uganda General Elections", a document supplied by the DP Secretariat, Kampala, and Bwengye, A.W.F.: The Agony of Uganda: From Idi Amin to Obote. London: Regency Press, 1985.
28. This was one major reason given for the July 1985 coup against Obote's government. Cf. General Tito Okello's Maiden Speech to the Nation carried by Radio Uganda 29 July 1985.
29. Military strongman Bazilio Okello, a close ally of General Tito Okello, was made Commander of Defence Forces. The Cabinet and appointments to top positions in parastatals clearly reflected Acholi dominance.
30. Again, a look at the ethnic composition of the Cabinet and top Commanders of the NRA will reveal the preponderance of people from the southern Bantu.
31. The discussion of the Nigerian federalism and its problems that follow is based largely on two sources: Awa, E.O.: Federal Government in Nigeria. Berkeley: University of California Press, 1964, and Oyovbaire, S.E.: Federalism in Nigeria. London: Macmillan Publishers, 1987.
32. At Independence and after the general elections of 1965, the Coalition federal government was made up by two regionally-based political parties, the NPC and the NCNC. The regions were so powerful and control of their government so much more attractive than control of federal government that the most powerful politician of the time, Alhaji Sir Ahmadu Bello, decided at independence to remain as the Premier of the Northern Region and to send his protegé, Alhaji Sir Abubakar Tafawa Balewa, to head the Federal Government as Prime Minister on behalf of the majority NPC party, of which Alhaji Sir Ahmadu Bello himself was the leader.

Abraham Kiapi

The Constitution as a Mediator in Internal Conflict

1. Introduction

We begin by defining our terms. The term "mediator" in this context means an intermediary who is regarded as a common friend between two opposing sides. He acts as a go-between, an arbitrator who pacifies parties who are at logger-heads, by using moderating influence between them. The term "conflict" as used here is not confined to armed confrontation; it also includes absolute difference, hatred and irreconcilable positions.

Throughout the world, in countries where conflicts have existed, constitutions have acted as mediators between the opposing sides. For example, the Magna Carta (1215), the Petition of Rights (1628) and the Bill of Rights (1688/89) resolved disputes between the English kings and their subjects. After the successful overthrow of a tyrannical monarchy, the French adopted a constitution of which the Declaration of the Rights of Man (1789) formed an integral part to safeguard possible future conflicts between the ordinary citizen and the state. Conflicts arose between England and the 13 American Colonies throughout the first half of the 18th century. In 1774, the American colonists decided to resolve the conflict once for all by declaring their independence from England. They drew up a constitution that set up the authority of the state and the rights of the people, and established a Supreme Court to resolve constitutional disputes between the citizen and the state.[1] More recently, in 1963, Kenya found it necessary to adopt a majimbo (regional) constitution to resolve conflicts between the smaller minority tribes and the three dominant groups - the Luo, Kikuyu and Akamaba.[2] It was for the same reason that Nigeria became a federation.[3]

Constitutions have acted as mediators of internal conflicts because, in the first place, they are like a peace treaty, laying down agreed arrangements on how the affairs of the nation are to be managed. For example, recently Tanzania had to modify its constitution radically to accommodate conflicting demands from the mainland and Zanzibar which enabled a Zanzibari to become the President of the Republic, and a person from Pemba to become the Head of Government of the Islands of Zanzibar and Pemba.[4]

2. Uganda's Experience

A constitution can also act as a mediator because it is usually a compromise between irreconcilable demands from various sections of the population. It attempts to accommodate as many views, desires, expectations and demands as possible. This was the most characteristic feature of the Constitution of Uganda, 1962.

There were two features of this Independence Constitution which were distinctive and tailored to the circumstances of the country, and it was on these points that the constitution acted as a mediator at its best. We must recall that Uganda was forged into a united country from a collection of tribes with varying history, tradition and customary institutions.

One of the distinctive features of the 1962 Constitution was the federal status given to Buganda within Uganda. Though the Constitution formally declared that Uganda was to consist of the federal kingdoms of Ankole, Buganda, Bunyoro and Toro and the territory of Busoga in addition to the "republican" districts, only Buganda had any substantial degree of autonomy within Uganda. In practice the other kingdoms and Busoga continued to be controlled by the central government, like any other district of Uganda. Powers given exclusively to them were limited to the position and the status of their rulers. But the relationship of Buganda to the rest of the country was truly federal.

Matters with respect to which the Buganda Lukiiko had exclusive powers were:

a) The Kabakaship;

b) the powers, obligations and duties of the Kabaka as such;

c) the status of the Kabaka's ministers as such and their powers, obligations and duties in addition to those conferred by or arising under a law passed by the Parliament of Uganda;

d) the public service of Buganda;

e) matters relating to taxation agreed to between the Kabaka's Government and the Central Government;

f) Buganda's public debt, public holidays and festival;

g) traditional and customary matters relating to Buganda alone.[5]

Matters reserved for the Central Government included foreign affairs, immigration, national defence, internal security, penal law, the judicial system, public finance, public health and the public service of Uganda. Matters over which the legislature of other "federal states" had exclusive powers to make laws were limited to the office of their ruler, his powers, obligations, and duties; public holidays and festivals; traditional and customary matters relating to that state alone. They could exercise jurisdiction over matters only after arrangement with the Central Government.

The second distinctive feature of the Uganda Independence Constitution was the procedure for amending the entrenched provisions of the Constitution. A Bill for an Act of Parliament to amend the Constitution had to be supported on its second and third readings by not less than 2/3 of all the members of the National Assembly. But if the act was to make provision for transfer of any part of Uganda from one federal state to another or to a district, then the district or federal state to which it was to be transferred had to consent to the transfer by a resolution supported by no less than 2/3 of all the voting members of legislative assembly or council of each of the states or districts concerned. The federal structure, the fundamental rights, and matters over which a federal state was given exclusive powers could not be changed by the central legislature without similar consent given by the legislative assemblies of those federal states that would be affected by the change. This all meant that the position of the Rulers, the Bill of Rights and the agreed boundaries of Uganda could not be changed unilaterally by the Central Government.

3. The "Lost Counties"

At the end of the last century all Bunyoro territory south of the River Kafu had been transferred to Buganda, and the Buganda Agreement of 1900 confirmed this transfer. Bunyoro called this territory the "lost counties".[7]

From that time many attempts were made by the Bunyoro to recover these counties from Buganda. In 1912 the Mubende-Bunyoro Committee was formed as a political organization whose main aim was the return of the counties to Bunyoro. In 1912 when speaking before a joint Parliamentary Commission investigating the desirability and the feasibility of closer union in East Africa, a prominent Munyoro complained to the Secretary of

State for the colonies about the loss of Bunyoro territory. But the Colonial Secretary refused to go into the question, maintaining that it had long been settled. When signing the 1933 and 1955 Agreements with the British Government, the King of Bunyoro made formal public statements reserving Bunyoro's claims to the lost counties. His claims were reinforced by five petitions addressed to the Secretary of State for the Colonies between 1945 and 1954. Several representations were also made by the Mubende-Bunyoro Committee between 1951 and 1955. But all were turned down.

In 1958 the Omukama (or King) of Bunyoro asked the Colonial Secretary to refer the dispute to the Judicial Committee of the Privy Council. This also was rejected, on the grounds that there were no justiciable legal issues which could properly be considered by the Privy Council. The Uganda Relationships Commission recommended that a referendum should be held in two of the disputed counties - Buyaga and Bugangaizi - and one other county to be chosen by Bunyoro. The Commission advised that if the people of the counties chose to join Bunyoro, the counties should be handed over at Independence. The recommendation of the Commission was rejected by the Kabaka's government and the Constitutional Conference of 1961. The Colonial Secretary accordingly appointed a Commission of Privy Councillors to investigate the dispute. The terms of reference of the Commission were:

> Having regard to the paramount need for the people of Uganda including Buganda to move together into independence in conditions which will ensure peace and contentment, to investigate the allegations of discrimination, to receive representations from those concerned and to advise whether any and if so, what measures, should be taken to deal with the situation.

The investigation was to be conducted in the counties of Buyaga, Bugangaizi, Buwekula, Buruli and Bugerere, and portions of Singo and Bulemezi. After its investigations, the Commission recommended that Buyaga and Bugangaizi should be returned to Bunyoro before Independence Day while the Governor was still in office, but that there should be no changes in the status of the territory east of Mubende District.

The recommendations of the Commission were considered at the Independence Conference of 1962 and it was there agreed that there was to be no transfer of territory before Independence; but the disputed counties of Buyaga and Bugangaizi were to be administered by the Central Government and that a referendum was to be held after two years to find out the choice of the people living in the disputed counties. They were to be given three alternatives: to remain in Buganda, to be transferred to Bunyoro or to remain a separate district within Uganda.

These conclusions of the Conference were incorporated into the Uganda Constitutional Instruments of Independence. Section 26 of the Uganda (Independence) Order in Council, 1962, provided that such a referendum should be held after 9 October 1964, on a day appointed by the National Assembly. Only those eligible to be registered voters for elections to the National Assembly would be entitled to vote in the referendum. The referendum was to be organized and conducted in such a manner as Parliament would describe. The choice of the majority of the voters in the referendum was to be implemented by amending the Independence Constitution by a simple majority in the National Assembly.

These measures were implemented in 1964 when a referendum was held. Two of the disputed counties, Buyaga and Bugangaizi, voted for their re-union with Bunyoro, and Parliament passed the necessary Bill for their transfer.[8] Here we see another victory for the Constitution as a mediator in internal conflict in Uganda.

4. Human Rights

Thirdly, a constitution may also allay fears on the possibility of the violation of fundamental human rights: the rich against their properties being unfairly expropriated; minorities against oppression; religions against discrimination, etc. To avoid such situations, most constitutions contain a Bill of Rights.

Government is the collective power of the people. Government exists as a service institution in order to ensure that the life of each individual in society is safe and that there is no unauthorized interference with his personal liberty, property, or other rights. Consequently, it is the function of every constitution to strike a balance between the power of the state and the rights of the individual. Most constitutions accordingly guarantee the fundamental rights of the individual and give him access to the courts if these rights are infringed by the government. And so did all constitutions of Uganda. Because of fears expressed by the various sections of the population, a Bill of Rights was entrenched in the 1962 Constitution of Uganda, and this has been carried forward by the 1966 and 1967 Constitutions as well.

More specifically, a Bill of Rights was considered necessary for the following reasons:

The Baganda were fearful as Independence approached. They had been the most outstanding tribe throughout the colonial period, enjoying more autonomy than the rest of the country. They had more educated people and a higher economic development, which made them a subject of envy by other tribes of Uganda. To make things worse, they were seen as arrogant throughout the rest of the country.

Besides tribal issues Uganda had also religious problems. The country is mostly Christian, divided into Roman Catholics and Protestants. Due to past differences and misunderstandings there was no love lost between members of the two denominations. This was openly reflected by their party alignments as Independence approached. The Catholics formed the Democratic Party, led by Benedicto Kiwanuka; Protestants and the minority Moslems formed the Uganda Peoples Congress, led by Milton Obote. There were therefore fears of religious persecution whichever party should come to power. Incorporating a Bill of Rights into the Constitution was considered to be the solution to allay such fears after Independence.

Though the Independence Constitution has since been changed beyond recognition, its fundamental rights provisions have largely been preserved. Under the present Constitution the fundamental rights are to be found in Chapter III of the Constitution. They provide that every person within the boundaries of the country must enjoy equal protection of the law, and the fundamental rights and freedoms of the individual: that is, right to life, liberty, security of the person and the protection of the law, freedom of conscience, of expression and assembly; and protection of home and other property and from deprivation of property without compensation. Section 22 of the Constitution provides that any person whose rights are being or are likely to be violated contrary to the fundamental rights entrenched in the Constitution, may apply to the High Court for redress. The High Court has original jurisdiction to hear and determine any application made by any person alleging infringement of his rights. The High Court is given full powers by the Constitution to make such orders, issue such writs and give such directions as it may consider appropriate for the purpose of enforcing, or securing the enforcement of, the provisions of the Constitution guaranteeing the fundamental rights. But if the High Court is satisfied that adequate means of redress for the contravention are or have been available to the complaint under any other law, then remedial orders or writs are not to be issued.

Successive post-Independence governments in Uganda generally failed to respect these fundamental rights of the individual, however. Indeed this was one of the reasons why the National Resistance Movement and its military wing, the National Resistance Army, were formed in 1981 and fought a bitter bush war against the government of Uganda until achieving victory in 1986.

After suspending the Constitution in March 1966, President Obote declared a state of emergency throughout Uganda, resulting in many people being arrested and detained without trial for long periods. He even went as far as to disregard court orders for the release of detainees after these had successfully applied for writs of habeas corpus.

In Ibingira V. Attorney General[9] five ex-ministers were arrested from the Cabinet Room and detained, but successfully applied for a writ of habeas corpus. Brought to Entebbe Airport from the Northern region of Uganda where they had been detained, they were met by the Permanent Secretary, Ministry of Internal Affairs, who informed them about the decision of the court and told them that "they were now free". On leaving the airport building, however, they were immediately re-arrested and detained under emergency regulations. Their contention that the government acted in bad faith was rejected by the Court of Appeal for East Africa.[10]

On its return to power, the Uganda Peoples Congress government resumed the old practice. Many people were arrested and detained illegally in various prisons and military barracks. They successfully applied for writs of habeas corpus; the High Court ordered for their release; and on leaving the High Court Building, they were immediately re-arrested by the police, bundled into police vehicles and taken back to prison. Lawyers and judges made many protests, but these fell on deaf ears.

Recently there was a row, not least within legal circles, when President Museveni issued a proclamation not only banning legal suits against the government for injuries suffered at the hands of security forces from September 1978 to January 1986, but also nullifying unsatisfied court orders which had awarded damages against the government.[11] This proclamation was successfully challenged before a Constitutional Court, which held it ultra vires, i.e. beyond the power of the initial proclamation of January 1986, which provided that laws were to be made by the National Resistance Council and signed by the President as evidenced by the public seal, and called "decrees". This later proclamation was not called a decree, it was signed by "Yoweri Museveni, Chairman, National Resistance Movement", and it purported to deprive individuals of their properties, to wit, judgement debts; thus, it was held ultra vires and void.[12] The government magnanimously bowed to the decision of the court and proceeded to pass a decree which was done in the manner initially authorized by the January proclamation and did not interfere with judgement debts (which have all since been paid by the government).

This case study shows that the courts can also by interpreting the Constitution resolve internal conflicts - provided of course the government abides by their decisions, as in this case.

5. Unitary and Federal

Every constitutional arrangement must enable every part of the country and every person living in it be given the opportunity to participate in decision-making on matters affecting him. For this reason a constitution is either unitary or federal.

A unitary state is organized under a single central government, and the constituent districts hold power at the discretion of the central government. The essentials of a unitary state are (a) the supremacy of the central government, and (b) the absence of subsidiary sovereign bodies. This means that all or most powers of government are concentrated in one Central Government. Examples of unitary states today are the East African countries, Great Britain, and France.

To enable local participation of the people in their governance, the country is divided into units (by whatever name called[13]) and each unit is given some form of functions to carry out. Such functions usually relate to matters affecting the people directly, matters which cannot be dealt with from the capital. For the sake of convenience and efficiency some functions are left to a local authority to deal with.

In a federal constitution, the powers of government are divided between the Central Government and the Constituent Governments in such a way that the government of each constituent part is legally independent within its own sphere. The Central Government has its own area of powers and exercises them without any control from the governments of the constituent parts of the country. The constituent parts of the country on their part exercise their powers without being controlled by the Central Government. The legislature of the Central Government and of the parts have limited powers. The indispensable quality of the federal state is, therefore, the distribution of the powers of the government between the federal authority and federating units. The country is organized under a single independent Central Government for some purposes, and under semi-independent regional, state, or provincial governments, for other purposes.

The question is: when should a country have a unitary or a federal constitution? Regardless of its size, where the country is populated by a homogeneous people having a common language, culture, history and background, there is no need for a federation. A good example is afforded by the Republic of France. Federation is usually preferred where there is fear of domination of a section or sections of the population by larger tribes - the position in Kenya at Independence. Similarly, where widely dissimilar peoples and tribes are grouped together under a single administrative system, federation may be desirable. Switzerland is a tiny country, but because each of the 22 cantons regards itself as separate and distinct, it is a federal state. Again where the fervour for integration and separation have been at odds with each other, the federal solution is a popular formula. This is partly why Nigeria is a federation: each state enjoys autonomy within unity. Another situation that calls for federation is where the different parts of a country have been enjoying autonomy for a long time but decide to unite into a single state. The United States, Canada, Australia, and the Federal Republic of Germany are federations for this reason. Some states, such as Malaysia, are federations because each federating unit wants to preserve its traditional cultures, that is the kingship system.[14] Federation provides a solution for winning political support for political and economic integration for a heterogeneous population.

There is also a middle way between a federation and a unitary state. This alternative combines devolution of power to regional governments with an over-riding authority exercised by the central government. This was the formula used to keep Nigeria one at Independence, and is still the position in the USSR, Yugoslavia and the Federal Republic of Germany.

Another choice is co-operative federalism, where the central and regional governments co-operate to carry out functions jointly, such as maintenance of law and order, regulation of the economy, and transport. This system operates in the United States, Canada, and Australia.[15]

What should be the choice for Uganda? Uganda is not a "nation", in that it does not consist of a population having a common language, culture, traditions and history. In that respect, it is a hotch-potch of heterogeneous tribes. On the other hand, however: have we not lived together enough to have acquired a common identity as Ugandans? Have we not inter-married and lived among tribes other than our own? Have we not mixed freely in schools, at work places, churches, public gatherings and social occasions? Does really one tribe feel it is so different and distinct from other tribes, even these days? Have we not learned each others' languages? Are English and Kiswahili not unifying factors?

Having considered all these questions, and to avoid reverting to the old days of tribalism, with duplication of facilities and tribal rivalries, this author recommends that Uganda should have a unitary constitution. However, the central government should be given authority to devolve as many powers as possible to the districts, so that they can be able to enjoy local self-government and carry out governmental functions which affect them directly - building and maintaining trunk roads, hospitals, secondary schools, public service, etc. To ensure that such functions are not neglected in any district, the Constitution should give concurrent powers over them to the central government and local authorities. A formula should be worked out to ensure that the more backward areas of Uganda receive priority in the allocation of funds, to enable them to catch up with the rest of the country.

6. Taming the Executive

The provisions of a Constitution can also forestall future conflicts by limiting the powers of the Executive. Now, the need to have a constitution arises from the necessity of having an organized society in which power is given by the people to a group of individuals to manage the affairs of the people, including the use of force against them. The expectation is that public power will be used in accordance with certain rules laid down by the people beforehand, and that the rights of the individual will be respected by both society as a whole and the government. Constitutions exist to tame public power by limiting it, so that it is used to promote the welfare of the people. Consequently, a constitution can be regarded as a contract between the people and the governors of the people: and these governors are the Executive.

The Executive is the branch of the government responsible for the administration of the laws and the affairs of the state. They are the people who wield actual power in the country; thus it is essential that the range and limit of their powers be laid down in the constitution. The constitution also defines the relationship between the Executive and the Legislature, as a constitution may create either a parliamentary or presidential form of government.

The parliamentary form of government has been developed in Britain over the years as the powers of the Sovereign have been gradually reduced by successive Acts of Parliament. Under this system, the legislature has supreme power. Parliament has the final say in legislative matters, taxation and public expenditure; indeed, a government can be forced to resign by a defeat in Parliament. The executive branch of the government is generally chosen among, and is responsible to, the legislature. The chief of state, whether a president or a hereditary monarch, has no real powers and is in fact a figurehead. Examples of countries with a parliamentary form of government include the Federal Republic of Germany, France, the United Kingdom, and the Nordic countries. In France power is shared between the President and the Prime Minister. Its variation is the cabinet government, where most decisions affecting the affairs of the people are made by a Cabinet. This is the type of government established by the Constitution of the Republic of Uganda, 1967. It is, therefore, not very easy to distinguish between the parliamentary and presidential forms of government.

The presidential form of government, as it exists in the United States, means that the executive and the legislative branches of the government are separately elected, each with its own clearly defined powers. The executive consists of an independent President whose Ministers are not members of Congress (Parliament) and who cannot be dismissed by the Legislature through a vote of no confidence or through loss of support in the legislature.[16] This form of government also operates in Tanzania.[17]

To avoid the danger of presidents degenerating into dictators, constitutions usually curtail the powers of the president or his tenure of office. Under the constitutions of the United States, Nigeria and Ghana,[18] political appointments by the president are subject to ratification by the legislature. No president can serve for more than eight years. In Switzerland, the Supreme Executive and governing authority is the Federal Council composed of seven members. The function of the President is to chair meetings of the Federal Council, and the President serves only a one year term.[19] In the Soviet Union, the Council of Ministers is the "highest executive and administrative authority of the USSR". The Council is formed by the Supreme Soviet and is responsible and accountable to it.[20]

Uganda has had both parliamentary and cabinet forms of government, and the experience with the former was not a very happy one. As an interim measure for a year after Independence, Uganda's head of state was the Queen of England represented by a Governor-General.

Uganda broke its constitutional links with the British Crown one year after Independence, on 9 October 1963, by the enactment of the Constitution of Uganda (First Amendment) Act, 1963.[21] The Act established the office of President, who was to be the supreme head of State and commander-in-chief of the Armed Forces. He was to take precedence over all persons in Uganda and not be liable to any proceedings whatsoever in any Court. The Act also created the office of Vice-President, who was to perform the functions of the President and enjoy the constitutional privileges of the President when the President was out of the country, or for some other reasons was unable to perform the functions of his office, or when the office of the President was vacant. If the President was unable to perform the functions of the President, these presidential functions were to be performed by the Chief Justice.

President and Vice-President were to be elected from among the traditional rulers of the federal states and the constitutional heads of districts by the National Assembly, for a term of office limited to five years. The President and the Vice-President could be removed from office by a resolution of the National Assembly, but such a resolution could normally be moved only by the Prime Minister. If it was moved by a member of the National Assembly other than the Prime Minister, the member moving the resolution had to satisfy the Speaker that not less than one half of all the members of the Assembly had signified in writing their intention to vote in support of the resolution. And finally, such a resolution for the removal of the President or the Vice-President would have to be supported by the votes of not less than 2/3 of all the members of the National Assembly.

The office of the President was purely constitutional, and he had no discretion to refuse assent to bills. Like the Governor-General, he had to act in accordance with the advice of the Cabinet or a minister acting under the general authority of the Cabinet. The President could act at his own discretion only when appointing a Prime Minister, when removing a Prime Minister from office after a vote of no confidence passed against him in the National Assembly, or when dissolving the National Assembly after the expiration of the term of the Assembly.

Where the President was required by the Constitution to do any act with the advice of any person and the Prime Minister was convinced that the President had neglected or declined to do so, the Prime Minister was given the power to inform the President that it was his intention to do that act himself, after the expiration of a period to be specified by the Prime Minister. At the expiration of that period, if the President had not done that act, the Prime Minister could lawfully do it himself. An act done under such circumstances by the President was deemed to be the act of the President himself. The practical effect of this was that the Prime Minister could assent to bills, make statutory instruments, appoint persons to public office, and exercise all the powers of the President, even if the latter had declined or neglected to act.

Sir Edward Mutesa, the Kabaka of Buganda, was elected first President of Uganda and Sir William Nadiope, the Kyabazinga (ruler) of Busoga, was elected Vice-President. The election of Sir Edward Mutesa was made possible by the alliance between the Uganda Peoples' Congress (UPC) and the ultra-traditionalist Kabaka Yekka (KY) (King Only) Party. The whole constitutional set-up was indeed an anomaly. The Head of State was styled "President" at national level, but to his Baganda tribe he was a King who was the Head of State of a nation composed of four kingdoms and eleven "republican" districts.

A year after his election, a power struggle ensued between the President and his Prime Minister, Milton Obote. Things came to a head on 22 February 1966, when the Prime Minister issued a statement to the nation, declaring that in the interest of national stability and public security and tranquility he had taken over all powers of the Government of Uganda. The statement continued:

> I shall henceforth be advised by a Council whose members I shall name later. I have taken this course of action independently because of the wishes of the people of this country for peace, order and prosperity.[22]

On 24 February 1966, the Prime Minister disclosed that he had been forced to take certain drastic measures because of events and unwelcome activities of certain leading personalities, who had plotted to overthrow the government by the use of foreign troops. He declared that "the Constitution of Uganda shall be suspended temporarily with effect from 7 o'clock tonight".

He then went on to enumerate those institutions of the government that were to continue functioning normally. In fact all were preserved except the offices of the President and Vice President. The effect was therefore to dismiss the President and Vice President. On 2 March 1966, Obote issued a further statement declaring that the functions of the President and Vice President were to be exercised by the Prime Minister by and with the advice of the Cabinet.[23]

On 15 April 1966, at an emergency meeting of the National Assembly, a resolution was passed declaring that "the constitution which came into being on October 9, 1962, be abolished and it is hereby abolished accordingly". The Assembly went on to adopt a new Constitution, copies of which they had not seen; they were told by the Prime Minister to pick them from their pigeon holes.[24]

Thus Obote started the chain of events that has led to conflicts in Uganda ever since. The lessons are clear. A parliamentary system of government requires conditions prevailing in mature democracies, where the population as a whole agree on the basic requirements of a democratic government. Uganda like most African countries suffers from a basic malady: an erratic attitude to politics. Politics is looked upon as a channel to acquire wealth, prestige and pomp. Once an African leader gains power, he tends to want to remain in power, if possible, till death. That was the root cause of the problem between Dr. Obote and Sir Edward Mutesa.

President and Prime Minister cannot go side by side in Uganda. It is therefore recommended that Presidential form of executive is the only solution for Uganda. However, safeguards must be entrenched to ensure that the President does not degenerate into a dictator. He should serve a maximum of two four-year terms; moreover, the political appointments and treaties he makes should be subject to ratification by the National Assembly, which should have the power to impeach him.

7. The Legislature

Experience of democratic countries has shown that conflicts can be resolved by discussing differences in Parliament. Parliament is a forum in which representatives of the people "let off steam" so that a situation likely to lead to a conflict can be diffused. That is partly why every constitution makes it clear who can make laws for the country; what the composition of the legislature should be; how the representatives of the people must be elected; in what manner they must make laws and to what extent the government must be answerable to the representatives of the people.

Legislatures may be either unicameral or bicameral. A legislature is unicameral when it is composed of one chamber only, and bicameral when composed of two chambers. In the latter system, power is shared by two more or less coordinate legislative organs. Normally, the lower house is more directly representative of the people, elected on a wider franchise. The upper house, the second chamber, is either elected on a restricted or derivative franchise or may contain nominated or hereditary elements or direct representatives of certain classes, interests or geographical divisions of the nation, the latter as in the United States. The two houses may or may not be of equal authority.

The creation of a second chamber is due to the belief that it is desirable to have a body generally less directly controlled by popular opinion, which may exercise delaying and supervisory powers over legislative proposals. Second chambers are also created to ensure that in a federal state, the constituent states can have an equal voice in national affairs. This is because the lower house represents the population of the Union rather than of the state. It is therefore possible for states as such to be underrepresented and out-voted in the lower chamber. The upper chamber is designed to off-set this disadvantage. The upper chamber is then composed of equal representatives from each state, thus giving the voice of the smaller states equal weight to that of the bigger states.

In the United States, the Senate, or the upper house, is representative. Each state is represented by two senators, elected by the people of that state. In the United Kingdom, the membership of the upper house, the House of Lords, was originally hereditary. Sons of the nobility who succeeded to their fathers' titles became members. Creation of life peerages, whereby a person is appointed a lord without his descendants succeeding to the title, is now also common.

Upper houses can be a cause of delay and deadlock in the legislative process. For this reason, some constitutions provide for joint sessions in case of a deadlock.[25] Others specify the period of time within which delays are allowed. In Britain, until 1910, the House of Lords was on par with the House of Commons in matters of ordinary legislation, with full powers of initiation and rejection. There was no arrangement for breaking deadlocks. The Parliament Act of 1911 took away certain powers of the

Lords. It provides that when a money bill has been passed by the Commons, it must be sent up to the Lords. If the Lords do not pass it within one month, royal assent must be given to it regardless of the views of the Lords. Thus, they lost all powers over taxation and appropriations for expenditure. In the case of other bills, these must also become law and the royal assent must be given to them if they have been passed by the Commons three times in three successive sessions within two years. At the extreme, then, the powers of the Lords are thus limited to holding up a bill for two years.

On the other hand, the constitution of some countries give the upper house sole powers with regard to certain matters. For example, in the United States, the Senate has the sole power of ratifying treaties and the appointment of senior public officers by the President.

A recurring question is always: What to do with a representative who loses the confidence of his constituents? Before they became de jure one-party states, Kenya[26] and Zambia had constitutional provisions requiring an incumbent member of the National Assembly to resign his seat and seek a fresh mandate from his constituents if he changed from one political party to another. In other words "crossing the floor" entailed resignation from the parliament.

Under Article 107 of the Constitution of the USSR, "Deputies who have not justified the confidence of their constituents may be recalled at any time by decision of a majority of the electors ..." Likewise, the constitution of the German Democratic Republic provides that a deputy who grossly infringes his duties can be recalled by his electors.

What type of legislature is ideal for Uganda? Because of varying densities of population - and constituencies reflect population densities - some districts will have more representatives than others in the National Assembly. To ensure that there is a forum in which every district is equally represented, it is suggested that an upper house should be created, consisting of three representatives from every district. As in the United States, members of either house may introduce bills, but to be passed, a bill must have majority support of both houses. The President should have no power to refuse assent to bills that have been passed by both houses by two-thirds majority, because the members of both houses represent the people.

Another matter to consider is executive interference with the electoral process. One of the reasons given by Mr. Museveni for waging a guerrilla war (which sparked off the current conflict in the north of the country) was that the 1980 elections had been rigged. This suspicion arose out of the fact that when members of the Democratic Party were busy celebrating their expected victory, Mr. Paul Muwanga, Chairman of the ruling Military Commission, issued a proclamation that no returning officer was to declare the results of any election without being cleared by him (Muwanga) personally. Heavy penalties were imposed for contravention of the proclamation. This was made possible because the Executive organized and conducted the elections. District Commissioners were made returning officers, directly under the office of the head of government. Since members of the government were very much interested in the outcome of the elections, they could scarcely be seen as acting impartially or fairly.

To avoid the recurrence of such a situation, it is proposed here as follows:

(a) A ruling political party must not be allowed to participate in the electoral process; that is, be responsible for organizing and conducting elections.

(b) The new Constitution should establish an Electoral Commission independent of the Executive, with power to sue and be sued, with its own secretariat and staff. It should be appointed by the President in consultation with the leaders of all political parties. Their appointment must be ratified by the constituent assembly in the first instance and by the National Assembly in the future. Each political party must be represented on the Commission, and the Commission should enjoy the same degree of independence as the judges of the High Court and the Court of Appeal.

(c) The Commission should be wholly responsible for drawing up constituency boundaries, registration of voters, counting of ballots, and declaration of results, independent of the Executive.

(d) The Commission should be responsible for conducting both general and local elections.

The Constitution should deal with "crossing the floor", i.e. when members of the National Assembly change their political allegiance from one party to another, without even consulting their electors. A member who changes his party political allegiance should be required to resign his seat and seek a fresh mandate from his constituents.

8. Political Party Systems

One of the Eighteen Points given by the Armed Forces for taking over power from Obote on 25 January 1971 was: "The lack of freedom in the airing of different views on political and social matters."

Just before the 1971 overthrow of the Obote regime, there was considerable uneasiness in the country. By the provisions of the Constitutions of 1966 and 1967, members of the National Assembly had prolonged their term by another five years. A state of emergency prevailed throughout the country, enabling the government to detain thousands of people without trial. The government did not allow criticism, but closed its ears to all constructive suggestions on how to solve the problems of the country. Amin had forbidden political activities, making it an offence for three or more persons to discuss together anything political.[27] Consequently his massacre of Ugandans went unchallenged within Uganda. Binaisa's "umbrella" policy whereby all political parties were to merge into one national organization led to his overthrow. All these events have shown that without political freedom, there can never be stability, peace and progress in Uganda. Political parties must be allowed to flourish. To avoid conflict, the public must be given the right to discuss matters affecting the nation. Pent-up feelings may flare up into violence otherwise.

What form of party system is then ideal for Uganda? Let us first examine the options.

One of the matters dealt with in constitutions is the method by which the people are to elect their representatives in the legislature and the head of state. For this purpose, most constitutions permit the freedom of association for political purposes. When such a right is given, people wishing to promote, establish or gain some acceptance for some form of government, policy or programme will band together and organize themselves into a political party. Political parties thus become a vehicle for choosing the government of the people. The voter is given the option to elect one candidate on the strength of the policy of the governmental programme he advocates through his party. It follows that where the nations is divided on what policies to follow or what kind of government programmes to adopt, two or more political parties will emerge, with each party striving to win acceptance for its views and promises.

Three types of party systems can be identified around the world. At the extreme end are those countries with only one political party, usually referred to as one-party states. These include Tanzania, Zambia, Zaire and Kenya in Africa - and the Communist countries of Eastern Europe including the Soviet Union. In the middle are the bi-party states in which only two parties dominate the political scene. The United States of America is the clearest example of such a bi-party state, as the only parties capable of winning elections are thc Democratic and the Republican Parties. Countries like Britain, Italy and West Germany are multi-party states today.

8.1. One-party Systems

Each country has its own peculiar reasons for preferring one-party state. In the Soviet Union, for example, the Communist Party has always held that it must remain the sole, undivided guiding star in Soviet society. Leadership of the party is the necessary condition for the stability and firmness of the Communist system, and it is held that only one party can achieve the goals of socialism. In Tanzania, the principle argument for having a democratic, one-party state has been that nation-building requires the combined efforts of all available manpower.

The existence of two or more parties would mean that section of the population belonging to the opposition parties would not participate in the Government or have a voice in national affairs. It has also been said that traditional African cultural attitudes and communal practices favour decisions by consensus. It is not African to organize society in such a way that one side exists to oppose another: instead, all participate in decision-making. Furthermore, multi-party systems are seen as artificial luxuries which tend to make a game of the management of the affairs of the nation. They also represent and solidify class divisions and inequalities.

Another reason advanced is that a priority in new nations is to forge national unity. Tribal and sectional divisions stand in the way of unification. With more than one party, political organizations tend to reflect religious, tribal or sectional divisions. But with a national movement identified with the nation as a whole, such opportunities for tribal grouping are eliminated. In multi-party states, each party represents only a section of the community, not the whole nation - and this is prejudicial to building a united nation. It has also been argued that in nation building, an essential factor is communication between the people and their government. This must be two-way traffic, from the people to the government, and from the government to the people. The only machinery that can achieve this satisfactorily is a national movement wholly identified with the people and the government. Hence the need for a one-party state. Through the machinery of the party, the government can pass its policies to the people, and the people can convey back their reactions to these policies.[28]

On the other hand, those opposed to one-party states argue that if there is only one political movement in a country, the regime will degenerate into a dictatorship. This is mainly because the government will not be able to listen to constructive criticism of its policies and will shut its doors to alternative solutions to national problems. Those in power may tend to entrench themselves regardless of the wishes of the people. This argument seems partly true of the socialist countries, where membership in the party is not open to everybody, and the regimes use the party to suppress any opinions contrary to its views. In the Soviet Union, for example, two general rules apply in recruitment to the party: An applicant must first serve a period of probation as a candidate before being finally admitted. To become a candidate and later be admitted to membership, a person must be sponsored by a party member of several years standing. Party membership is consequently selective and not universal.

This is quite contrary to what is happening in Tanzania, for example. In Tanzania, membership of the CCM is open to all citizens who accept the beliefs, aims and objects of the party.[29] Once within the party, a person can oppose, criticize and make suggestions freely, provided these fall within the broad policies of the party. Moreover, at elections, the citizen is given a choice of two rival candidates to vote for. And should public officials violate his rights, he can resort to the Permanent Commission of Inquiry (the country's ombudsman) and lodge a complaint. Thus, the Tanzania example shows that one-party system can be truly democratic.

In conclusion, we may say that one-party states degenerate into dictatorships not simply because they are one-party, but because of the policies of those who manipulate the political machine.

Another argument advanced against one-party state is that it tends to disfranchise the electorate. In genuine elections, the argument goes, the electorate votes on the policies of two or more political parties and has a choice of candidates. But in one-party states, the voter is given Hobson's choice: either take and accept the policy, or leave it. Though this argument is valid, the Tanzania electoral system has shown that it is not always accurate. In Tanzania, for instance, voters are limited only in the types of policy to vote for. As mentioned, they are given the choice of two candidates to vote for. However, they are limited in the election of the President, because only one candidate is put forward by the Party. Even here, if the majority of the votes cast is against the presidential candidate, the party must place another candidate before the voters.[30] Franchise in a one-party state can, therefore, be democratic, depending on the style of the political system.

Perhaps a more valid argument against a one-party system is that it tends to restrict unduly the freedom of the people to associate for political purposes. Since the constitution provides that only one named party is to be the sole party in the state, those citizens who do not share the beliefs, aims and objectives of the legal party have no right to band together and form their own party to advocate different beliefs, aims and objectives. They are altogether excluded from exercising their political rights.

This leads to another disadvantage of the one-party system. Those who do not belong to the party may become objects of discrimination and victimization, in appointments to public posts or in the administration of public services generally. In Tanzania, for example, only party members can stand for public elections of any kind - local or national. Public servants who hold positions of responsibility must also abide by the leadership conditions laid down by the party. It is a disciplinary offence for civil servants or members of the armed forces and the police not to abide by the leadership code. Thus, party and government have merged.

8.2. Multi- and Bi-party Systems

As opposed to the one-party system, multi-party and two-party systems have important advantages. Normally one or more parties will form the government while the other(s) will remain in opposition. It is the duty of the opposition to make constructive criticisms of the performance of the party or parties in power, thereby helping to ensure good government, as the government will then strive to avoid mistakes and meet every reasonable point of view. By contrast, in one-party states, where organized opposition does not exist, there is no opportunity for open discussion of the actions and measures of the government, so the government and the public do not benefit from responsible criticism.

Another advantage of the multi-party system is that national differences can be compromised in Parliament. In one-party states, no such opportunity may exist, as the only and ruling party has the sole voice in national affairs.

As opposed to multi-party states, two-party states enjoy one major advantage. Normally one party wins an election, forms the government and remains in office for up to five years. The party is, therefore, able to carry out its programme. On the other hand, in multi-party states it may happen that no single party wins an absolute majority. This means a coalition of parties with contradictory policies for the government. This has two serious disadvantages. Each party is unable to fulfil all its promises to the electorate as it has to make concessions to the other parties. Secondly, disagreements abound in coalition governments, so the government may not last long. A succession of short-lived governments may result, which is not conducive to the political stability so essential for other types of development.

So far Uganda has five political parties: the Democratic Party, Uganda Peoples Congress, the Conservative Party, Uganda People's Movement and the Federal Democratic Party. Experience of the last general election shows that only the first two are capable of winning elections outright. Coalitions can therefore be avoided. It is proposed that the new constitution should recognize these political parties. As mentioned, a one-party system denies the public the right to associate for political purposes, to propagate different political beliefs and philosophies, and may lead to discrimination against non-party members. It is accordingly recommended that Uganda should continue with its present multiparty democracy.

9. Constitution Making

The next question to consider is how to make a constitution that can resolve the present conflict in Uganda. A constitution being a document containing rules in accordance with which the people's affairs are to be managed, it must be tailored to suit the conditions and circumstances of the particular country. A constitution that is good for one country is not necessarily suited to another. It must be home grown and home made, acceptable to the people, understood by them and respected by them. Every citizen has the right to participate in making the constitution.

It is accordingly suggested that the Government and forces fighting it must lay down their arms, sit at a round-table conference and discuss each other's stand. Once an agreement has been reached, the Government should call a national conference to discuss the Uganda the people want, a conference to be attended by representatives of all ethnic groups in Uganda. Soon after the conference the Government should appoint a constitutional commission to travel all over the country to receive views from the members of the public on the type of constitution they want. After that, the Commission should make a report in the form of a draft constitution, to be submitted to the people for further debate. The people should then elect their representatives to a constituent assembly which considers the draft. All representatives must remain in close touch with their constituents, so as to reflect their views accurately. The constituent assembly must pass the draft by two thirds majority for the Constitution to become adopted.

The 1966 Constitution was imposed on the people by Obote. It triggered off a serious strife between Buganda and the central government. The 1967 Constitution was imposed on the people by a National Assembly whose legal term of office had expired, which is why it is not popular with most Ugandans. One way to resolve conflicts through a constitution is to allow the people to participate in making it.

10. Amending the Constitution

A constitution is expected to enjoy a maximum degree of sanctity and respect. It should not be changed, modified or abrogated merely to suit the policies of successive governments; it must not be amended so often that is loses its peculiar character of being the source of all laws and governmental powers.

That is why in many countries the constitution is more difficult to amend or change than other laws. In other words, some constitutions are rigid, as for example the constitution of the United States. Under Article V of the US Constitution, any constitutional amendment must be proposed and ratified on a national basis. Either 2/3 of both Houses propose the amendment or the legislatures of 2/3 of the 50 States petition Congress to call a convention for proposing an amendment. In both cases, ratification must be by a 3/4 majority: either 3/4 of the legislatures or by conventions of 3/4 of the 50 States. Normally, amendments have been by proposal by Congress and ratification by the legislatures of the States. The US Constitution has been made deliberately rigid to ensure that successive Administrations or Congresses will not be able to tamper with certain fundamental institutions of the Union. These include the federal structure, the constituent States, the central management of matters like interstate and foreign commerce, and the rights of the individual.

In some other countries, any proposal for amending the Constitution is referred to the people for approval in a referendum. The people are given the power to reject or ratify proposed amendments. In Australia[31] and Switzerland,[32] for example, this procedure is mandatory. These two countries, like the United States, are federations. In a federation where the interests of the state and federal governments are set against each other, agreed arrangements entrenched in the Constitution must be protected from rash or sectarian alterations. The Constitution will accordingly require special majorities and procedures for amendments, to avoid the possibility of a legislature destroying the whole fabric of the Constitution by a single enactment.

Uganda should follow this approach. Since her new Constitution will be made with the participation of all citizens, all citizens should participate in any changes to it. It is accordingly recommended that all proposals for amending the Constitution should be put to the people in a referendum, and that these may be passed only with a 4/5 majority.

11. Summary and Conclusions

A constitution can resolve conflicts because:

(a) It is like a peace treaty, laying down agreed arrangements on how the affairs of the nation are to be managed;

(b) It is a compromise, attempting to accommodate as many views, desires, demands and expectations as possible;

(c) It tries to allay fears by incorporating a Bill of Rights;

(d) It can eliminate future conflicts by limiting the powers of the Executive;

(e) It can enable every part of the country to participate in the government.

For these reasons it is here recommended that Uganda should adapt a unitary constitution with devolution of powers to the districts. This constitution should establish a presidential form of government, with checks and balances provided by the judiciary and by the legislature. The legislature should be bi-cameral so that the voice of every district can be equally heard. The constitution should set up an independent electoral commission, representative of all political parties. The present multi-party system should continue. All citizens should participate in making the new constitution for Uganda. And, finally, any constitutional amendment must be approved by the people in a referendum.

Notes

1. The Constitution of the United States of America.
2. The Independence Constitution of Kenya, 1963, since replaced by the Constitution of the Republic of Kenya, 1969, which set up a Unitary State after fears of the minority subsided.
3. The Constitution of the Federal Republic of Nigeria, 1979.
4. The Constitution of the United Republic of Tanzania, 1977, as amended by Act 15 of 1984.
5. Constitution of Uganda, 1962, schedule I.
6. Ibid., schedules II to V.
7. Report of the Privy Councillors on the Dispute between Bunyoro and Buganda. Entebbe: Government Printer, 1962.
8. Constitution of Uganda (Third Amendment) Act, 1964 (Act 30 of 1964).
9. (1966) E.A. 306.
10. (1966) E.A. 445.
11. Legal Notice 6 of 1986.
12. Sempebwa V. Attorney General (Unreported, Constitutional Case No. 1 of 1987).
13. In the United Kingdom they are called "counties", in France "prefectures", in Nigeria "local government areas", in Tanzania "regions", in Uganda and Kenya "districts".
14. It was for this reason that the Constitution of Uganda, 1962, was semi-federal.
15. Wheare, K.C.: Federal Government. London: Oxford University Press, 1945.
16. See the Constitution of the United States of America, Art 2.
17. Constitution of the United Republic of Tanzania, 1977, as amended by Act 15 of 1984.
18. The relevant provisions of the Constitution of Nigeria and Ghana have been suspended.
19. Constitution of the Swiss Confederation, Arts 95-99.
20. Constitution of the USSR, Act 128.
21. Act 61 of 1963.
22. Uganda Argus, 23 February 1966.
23. For these statements see Uganda v. Commissioner of Prisons, Ex. Parte Matovu (1966) E.A. 514.
24. Constitution of Uganda, 1966.
25. Provisions of Art. 55 of the Constitution of the Federal Republic of Nigeria.
26. Constitution of Kenya, Art. 40.
27. Prohibition of Political Activities Decree, 1971.
28. Nyerere, J.K.: Freedom and Unity. London: Oxford University Press, 1967, pp. 195-205.
29. Constitution of Chama Cha Mapinduzi, Art. III.
30. Constitution of the United Republic of Tanzania, Chapter II.
31. The Constitution of Australia Act, 1900.
32. The Swiss Constitution, Art. 120.

Dan Mudoola

Communal Conflict in the Military and its Political Consequences

> Ugandans are gentle people; they are law abiding. It is the Government which has staged a revolution against the people. Ugandans have not staged a revolution against the Government. But every human quality has a limit. There may come a time when the people of Uganda will be forced to stage a peoples' revolution. Do not misuse our army, do not misuse the police. Do not make them hated by their own fathers, mothers and sisters.
>
> Martin A. Okello
> MP, West Nile and Madi Central, 1967

1. Introductory Remarks

On the eve of Independence and immediately thereafter, a euphoric atmosphere prevailed in Uganda. The nation had recovered her independence with all the trappings of constitutionalism. A constitution had been worked out, the result of protracted negotiations among the major political actors - the major parties, the Kingdom areas and Busoga, the districts and the retreating colonial power. Constitutional arrangements sought to work out political formulae for balancing the conflicting interests of the major political actors. These formulae involved a periodically elected Parliament, a Cabinet drawn from and responsible to Parliament, federal and quasi-federal status for Buganda and the Kingdom areas and Busoga respectively; and clearly defined powers of the major organs of government, the civil service and the judiciary. On the first anniversary of Independence, this original constitution was amended to provide for a ceremonial president to replace the Governor-General.

On the opening of the first Independence Parliament, the Queen's representative, the Duke of Kent, members of the coalition UPC-KY government and, to some extent, members of the Opposition were in a sanguine, self-congratulatory mood. The Duke of Kent promised that his Government "would foster the spirit of tolerance and goodwill between all the peoples of Uganda. It would pay due heed to the traditional beliefs and customs of the diverse peoples of Uganda. It would respect individual rights of the common man. It would recognize the special status and dignity of the Hereditary Rulers of the Kingdoms and of the Constitutional Heads of the Districts".[2] In equal measure, the Prime Minister, Apollo Milton Obote, believed that "traditional institutions would form a firm foundation upon which our newly independent state could be advanced".[3] The Opposition leader Basil Bataringaya, however, cautioned against "tribalism and factionalism, our two most deadly enemies - and unless we can acquire a sense of common purpose we can never be sure that our future path will be entirely smooth".[4]

Within the space of less than four years, another actor who had never been part of the political calculations leading to Independence was to come on the scene. This was the Uganda Army. On 25 January 1964, there was an army mutiny whose objectives were apparently limited; it was suppressed. In 1966, with an army purged of his opponents and after a confrontation with Sir Edward Mutesa, Milton Obote overthrew the 1962 constitutional arrangements. He chased out Sir Edward Mutesa II, who was both Kabaka of Buganda and President of Uganda, introduced an Interim Constitution (to be followed by the 1967 Constitution) and ruled, basically with army support, until overthrown in the 1971 January coup. Next, from 1971 to 1978, Idi Amin used the army as an instrument of rule until he, too, was overthrown, by a combination of Tanzanian and Ugandan forces. Despite misgivings about the activist role of the military in politics and some apparent efforts to define its place in Uganda by the National Liberation Front regimes, the Uganda military has continued to be actively involved in Uganda's political processes. From 1981 until July 1985, Uganda was embroiled in a Civil War, with the National Resistance Army seeking to overthrow Obote. Under NRA harassment, Obote was overthrown by the Uganda National Liberation Army led by "the Okellos" who, in turn, were to be swept out by the National Resistance Movement.

The objective of this paper is to explain the circumstances that have given rise to such a political activist role of the Uganda military. S.P Huntington, in his incisive study from 1968,[5] attributes the interventionist role of the military in the politics of changing societies to a state of political and institutional normlessness - a situation lacking widely accepted and legitimate procedures for resolving conflicts, short of physical show of force. In such a situation, social and political forces become highly politicized, all competing to advance their own interests through rules of the game they seek to dictate to other competing social and political forces. The military dramatically enter the political arena simply because they happen to have the advantage of the means of coercion.

> Each group employs means which reflect its peculiar nature and capabilities. The wealthy bribe; students riot, workers strike, mobs demonstrate and the military coup. In the absence of accepted procedures, all these forms of direct action are found on the political scene. The techniques of military intervention are simply more dramatic and effective than the others because, as Hobbes puts it, "when nothing else is turned up, clubs are trumps". (Huntington, p. 196)

Huntington's model can go a long way to explain the circumstances that have led the Ugandan military to play a political activist role on the Uganda political processes. The major argument of this paper is that such a role has been the result of failure on the part of successive Uganda political leaderships to work out widely-accepted institutionalized means of resolving conflicts by peaceful means.[6] Political leaderships operate within the formal rules only to the extent to which these rules are tactically useful to them: they are only too ready to operate outside these rules when it serves their interests. The Uganda military is not insulated from this institutionless arena. It became a political actor when competing socio-political forces, in a bid to tilt the balance in their favour, sought the support of the military. The result was that the Ugandan military, after Independence, was built, expanded and equipped in response to internal political cum military crises which, in turn, ultimately led to its markedly activist role on its own terms.

2. The Uganda Military in the Making

On Independence Day, the presence of the Uganda military was marked only by a few troops which took part in the ceremonies and by a young officer, Karugaba, recently from the Royal Military Academy at Sandhurst. Karugaba was acting as aide-de-camp to the Duke of Kent, the Queen's representative at the Independence ceremonies. At Independence, the Uganda Rifles, the successor to the colonial army, consisted of only one battalion of about a thousand men, mostly recruited from the then Northern Province, especially from Acholi. The Rifles were at that time still officered by British officers, seconded from their metropolitan units.

For its size and equipment, the Uganda Rifles had overwhelming tasks to perform. It was deployed to maintain law and order in various parts of the country where there were tensions arising from secession attempts among the Bamba/Bakonjo from the Toro Kingdom, cattle rustling in Karamoja, and the spillover effects from civil disturbances in the Congo, the Sudan and Rwanda.

It was in response to the above tasks as well as, probably, for symbolic reasons that the new Ugandan leadership saw a need to expand and equip the Uganda Rifles. Initially, this expansion was characterized by goodwill from both the Government and the Opposition, accompanied, however, by some apparent caution with regard to expenditures involved and maintenance of standards.[7] A programme for expanding the army and training an officer corps was launched. In the budget for the fiscal year 1962/63, army estimates were doubled in order "to meet the full cost of maintaining our First Battalion - for a full financial year" and in order to build up another battalion in Moroto. Provisions were made to establish a training wing at Jinja for officer cadets, and arrangements were made with the British government to have Ugandans trained at Sandhurst and at the school for officer cadets in Aldershot. Already by mid-1963, according to Felix Onama, Minister of Internal Affairs, there were 28 Ugandan officers serving in the army, with a further 30 undergoing training.[8]

There was goodwill all around to expand the army and train a Ugandan military officer corps. Onama's programme was endorsed by the Leader of the Opposition, who, however, felt uneasy about the alleged political and regional "high-handedness" of the expatriate officers with "other officers and the alleged political and regional considerations going into recruitment of the Ugandan officer corps in the making".[9]

But for all this programme of expansion and training, the Government appears to have been in no hurry to fully Ugandanize the officer corps, as evidenced in the President's speech:

> The expansion of the Uganda Army continues to go ahead as planned. It is the government's hope that by the end of 1964 eight Company Commanders will be Ugandans and that by the end of 1965 two Battalion Commanders will be Ugandans. It will be seen that if this plan comes to fruition then the roles of those officers seconded to us from the British Armed Forces will gradually change and it is hoped that they will remain in an advisory capacity.[10]

Thus, according to the President, a Uganda Army fully commanded and officered by Ugandans was timetabled to take a couple of years from the date of the President's speech. But on 25 January 1964, Government leaders were rudely jolted out of their timetable when men of the First Battalion refused to obey orders, demanding pay increases and general improvements in their conditions. Details of what happened need not detain us here;[11] the significance of the mutiny lies in the Government's reaction to the incident, their interpretation of the events and the politico-military consequences arising from the incident at Jinja.

The Government at once approached the British Government for military assistance to quell the mutiny.[12] The British promptly sent a battalion from the Staffordshire Regiment who took control of the situation immediately on arrival and disarmed the mutinous troops. Men of the Headquarters Company and "A" Company were dismissed, and a court-martial was set up to try the ringleaders. By 14 March 1964, men from the Staffordshire Regiment were ready to leave.

It now remained for the leadership to make a post-mortem of the January events. Abdala Anyuru introduced a motion in Parliament deploring the events in Jinja but noting "with great appreciation and satisfaction the promptness with which the government had dealt with the situation".[13] The official interpretation is worth remarking on: The event had no political implications; it was an isolated incident involving men of the Headquarters Company and "A" Company who had gone on strike over pay; therefore, their deplorable behaviour could not be generalized with respect to the Ugandan military as an institution.[14]

The occasion, however, provided Members with an opportunity to air their views about their army, with particular reference to its especial role and to regional imbalances within the military. Martin Okello was not happy with the way the governing party had allegedly ingratiated itself with the military during the pre-

Independence election, to which he attributed the unhappy events at Jinja.[15] Ali Kisekka was unhappy about the regional imbalance in the army which favoured the Northern region; in this he saw negative implications for nation-building.[16] But the Northern members were all out to defend the doctrine of ethno-functionalism[17] with particular reference to the military. For in words of Lakidi:

> Some people are born to be good traders, some are born to be very good civil servants, some are born to protect this country. The North has been heavily accused that the recruitment is all the time going to the North. I think many people should be grateful to the North, and particularly to my tribe, Acholi. The Acholi have pledged themselves to protect this country. If they are in the army they have got to be supported. If people are beginning to speak in this House to discredit them, their morale in the army, the police and prisons would be lowered.[18]

In the aftermath of January events, the military gained more than they had bargained for. They did obtain their pay rise. Moreover, at the time of mutiny, "there had been 55 officers, including 2 majors and 14 captains and the rest lieutenants".[19] Immediately after the mutiny, command of companies was taken over by Ugandans. Seven months after the mutiny, there was a big promotion exercise in which 19 Ugandan officers were promoted. Shaban Opolot was promoted to Brigadier and appointed Commander of the Uganda Army; Idi Amin was promoted to Colonel and made Deputy Commander. The rest were promoted to ranks ranging from Lieutenant Colonel to Temporary Major and Temporary Captain.[20]

In the light of subsequent complaints about a predominantly Northern officer corps, in this promotion exercise, it is worth noting that ethnic representation appeared reasonably balanced: 6 Iteso, 3 Nubians, 4 Banyankole, 2 Banyoro, 2 "West Nilers" and 1 Langi.

What were the politico-military consequences of the mutiny? We have already noted that the Government tended, at least in public, to regard the mutiny as of limited consequence. The mutiny reflected the fragility of the politico-civilian institutions in the making; after the mutiny, inevitably, politicians had to reckon with the military as part of their political calculations for survival; but there was still no serious effort to work out political mechanisms for ensuring that civilian supremacy would prevail over the military.

During the critical January days, the actors in containing the mutiny were confined to Obote himself and a few colleagues, the British government and men of the Staffordshire Regiment. The political parties had to content themselves with sending congratulatory messages after the event, and Parliament had "to note with appreciation and satisfaction the way the government had handled the situation". There had been no single civilian political force to stand in the way of the mutineers. Obote had to swallow his pride and invite the erstwhile colonial power to protect the civilian institutions - or so he hoped.

Despite all appearances, the new visibility of the military was not lost to politicians. They took care not to condemn the military as an institution. Their speeches in Parliament were punctuated by words of gratitude to those who had remained loyal. This should have been the time for reflection to see how the role of the military could have been redefined in the new nation state. After such similar events in Tanzania, the Tanzanian government had taken steps to ensure that civilian supremacy would not be questioned that easily. To de-mystify the monopoly of use of arms, national military service was introduced in Tanzania; the whole army, at least officially, disarmed and disbanded; the new army was to be socialized and politicized into its roles. It was made clear where, ultimately, legitimate power lay - within the ruling party in Tanzania.

In the Ugandan case, however, in civilian-military relations the leadership stuck to and invoked the simple command-obey model in which the military were an instrument of the state; the military had to be disciplined, and had a clear chain of command. But the Government seemed to have no idea how this could be operationalized. The absence of an official operational formula for domesticating the Uganda military meant that in their factional bids for power, groups would have to work out their own private agenda for politicizing the military on their own terms - which, as we shall see, has had tragic consequences for the country.

Expanding, equipping and training the army proceeded uninterrupted between the years 1964 and 1970. In the course of six years, four battalions were established - the First Battalion at Jinja, the Second at Moroto, the Third at Mubende and the Fourth at Mbarara. In addition, there were other formations. An Ordinance Depot was established at Magamaga; an Artillery Regiment and Signals Training Wing at Masindi. After the confrontation with Sir Edward Mutesa, the Malire Mechanized

Specialist Reconnaissance Regiment was established in the former Kabaka's Palace in the centre of Kampala. This was an elite mobile regiment well equipped with armoured personnel carriers, Sherman tanks and recoilless guns. Brigade headquarters were established at Mbale for the First Infantry Brigade and at Masaka for the Second Infantry Brigade; a Training Wing for recruits and Senior NCCs at Jinja, and a school for paratroopers at Lubiri. With Israeli assistance, an Air Force was established early in 1965.[21]

This expansion and equipment of the army was basically a response to internal and border problems. At the height of the expansion, there were troubles in Karamoja; in the "lost counties"; in the heartland, Buganda, where a State of Emergency had been declared after the events of 1966. It is worth noting that some of these battalions were established in or near the epicentres of trouble-Mbarara close to Bakonjo/Bamba county; Mubende in the "lost counties"; Moroto in Karamoja.

The consequences of such a relatively large military establishment within so short a time are not hard to imagine. The army emerged as a highly visible institution with a status it had never enjoyed before. The political leadership spoke of it endearingly and were only too ready to give it whatever could be afforded.[22] This in turn must have generated into the army a growing sense of functional indispensability. The Ugandanization of the officer corps had not gone quite according to the leaders' original timetable, as Felix Onama, Minister of Internal Affairs, had to admit. "Our Ugandan officers are, therefore, plunged into work and responsibility far larger than they could have expected in the normal course of an army career".[23] Before the officer corps found themselves drawn into the power struggles of the mid-1960s, they had not quite managed to settle down to an esprit de corps which, one might hope, would have insulated them from political pressures.

3. Political Crises - the 1966 Crisis

From 1964 onward, tensions erupted within the civilian political institutions, turning Uganda into a virtually institutionless arena, with groups ignoring the formally established rules and seeking to impose rules only they themselves understood. The period 1962-1966 was one of apparent peace, not necessarily because the leaders were committed to working within the formally established constitutional framework, but simply because none of the leaders and the groups they represented felt strong enough to overthrow the rules of the game. Within a few months after Independence there were already signs that groups would play the game only to the extent their interests could be served. Addressing a press conference in April 1963, Obote said: "The Uganda People's Congress will never be dislocated from power by any mathematical manipulations".[24] What, however, if these mathematical manipulations were carried out according to the established constitutional rules? Obote himself was to provide the answers early in 1966.

Tensions which ultimately undermined constitutionalism arose from conflicting interpretations of Buganda's autonomy, conflicting interpretations of constitutional rules of the game; the "lost counties" issue, and cleavages within the Uganda People's Congress, the ruling party. The sum total of all these crises was that constitutionalism was undermined, and that the military would be brought into the political arena, with contending political actors vying for support within the army.

The alliance between the Uganda People's Congress and the Kabaka Yekka had arisen out of a desire on the part of the two parties to reap maximum advantages. Soon after they formed the coalition government, conflicting interpretations of the constitution arose, with Buganda seeking to take over central government police stations in Buganda. With relations somewhat strained, the Buganda leadership believed they could play a game by taking the central government to court and/or withdrawing from the alliance, which provoked Obote into making the "no mathematical manipulations" statement referred to above.

Through "crossings" in Parliament from the Democratic Party and Kabaka Yekka, Obote was numerically strong enough by October 1964 to allow the plebiscite to take place in the "lost counties" of Buyaga and Bugangaizi - to the extreme annoyance of the Buganda Government. The population voted for return of the counties to Bunyoro. Announcement of the result of the referendum was followed by the resignation of Michael Kintu's government at Mengo and widespread rioting in Buganda. To contain the situation, Obote warned that "maximum force" would be used to quell any disturbances, which was interpreted literally by some men of the Special Force, a para-military organization. At Nakulabye, in the suburbs of Kampala, Special Force men opened fire and killed an indeterminate number of people

The Nakulabye massacre, as it has been called, is notable for a number of reasons. It marked the beginnings of use of naked force in the Uganda heartland. True, force had been used in the troubled marginal areas - Toro, Karamoja and on the borders- but never so close to Kampala. The incident also marked the beginnings of alienation between Buganda and the Obote government, worsened by the provocative statements of Onama, the Minister of Internal Affairs, and his overprotectiveness of the atrocious behaviour of the security forces in Buganda. Although a Commission of Inquiry was set up to investigate the Nakulabye massacre, relations between Buganda and the central government were never to be the same.[25] The UPC-KY alliance came to an end.

Nor had all been well within the leadership of the Uganda People's Congress since the 1964 Gulu UPC Delegates' Conference, where populist Secretary General, John Kakonge, had been ousted and replaced by Grace Ibingira.[26] With the break-up of the UPC-KY alliance and massive "crossings" to the government party, numerically the UPC looked formidable - but there were inherent seeds of instability. Cleavages emerged, mainly along regional lines. The anti-Obote supporters took advantage of a motion alleging that Obote, Colonel Idi Amin, Nekyon and Felix Onama had amassed wealth during Uganda/Congo border clashes, to censure the Obote Administration. The motion sought a Commission of Inquiry into these allegations and suspension of Army Commander, Idi Amin, from duty. With the support of the UPC parliamentary group, the motion was passed.[27]

Clearly this was a revolt against Obote. In the normal course of events, strictly within the constitutional rules of the game, various courses of action would have been open to Obote. He could have dissolved Parliament and called for new elections to seek a new mandate; formed a new government pending new elections, the date of which he would determine; called for an emergency UPC Delegates' Conference to explain his case and thereby "corner" his opponents; or he could simply have awaited the outcome of the Commission of Inquiry. But Obote chose the perilous but apparently easier path of arresting and detaining his five ministers and the Commander of the Army, Shaban Opolot, suspending the 1962 Independence Constitution, declaring himself President, and introducing an Interim Constitution. The lone voice to react against all this was the Buganda government, which called on Obote and his government "to remove themselves from Buganda soil". This provided Obote with a neat casus belli- he sent troops to attack the Kabaka's Palace, which he occupied after some fighting. Sir Edward Mutesa fled into exile. Buganda was declared a Disturbed Area.

Clearly, Obote was operating outside the established constitutional rules of the game. He had ignored the civilian institutions - he had not resolved the crisis within Parliament, nor through the party. He was able to do this only because he had won the support of a faction within the army under Commander Idi Amin. While the civilian political institutions were under strain through the cleavages outlined above, these cleavages spilled over into the Army, with factions aligning themselves with their civilian counterparts. Before his arrest, Shaban Opolot was reported to be aligned with some "Bantu" officers with Sir Edward Mutesa and the detained ministers. Obote had moved fast to purge the Army of suspect officers, winning the full support of Idi Amin. Thus he was able, with critical Army backing, to resolve a basically constitutional issue by military means. The Army had mounted the political stage.

4. Obote's Search for Legitimacy - the Way to the 1971 Coup

After the defeat of Sir Edward Mutesa and his opponents within the party, Obote proceeded to define his own rules of the game. He drafted the 1967 Constitution and presented it to Parliament. However, their options were severely circumscribed, for any casual observer could see that the military were the meaningful power behind the scene. Uganda was declared a Republic; monarchies were abolished; a Presidency, of which Obote himself was the incumbent, was established. Briefly, this was a unitary constitution.

With the defeat of his opponents, the party in disarray, and a cowed Parliament, Obote was at the height of his power. Dizzy with success, he told his Parliament:

> Hon. Gentlemen, there is nothing to regret; what we have to deal with is clear. What we have is determination and in the Government we are determined - I have given you a full statement, it is up to you to give the necessary support. You have a big responsibility, all of us have a big responsibility. Some philosopher once said "The midwife of an old society pregnant with a new one is force". It is my view that Buganda is an old society pregnant with a new one.[28]

In some sense, however, Obote as a prisoner of his own success, as so often happens in such situations. The net effect of his success was to undermine precisely those politico-civilian institutions which he so badly needed to legitimize his rule. Obote acquired a "conqueror mentality",[29] as reflected in his speeches, actions and actions of his troops occupying Buganda. The Kabaka's Palace (Lubiri) and the headquarters of the Buganda Lukiiko (Parliament) were regarded as war booty and were converted into barracks and army headquarters, respectively, the latter to be renamed "Republic House". The atrocious behaviour of the troops in Buganda was a subject of bitter comments by Baganda members of Parliament, some of their relatives having been victims, but this only drew sarcastic barbed remarks from Mr. Onama, the Minister of Defence.[30]

For some two years Obote nursed the army as his critical power constituency. He took salutes at passing out parades, attended weddings of high-ranking officers, witnessed army exercises and, of course, made speeches on these occasions. In a space of about one and a half years, Obote visited various military installations six times.[31] All these, in the normal course of events, would not have been out of the ordinary since he was the Commander in Chief, but they are telling in the context of the times we are discussing. His officers were well rewarded. In April 1968, Amin was promoted to Major-General and appointed Chief of Defence Staff and "Principal Military Advisor to the Cabinet and the Minister of Defence"; Colonel Suleiman Hussein and Colonel Pierino Yere Okoya were promoted to the rank of Brigadier.[32] In general, the military were amply provided for, materially.

The net effect of introducing the new constitution by extra-legal means was a politico-institutional void which Obote saw had to be filled. He must have realized that he was riding on the back of a tiger and would have somehow to devise means of domesticating it by "re-organizing" the Uganda People's Congress on his own terms, introducing formal politico-cultural norms to sustain him in power and by building countervailing forces to neutralize the military.

We have already noted that immediately before and after the 1966 crisis, the Uganda People's Congress was in disarray. The major political question of the day had been resolved by the sword. In 1968, Obote called a Delegates' Conference, the first since 1964, and defined the rules on his own terms. From past experience, he realized that the party could provide an independent power base. He now sought to strengthen his hand over the party. At this conference, he was "re-elected" President of the Party for a seven year term and was given the power to nominate officials to hold office only at his pleasure.[33] In this way the party was dependent on Obote, not vice-versa. For the next three years, until he was overthrown, it cannot be said that high policy decisions originated from party organs: the party simply served as a forum through which policies worked out by Obote were legitimized. It is worth noting that the Common Man's Charter and the accompanying "Move to the Left" documents had all been drafted outside party organs, and were then "debated on" and approved within party fora. The critical nerve centre of power remained the Army.

The introduction of the 1967 Constitution and abolition of the monarchies had left a politico-cultural void. A political system cannot long depend on show of physical force alone; it must be backed by a core of political values, at least, among the politically significant social forces. With his opponents in prison or dead, or in exile, or vengeful, Obote made some attempts to introduce documentary ideological bases for the new order in a latently hostile political environment. This he did by trying to identify the "enemies" and by introducing the Common Man's Charter and the attendant documents.[34]

We have already seen that the 1966 crisis had been sparked off by a revolt within the UPC leadership. Basically the crisis had been over Obote's leadership, and his colleagues had been out to have him removed. In control of the mass media, the regime set about portraying the 1966 events as a revolution against forces of "Imperialism", "Feudalism" and in defence of the "Common Man", with Sir Edward Mutesa as the scapegoat. The semi-official ideologue of the new regime was Akena-Adoko, head of the intelligence service, euphemistically called the General Service Unit. In his book, The 1966 Crisis, he provided the ideological rationale for "Revolution".[35]

The Common Man's Charter and the Move to the Left documents were meant to herald a new political era in which the Common Man's interests would be paramount, in which the gap between rich and poor would be narrowed or closed altogether, and one in which there would be meaningful political participation. A theoretically ingenious formula for electing members of Parliament and the President was worked out.

The establishment and strengthening of the General Service Unit and the Special Force in the late mid-1960s was an apparent attempt to make them countervailing forces to the military. Much as the Army had been pampered, Obote was not quite too sure of them. Originally the General Service Unit had been set up as a "counter-espionage" organization, especially to watch over the activities of foreign missions. But as internal political crises intensified, its activities became increasingly domestic. Members of the service had been trained in the Soviet Union, Czechoslovakia and Israel. The Special Force had been built under colonial rule to deal with domestic problems too big for the police. After Independence, as domestic problems became more intense, the Special Force was expanded and equipped in military fashion. Nor was this building up of the General Service and the Special Force easily lost to the military. With Buganda subdued and without any active or potential power centre to challenge Obote's rule, the military must have come to very uncomfortable conclusions. In the last two years before the 1971 coup, relations between the General Service Unit and the Special Force on the one hand and the military on the other became strained. (Immediately after the January 1971 coup, members of the General Service Unit and Special Force were in fact to be rounded up and the two organizations were disbanded.)

Obote's attempt to reorganize the party, to introduce new political formulae and build countervailing forces to neutralize the military did not go far to regularize his regime and make it less dependent on the Army. This failure may be attributed to a political environment that was latently hostile or apathetic to the highly personalized civilian institutional arenas for handling conflicts and the power struggle shift from civilian to military institutions.

Despite his military victory over Buganda, Obote never quite made any political inroads into Buganda. The Baganda remained subdued, bitter and sulky. Until the 1971 coup, Buganda was in a state of emergency. And this is the economic, cultural and political heartland of the country. Because Buganda was either politically demobilized or subdued, this left the legitimacy of the Obote regime rather tenuous. Professor Gingyera-Pinycwa, lamenting the quarrel between Obote and Amin to which he particularly attributes the January 1971 coup, does not see any correlation between the political marginalization of the Baganda and the coup.[36] True, the Baganda had been disarmed, but the state of emergency in Buganda made Obote more unduly dependent on the Army for fear of domestic upheavals; and this, in turn, generated within the military a sense of politico-functional indispensability, relegating to the background the crucial importance of civil political institutions as legitimizing instruments. The way the Baganda were to cheer Amin immediately after the coup was to help legitimize the Amin coup domestically and internationally.

The political organs within the ruling party and Parliament had been either so personalized or cowed that no meaningful resolution of political conflicts could have taken place. The ascendancy of the military might have been contained if the institutions had been meaningfully strengthened, but such strengthening of civilian institutions would in itself have undermined Obote's power position. Meaningful power struggles shifted from civilian political institutions to the military. Here, Obote was placed at a tremendous disadvantage in that this arena was closed to him to operate freely. Too long had he left two of his closest supporters, Onama and Amin, in strategic positions. As relations between Amin and Obote soured, other institutional, civilian social forces simply assumed spectators' roles. Obote probably could have saved himself if he had played the game Stalin and Krushchev had played on Marshall Zhukov: removing the hero precisely at the pinnacle of his success.[37]

Tensions within the military, tensions which were to culminate in the January 1971 coup, arose from inter-service rivalries, generational cleavages within the officer corps, popularization within the military along ethnic lines and clumsy attempts on the part of Obote to have Amin neutralized in the Army. We have already touched on the rivalries between the Special Force and the General Service Unit on the one hand and the Army on the other. Strengthening of the General Service Unit and Special Force naturally alienated some elements within the Army further.

As the Army became more functionally complex, there was a need to recruit and train officers with relatively higher education. There were signs that some of these younger men were increasingly coming closer to command positions. Tensions within the officer corps between the new relatively well educated officers and officers from the ranks were common knowledge at the time. Coupled with this was ethnic polarization. By the late 1960s there were indications that Obote was seeking to build a smaller and hopefully more reliable base among the Acholi and Langi, as evidenced by the strategic command positions members of these groups held and by the elite units the men manned. Amin responded by carrying out recruitments of his own and by surrounding himself with officers he could trust.[38] There then followed the mysterious murder of Brigadier Okyoa and death in a car "accident" of Lieutenant-Colonel Omoya.

In late 1970s, Obote took advantage of Amin's absence abroad to carry out promotions within the Army, promotions leaving no doubt that Amin was on the way out. At this stage, with the army highly polarized, it was a question of who would strike first. While Obote was away in Singapore, attending the Commonwealth Heads of State Conference, Idi Amin staged his military coup.

In the light of the processes by which the military had acquired visibility and assumed a nakedly activist role in Uganda politics, we may argue that the Amin coup, and the politics Amin pursued afterwards, simply pushed to a logical conclusion trends already set by Obote - trends which increasingly rendered powerless any political institutions for resolving conflicts. By the time Amin assumed power, such institutions were so fragile that it needed only a simple announcement to have them banned. Party political activities were suspended and Parliament was dissolved; for the next 8 years all institutions - civilian and military - were subject to the dictates of Idi Amin.[39]

The Amin regime was to last some 9 years and yet it did not operate through institutions for resolving conflicts, short of use of force or terror. Terror was used as an instrument of domestic policy. Again, this pushed to a logical conclusion a precedent set by Obote, when he used the army as an instrument of domestic policy. True, Obote had been relatively more sophisticated in giving his courses of action some semblance of legitimacy through formal organs of the party and government; but the precedent was set.

5. The Military in the Post-1979 Regimes

The removal of Idi Amin did not relegate the military to the background. After all, Amin had been removed by military means - by a combination of the Tanzanian People's Defence Force and Uganda troops. Here we shall discuss the politics of the Uganda National Liberation Front and the Obote regime only to the extent that the military influenced the politics involved.[40] In these regimes, the military was virtually king-maker until with the entry of the "Okellos", the king-maker was to become King. Yusufu Lule and Godfrey Binaisa were removed partly because they had alienated the king-makers, and Milton Obote reassumed the Presidency mainly with support of the Military Commission. The orchestrated December 1980 elections were simply meant to legitimize the de facto state of affairs.

After the 1978/79 "Kagera War", Uganda leaders were highly ambivalent towards the military. With the defeat of Idi Amin's army, there was some chance to re-define the role of the military in the newly "liberated" country. On the one hand, leaders saw the military as the most effective instrument in the removal of Idi Amin and as a critical factor in the ensuing power struggles; on the other they also saw the military as a monster that could swallow them if not domesticated. As a liberating instrument, the new Uganda National Liberation Army enjoyed a honeymoon relationship with leaders and civilians alike. As a critical factor in the ensuing power struggles, the Army was to become the object of ingratiating attention from various political forces. Hence, such labels as "Museveni's", "Obote's" and "Muwanga's" soldiers were freely bandied out.

Ugandan leaders' varying attitudes towards the military as a liberating instrument, as a critical factor in the power game, and then as a monster to be domesticated were of course highly contradictory. Factional vying for support within the military implied a sense of political helpless and hopelessness in the absence of viable civilian political institutions to contain the military. Under the UNLF, steps were taken in an apparent effort to subordinate the military to civilian control. Many UNLF leaders felt that a future Uganda military "monster" could be prevented from emerging only if efforts were made to strengthen the UNLF as an organization by proportional ethnic representation, by having a literate army with an educated personnel, by politicizing the army and building a people's militia as a countervailing force.

Tentative steps or ideas to domesticate the new army either generated hostility from various political forces or were introduced into an environment that completely misunderstood the ideal underlying objectives. The apparent assumption behind strengthening the UNLF vis à vis the military was the Army could be neutralized only if there was a strong civilian organization. But, as we have discussed elsewhere,[41] factions within the UNLF had little in common beyond the overall label. Proportional ethnic representation was the idea of Lule, first President in the first UNLF government.[42] His opponents were quick to point out that, since Buganda and the Southern areas were generally numerically powerful, these areas would come out at greater numerical advantage, and that this would be a blatant way of one group establishing hegemony over the army. The area most adversely affected, if Lule's ideas had been implemented, would have been the North generally, and Acholi and Lango specifically. This inevitably would have entailed a change in the balance of military and political power, for which the Northern leadership were not prepared. Henry Makmot clearly echoed these fears in the National Consulative Council, invoking the doctrine of ethno-functionalism:

> There are tribes which are much, much bigger than others, so you could expect about half of the army coming from that tribe or the tribe which is more fortunate or tribes which are related - and in Uganda -I stressed this when I contributed to this debate much earlier in May/June - that there are sections of the population who just cannot fight even if they are soldiers. (Interjections) And I will stress this that there is evidence to that effect. Even in the recent fighting there is evidence that some people just could not stand fires. (Sic.) This I am stressing because practice is different from theory.[43]

The search for a literate army and an educated officer corps was a response to the low levels of literacy and education in the Amin army and its officer corps, to which some leaders attributed the brutality of the Amin's army. Opposition to this proposal, muted as it was, was based on particularistic considerations. Political groups, making a rush for support within the army and seeking to establish their bases within, could hardly have education and general literacy as important criteria, particularly if they considered them politico-military disadvantages. Certainly, Lule earned the active hostility of the predominantly Northern core of the UNLF who had marched from the Uganda/Tanzania border. Likewise, implementation of the educational criteria would have entailed a change in the politico-military balance of power, to the disadvantage of the Northern leadership.

The UNLF leaders in Moshi saw that they had to come to grips with reality by recognizing the UNLA in the making as an interest group. Not only would interests peculiar to the military be taken care of by military representatives, but military representation would also enable the military to participate in the decision-making processes in the top civilian organs. But this was simply an ideal. In the struggles that ensued within the UNLF and UNLA, the military representatives identified themselves with factions or parties they supported. In Obote's bid for power, critical elements within the Military Commission clearly demonstrated where their sympathies lay by supporting Obote.

Politicization of the military and the establishment of a people's militia were ideas held by Yoweri Museveni, when he was Minister of Defence in the first UNLF government. In his policy paper submitted to the National Consultative Council he argued for a politicized army and a people's militia, on the grounds that all armies are necessarily political and that a people's militia was one of the surest guarantees for domestic stability, security and democratization of the instruments of coercion - all of which would make it difficult for any adventurer to hold the population to ransom by staging a coup d'etat.[44]

Given the factional politics of the UNLF and the fragmented nature of the UNLA, Museveni's ideas of a politicized army and a people's militia were somewhat too advanced at the time. True, his ideas were supported in the National Consultative Council, but such expressions of support were simply declarations of intention, not any closer to the political and military realities prevailing at the time. The underlying assumption of a "politicized" army is that there is either a hegemonic party or a residual consensus of internalized political ideas which can be inculcated to hold the military together as an institution, and that the military will be ready, as a result, to accept the supremacy of civilian political institutions. In the case of a people's militia, where this was implemented, especially in Acholi, the militia were simply personal followers of individuals or factions; they became sources of instability, as events were later to prove.[45]

That efforts by the UNLA to domesticate the military had failed miserably was illustrated by the assumption of power by the Military Commission, whose political sympathies, as we have seen, lay with the Obote UPC. The military were, thus, able to demonstrate that they still had the veto power to determine which rules they preferred.

On his second assumption of power, Obote found himself in the same old trap, that which ultimately had led to his downfall: namely, having to use the military as his critical basic constituency. True, he had assumed power through the appearance of an election which his party had "won": but the critical power behind the throne was the military. The Uganda People's Congress continued to play at the functions of legitimization as it had done before the 1971 debacle.

Within a few months of assuming office, Obote was saddled with a guerrilla war of attrition in Buganda. In his second struggle for power, he tried encircling Buganda, a strategy which had paid off well in his first bid for power during the early 1960s.[46] As a result of this strategy, Buganda had been forced to break out of the encirclement by seeking an alliance with the UPC - an alliance which at the time was tactical, but which proved disastrous for Buganda and, eventually, for Uganda. But

Buganda of the 1980s was radically different from that of the 1960s. Surrounded as they were during and immediately after the December 1980 elections, the Baganda were not prepared to seek a parley with Obote to break the encirclement. Instead, they attempted armed uprisings led by various groups, the most prominent of which, it turned out, was the National Resistance Movement led by Yoweri Museveni. Obote swallowed the bait by seeking a military solution to the uprising, which proved a disaster for him. Indeed, the 1980s were not the mid-1960s, when Obote had depended basically on the military to rule.

The 1980s were different for a number of reasons. Firstly, force was too dispersed for Obote to use it effectively as an instrument of domestic policy; secondly, for all the appearances of elections, legitimacy was too tenous in the strategic heartland; thirdly, Obote's clumsy attempts to build the Army as a critical basic constituency boomeranged; fourthly, resources were too scarce to be allocated to his civilian friends and enemies and to the Army to be of political utility; and, fifthly, the guerrilla war took such a heavy toll on his military supporters that this led to polarizations within the military, culminating in the July 1985 coup.

From the Uganda experience of the mid-1960s up to the fall of Idi Amin force could be used successfully, to a limited extent, as an instrument of domestic policy when the target groups lacked relatively free access to instruments of coercion. For some 70 years the Baganda had been disarmed and demilitarized, when Lugard used his Maxim gun on Kampala Hill. Obote's Amin had only to fire a few volleys into Sir Edward Mutesa's Palace and the game was up for Mengo. From 1966 until he was overthrown, Obote could enjoy almost carte blanche in Buganda under a state of emergency. With the defeat of Idi Amin, political forces in Uganda generally - and Buganda specifically - came to realize that force was a highly critical element in the political jungle that was Uganda. Thus, when Obote reassumed power, he found a heartland group already prepared or preparing to meet him militarily. In such a situation, force was of limited political utility. True, Obote had, during the mid- and late 1960s, ruled Buganda under a state of emergency even when his legitimacy was tenuous, but this tenuousness was then of no consequence, as he ruled a disarmed and demilitarized people.

Now Obote's military arm was different from that of the 1960s. In the mid-1960s, it had been a relatively smaller, compact, disciplined and well provided for army. The material and status advantages he showered upon the Army had made it relatively easy to win their loyalties. During the 1980s, although General Tito Okello and Brigadier Oyite-Ojok made sure that the UNLA was made up of troops ethnically close to Obote, it was not so cohesive any longer. After Brigadier Oyite-Ojok's mysterious death in a helicopter accident, the Acholi officers, whose tribesmen were dominant in the army, sought one of their number, Brigadier Bazilio Okello, to be Chief of Staff of the Army to succeed Oyite-Ojok.[47] But this did not go down well with Obote. It took almost a year before the Army had a Chief of Staff. Obote stumbled onto his politically and militarily inept fellow tribesman, Smith Opon-Acak, as Chief of Staff, which left the Acholi rank and file disgruntled. Smith Opon-Acak then took it upon himself to disarm and purge the army of Acholi, who simply reacted by retreating to their home-land, to dig for better or worse.

Probably even with a militarily prepared Buganda where his legitimacy was tenuous and with an army whose loyalty he was not sure of, Obote would have muddled through, had he had sufficient resources to silence his opponents or reward his supporters. But resources were either too limited, or were dissipated in the corruption orgies going on under his very eyes.

Meantime the guerrilla war was going badly for Obote's war machine, a war machine that was already disgruntled and bearing the brunt of the fighting, especially the Acholi officers and men. The Acholi retreat from Kampala left a virtual military power vacuum in the Southern areas, south of Lake Kyoga, which Museveni's NRA were only watching with amused interest. Whether by default or intentionally, we have yet to know, the NRA left a corridor through which the troops of the Okellos (Bazilio Okello and Tito Okello) could drive to take Kampala on a Saturday morning, 27 July 1985.

6. Conclusion: The "Okellos" and the NRM Victory

In this paper we have argued that the political visibility and the activist role of the military in Uganda have been the result of failure on the part of Uganda's leaders to build institutions capable of domesticating civil conflicts. Instead, they have chosen to build the military in response to internal politico-military crises. With the institutional vacua created by Obote and Amin, the military assumed such roles that it could either play king-maker or play king. The entry of the Okellos in July 1985 created a highly polarized politico-military situation in which the antagonistic politico-military forces, the Okellos and NRM, appeared so evenly balanced that Uganda seemed to be in for a prolonged civil war.

The Nairobi Peace Talks which dragged on for some four months arose partly because the contending forces realized that, for the time being, they could not dictate terms, and partly in order for the antagonistic forces to mobilize resources for a final showdown. With forces apparently evenly balanced, and without a formula to regulate relations between them, the Nairobi Peace Talks were aimed at working out some kind of modus operandi. However, the terms of the peace accord which were eventually signed were so complicated for the contracting parties, and involved so much give and take that none of the groups could have adhered to the accord under the circumstances prevailing.

The Nairobi Peace Talks did give time to the parties to prepare for a final showdown. In their pronouncements and their actions, the Okellos demonstrated that, given a chance, they would prefer a showdown and then dictate their own terms. They effected political and military appointments designed to keep out the NRM, they sought alliance with military groups hostile to the NRM, and carried out large-scale mobilization. However, the NRM and their military arm, NRA, were not caught napping. Also they used the Nairobi Peace Talks to internationalize their message, carry out large-scale mobilization, and extend their control of areas. By the end of December 1985, they were poised on the outskirts of Kampala.

A number of implications arise out of the NRM victory, implications likely to have a strong bearing on civilian-military relations and the building of political institutions. The armed uprising was a reaction against the use of the military as an instrument of domestic policy, dating back to 1966; the movement grew because of a symbiotic relationship between the National Resistance Army and the civilian population. Moreover, the NRM victory has exploded the myth of "martial tribes", a myth propagated by Colonialism and echoed by the Odas, the Lakidis and the Makmots; and has marked a shift in the balance of politico-military power from marginal groups to groups from the strategic heartland.

Throughout this paper we have seen that the military has been a critical actor in political developments in Uganda since 1966 and this eventually provoked an armed uprising from the population. Martin Okello's prophecy has indeed been fulfilled. The movement succeeded because civilians realized it was, ultimately, in their own physical interest to support such a guerrilla movement.

This early symbiotic relationship then may provide the basis for an integrated civilian-military relationship. In turn, this may change the role of the military which up to now has been predatory. Coupled with this, the NRM victory has wrested the monopoly on the use of force away from marginal groups in whose interest it was not to build viable political institutions.

The result may be a situation in which there is a balance of socio-politico-military forces, where no one group will feel confidence that it can dictate terms because it has a monopoly on the means of coercion. Such a situation augurs well for building viable civilian political institutions that can domesticate conflict. The experience of the past 20 months, since the NRM assumed power, has shown that the National Resistance Movement has also realized that in the final analysis they cannot dictate terms. Rather, they are in the process of working out a formula to accommodate conflicting interests. Stability will depend on whether conflicting socio-politico-military forces can realize that using coercion to settle domestic conflicts is self-defeating - as Obote has, one may hope, learnt at the cost of his "throne".

The role of the military in Uganda and its consequences may be summed up by going back in history, to Edward Gibbon's observations of the consequences that arose out of the activist role of the Praetorians in the politics of ancient Rome:

> By thus introducing the Praetorian guards into the palace and the Senate, the emperors taught them to perceive their own strength, and the weakness of the civil governments to view the vices of their masters with familiar contempt - and their pride was nourished by the sense of their irresistible weight.[48]

Notes

1. Uganda Parliamentary Debates (henceforth termed Hansard), vol. 71, 1967-1968. Entebbe: Government Printer, p. 163.
2. Hansard, vol. 1, 1962-63, p. 2.
3. Ibid., p. 3.
4. Ibid., p. 34.
5. Huntington, S.P.: Political Order in Changing Societies. New Haven, Connecticut: Yale University Press, 1968, p. 196.

6. For a detailed discussion of the problems of institutionalization in Uganda, see Mudoola, D.: "Post-colonial Politics in Uganda - An Interpretation", in Mawazo, vol. 6, no. 2, December 1985.
7. Hansard, vol. 14, 1962-63, pp. 663-4.
8. Idem.
9. Hansard, vol. 18, 1962-63, pp. 402-3.
10. Hansard, vol. 19, 1963-64, p. 6.
11. For details as officially given, see the debate on a motion introduced by Abdalla-Anyuru in Hansard, vol. 23, 1963-64, pp. 861-989.
12. Ibid. See Obote's version of events, pp. 938-39.
13. Ibid., pp. 861-62.
14. Ibid. Obote's speech, p. 934.
15. Ibid. Okello's speech, p. 887.
16. Ibid. Ali Kisekka's speech, p. 954.
17. For an elaboration of this concept see Mudoola, D.: "Post-war Politics in Uganda". Paper presented at the Conference on "Crises of Development in Uganda", Roskilde, Denmark, 25-28 December 1985.
18. Hansard, vol. 23, Lakidi's speech, pp. 959-60.
19. Ibid. Obote's speech, p. 934.
20. Uganda Argus, 9 September 1964. Among those promoted was a Lieutenant Oyite-Ojok to "Temporary Captain". Incidentally, at the height of Oyite-Ojok's military "triumphs", the mass media reported him as "Sandhurst trained", but according to the Uganda Argus 22 November 1963 he had been trained at the Mons Officer Cadet School, Aldershot. He appears in a group photograph, in the Argus issues, with Katabarwa Matovu, J.E. Ebittu, Z. Ariko, B.M. Ekiring, E.B. Kamara, B.J. Kisira, and S.E. Lukawama.
21. For all this information on these military formations, I am grateful to Major Gideon Lusweswe, formerly Deputy Quartermaster-General, Uganda Army.
22. Compared to their civilian counterparts, the life of Ugandan officers in the 1960s was one of comfort. It was "trendy" for society Uganda girls to marry young Lieutenants, Captains and even Brigadiers, although there were of course too few to go around.
23. Hansard, vol. 28, 1963-64, p. 2060.
24. Uganda Argus, 12 April 1963. Obote addressing a press conference in Kampala.
25. For more details about and reaction to the Nakulabye Massacre, see Hansard, vols. 41, 42, and 43.
26. For a comprehensive preview of the UPC as a party in government see Mujaju, A.B.: "The Role of the UPC as a Party in Government", in Canadian Journal of African Studies, vol. 10, no. 3, 1977.
27. Hansard, vol. 58, 1965-66, pp. 995-1046, for details of "The Ocheng Motion".
28. Hansard, vol. 60, 1966-67, p. 59.
29. I am grateful to Professor Mujaju for this concept which neatly sums up the attitudes of Uganda rulers towards "target" groups.
30. For example, see his reactions during the Debate on the Nakulabye incident, Hansard.
31. For example, note his visit to Mbarara Barracks, reported in Uganda Argus, 18 July 1966; to Gulu Army barracks, 25 August 1966; to Arua "to attend the wedding of the Army Chief of Staff, Col. Amin"; to Kabamba Army Training School, in Uganda Argus, 25 March 1968; his visit to Karamoja, "inspecting recruits" 9 April 1966; visit to Army headquarters, 13 April 1966; address to Air Force personnel at Gulu Air Base, 6 May 1968.
32. Uganda Argus, 10 September 1964.
33. Also see Gingyera-Pinycwa, A.G.G.: Apollo Milton Obote and His Times. New York: NOK Publishers, 1978, pp. 65-66.
34. The "Move to the Left" documents were Common Man's Charter, Nakivubo Pronouncements, and the National Service Proposals.
35. Akena-Adoko: 1966 Crisis, published by Milton Obote Foundation.

36. Gingyera-Pinycwa, op.cit., see especially pp. 231-45.
37. On his return to the Soviet Union, after commanding Soviet forces in Germany, Zhukov was immediately relegated to the background by Stalin, but later, Krushchev recalled him from oblivion to be Minister of the Defence. During Krushchev's struggles for power in the Central Committee of the party, Zhukov made his tanks conveniently available in and around Moscow in support of his patron, who immediately after his problems accused Zhukov of "Bonapartist" tendencies and removed him from office.
38. Some of these officers took care to keep Amin informed of domestic developments and his impending arrest while he was in Egypt attending Nasser's funeral and provided him with a strong military escort from Entebbe Airport where he arrived from Egypt, unannounced. Among the escort were Major L. Ozi (later to be his Chief of Intelligence) and Mustafa Adris (later to be his Chief of Staff and Minister of Defence).
39. There is now substantial literature on the Amin regime, including Lofchiem, M.: "The Uganda Coup: Class Action by the Military", in Journal of African Studies, vol. 10, no. 1, 1972; Southall, A.: "General Amin and the Coup", in Journal of Military Studies, vol. 13, no, 1, 1975; Martin, D.: General Amin. London: Faber and Faber, 1974; Kyemba, H.: The State of Blood. London: Paddington Press, 1977; Mazrui, A.: Soldiers and Kinsmen. Beverly Hills: Sage Publications, 1975.
40. On the politics of the UNLF, see Mudoola, D.: "Post-war Politics in Uganda", op.cit.
41. Ibid.
42. National Consultative Council Debates, vol. 1 (unpublished). President Lule's speech to the National Consultative Council, 22 May 1979.
43. National Consultative Council Debates, vol. 4 (unpublished). Makmot's speech, p. 755.
44. National Consultative Council Debates, vol. 3 (unpublished). Museveni's speech, pp. 684-92.
45. Acholi militia men were among Tito and Bazilio Okello's group which swept on to Kampala on 27 July 1985.
46. Also see Mudoola, D.: "Post-war Politics in Uganda", op.cit.
47. For this information, I am grateful to a colleague who was well placed to follow these events.
48. Gibbon quoted in Hartman, T.R.: Palace Politics. New York: McGraw-Hill Book Company, 1980, p. 1.

Edward Khiddu-Makubuya

Paramilitarism and Human Rights

1. Introduction

The main objective of this paper is to raise certain human rights issues related to significant human institutions which usually receive scant treatment in legal and/or social science literature. I refer here to the theory and practice of paramilitarism and the institutions through which it is normally practically manifested. After a general survey I will raise specific issues pertaining to Uganda and human rights.

Policy makers, scholars, and indeed, ordinary people throughout the ages have paid significant attention to matters military. In the same way, the regular police and their operations receive considerable attention from policy makers, scholars, ordinary people (who are usually at the receiving end), advocates of civil liberties etc. There are national laws and international norms governing military and police work. The same is, however, not strictly true of paramilitary institutions.

What, then, are paramilitary institutions? As a paramilitary institution could take many forms, it will naturally be difficult for any group of scholars to agree on a standard or uniform definition. While the principle of paramilitarism is universal, its practical implementation varies from country to country. Add to this the characteristic reluctance of many people to discuss the issue at all or to supply information. It is neither a regular police nor army. Operatives of a paramilitary institution are assumed to have received police or army training, to which they are presumed to have additional training in special skills that make them especially qualified for paramilitary tasks. Since a paramilitary organization is, inter alia, an intelligence unit, disguise and camouflage are part of its operational principles. This means that operatives should be not easily identifiable. Hence the necessity to get by without uniform.

It is often claimed that a paramilitary organization has a non-specific functional brief. This, however, is strictly not correct: critical inquiry will soon reveal that the bosses and the line operatives within the organization will, between them, be articulate on the specific functional briefs of their organization. While the functional brief is specific and known within the organization itself, the brief remains specifically undisclosed to the public except in the few instances when astute observers may be able to read between the lines of the practical operations of the organization. The powers and operational codes of the regular army and the police will normally be spelt out in national laws and international norms; and military manuals and police handbooks tend by definition to be public documents.

By contrast, the powers and operational code of a paramilitary organization essentially remain unpublished. In this sense, then, a paramilitary organization has undefined and practically unlimited powers. The regular army and police are usually amenable to some form of public control or collective scrutiny: not so a paramilitary set-up. Rather it is normally under the control of the Head of the Executive or an officer who is, in turn, under the Head's direct control. In many countries paramilitary organizations conduct themselves as though they were above the law, and indeed, much of the public will believe them to be above the law.

The apparently unlimited power of paramilitarism and the absence of a published operational code has promoted another tendency - unusual, unfamiliar and/or irregular methods of operation. Enlightened publics would normally be familiar with police values, and military values and their usual modes of expression and operationalization. The same publics are often puzzled in the face of the unusual methods employed by paramilitary operatives. And indeed, correct information about paramilitarism is hard to come by. Even in the best of circumstances, one has to deal with a great cloud of myth and fore about paramilitarism - occasionally promoted by the paramilitary organizations themselves.

Plate and Darvi (1983) acknowledge the enormous powers normally wielded by paramilitary agencies. They contend, however, that paramilitary agencies are "also like any government bureaucracy. They are capable of incompetence as in the post office". And also that if the paramilitary agencies have all the powers necessary to do the job, "their powers sometimes exceed their talents".[1] To some extent, the effectiveness of paramilitary operatives depends on myth and their unlimited power. But it must also be acknowledged that countries pour a good deal of resources into training, equipping and deploying paramilitary personnel. This exposure to organizational, management and/or operational skills must, in the first instance, be regarded as a significant factor in their effectiveness and practical success.

In theory, paramilitarism is supposed to execute duties of a "counter" nature, to protect and safeguard the security of the state against its supposed external enemies. In practice, neither the paramilitary operatives themselves nor their publics have found it easy to distinguish between the requisites of state security and the essence of individual political survival of the politicians of the day. In practice, "counter" duties have tended to recede into the background while paramilitarism has increasingly become the practical implementation of the Machiavellian principle that in the dynamics of state craft, it is better to be feared than to be respected. Consequently, paramilitarism ends up as an instrument of state coercion and political terrorism.[2]

Paramilitarism has often been a major factor in the generation of war mentality, especially in times of peace. Paramilitary operatives have turned into security missionaries who see themselves as being at war with the supposed enemies of the state. In this set-up, it becomes more or less natural that paramilitary operatives be given all the power they need and that their claim to resort to unusual methods of operation become easy to concede.

In short, paramilitarism has become a significant factor in undermining the rule of law and in actual violations of human rights. This is really an understatement. In many situations of gross violations of human rights it is neither the regular army nor the police which has been at the forefront, but the paramilitary. Herein lies the necessity of focusing sufficiently on paramilitary phenomena if one is seriously to promote and protect human rights.

I must emphasize that paramilitarism is universal. Paramilitary institutions exist all over the world today. Indeed, every country must have at least some of the characteristics referred to above. Paramilitarism exists in the so-called developed and underdeveloped countries. It also exists in the Communist and the "Free" World.[3]

2. Models from Uganda

What then has been the position in Uganda? At Independence in 1962, the country inherited a colonial army and colonial police force. Ever since then, however, the country has experienced unprecedented violations of human rights. If Uganda has any reputation in the contemporary world, then it is the notoriety of a country where governments have, for years, not respected fundamental human rights. Moreover, the country has had three constitutions - 1962, 1966 and 1967 - each with a comprehensive Bill of Rights.

And yet, the situation has not always appeared to be so negative. Winston Churchill claimed in My African Journey (1908) that "Uganda is a fairy tale. You climb up a railway instead of a beanstalk and at the top there is a wonderful new world. The scenery is different, the vegetation is different, the climate is different, and most of all, the people are different from anything elsewhere to be seen in the whole range of Africa ..." Over the years Ugandans have believed that their country was "the Pearl of Africa". However, most of this has turned out to be wishful thinking. Of late Uganda has almost certainly been "The Sick man of Africa", characterized by widespread state-inspired murder and terror, ethnic and religious strife internal war, violent politics, massive expulsions and displacement of peoples.[4]

Nor has there been anything accidental about such massive violations of human rights, inhumanity and brutality in Uganda. This phenomenon was the clear consequence of a certain configuration of factors and forces in Uganda's contemporary history: the multi-faceted colonial legacy, ethnicity and ethnic identity, religious identity, differential development regimes, massive poverty, poor political leadership, neo-colonialism and political underdevelopment.[5]

Recently the role of the Uganda military in the public life of Uganda has begun to receive serious and systematic treatment in the literature.[6] However, the role of paramilitary institutions is yet to receive similar attention: yet paramilitary institutions have played a significant role in the massive violations of human rights, inhumanity and brutality wrought in Uganda over the years. The paramilitary institutions I am here thinking of have included:

General Service Department
Special Force
Public Safety Unit
State Research Bureau
Anti-Corruption Unit
Anti-Smuggling Unit
Military Intelligence
National Security Agency

Recently, some information has begun to emerge which might in future permit detailed analyses of the above eight agencies. Meanwhile, I can give only a few particulars on three of them: the General Service Department, the State Research Bureau (SBR), and the National Security Agency (NASA).

General Service Department

As early as in 1964 it seems that the then Uganda Government woke up to the need for trained staff working under a "Counter-spy organization", due to the number of alleged foreign spies said to be operating in Uganda. It was also claimed that the government was using too many untrained informers who were providing false and misleading information. By mid-1964, it became known that some Ugandans had already been dispatched for counter-espionage training in Israel. On their return to Uganda, this first group of so-called "Israeli Boys" took up their paramilitary duties enthusiastically. However, the quality and calibre of this first group has been highly doubted by the second chief of the General Service, Akena-Adoko. He asserts that the people

> who formed the nucleus of the (general) service were recruited on the recommendations of politicians and trained in Israel. Many of them were ill educated, unemployed and greedy for just any type of job. The ground for employing some of them seemed to have been their unworthy compliance with the wishes of the politicians who had recommended them. However exalted in personal qualities they may have been, it was clear that they were neither fit to be the leaders of a security organization nor to form part of it. Their leader ... had fantastic ideas about the secrecy that should surround a security organization. He talked to his officers in whisper and met them in secret places to pay their salaries. They soon became notorious and they were called "Israeli Boys".[7]

Adoko goes on to state that the General Service Department (GSD) started in 1964 with his appointment as Chief General Service Officer. And he proceeds to praise himself on how he recruited "the best brains" into the General Service Department and trained them into efficient security officers.

There is no indication of a training programme. The Department was directly under the office of the Chief Executive, Prime

Minister Obote, who later became Executive President. There was no particular Act of Parliament setting up the General Service Department. It appears to have been set up by administrative instructions emanating directly from the then Prime Minister's office. The functional briefs of Department covered both internal security and external security, but by 1971, it appeared to have been concentrating more on internal than external security. The Department had grown in size, had acquired powers of arrest and imprisonment, and its personnel could interrogate, harass and torture without hindrance. This terror could be wielded on civilians, but it also made the regular armed forced uneasy. The notoriety of "Israeli Boys" had been transformed and indeed overtaken by the notoriety of the General Service Department generally.

Shortly after the overthrow of first government of Obote (1962-1971) the General Service Department was described as follows:

> Throughout the Obote regime increasing use was made of the General Service Department and the C.I.D. as political weapons. Members of the General Service spy service infiltrated into all spheres of Government and all areas of life including the Law Society and the national press. The head of the service was not accountable for the funds allocated to him. Many persons who revealed an independence of mind found themselves questioned in degrading circumstances by the General Service and intimidated. The C.I.D. spent so much time investigating crimes of a political nature that their other important work suffered. Consequently armed robbery and murder were daily increasing at an alarming rate.[8]

The paramilitary activity of the General Service Department irritated the armed forces so much that they made it one of the excuses for overthrowing Obote's first government. Writing about the estrangement between Obote and the then Uganda Army, Gingyera-Pinycwa has said:

> But even more offensive in some army quarters was what the General Service, headed by Akena-Adoko, came to do in the last days of the Obote regime. This was the training of people intended ostensibly to serve as bodyguards in military techniques and maneuvers. The army saw in this the rise of a veritable rival to itself. As they put it in their statement to the nation on January 25, 1971: "The Cabinet office, by

> training large numbers of people (largely from Akokoro County in Lango District where Obote and Akena-Adoko, the Chief General Service Officer, came from) in armed warfare, has been turned into a second army. Uganda therefore has had two armies, one in the cabinet, the other regular."[9]

If the Army itself felt threatened by the mere existence of the General Service Department, ordinary members of the public against whom it was regularly deployed were even more badly and adversely affected. The general feeling about the GSD was illustrated by an article published in the Kampala newspaper The Economy dated 19 December 1979 under the headline: "Bad News: Akena-Adoko Is Back". The article graphically described some of the terror that the General Service Department had instilled among Ugandans in the 1960s and sadly regretted that its former head, Akena-Adoko, had returned to post-Amin Uganda from exile, presumably with a view to resuscitating what the paper called "The spying Octopus".[10]

The State Research Bureau

The State Research Bureau (SBR) was one of the many paramilitary agencies which propped up Idi Amin from 1971 to 1979. Although Amin was fond of enacting decrees to cover his government operations regardless of their sordidness or nefariousness, he did not enact any decree to establish the SBR. Rather, it was established by administrative action in 1971 and was first described as a Military Intelligence Unit under the President's Office.[11] At first it was manned by army personnel plus a few civilians, with its director directly answerable to the President. Evidence available shows that the ordinary personnel of the SBR were military and/or military intelligence personnel who were assisted by specially detailed civilians. The SBR gave additional training to its personnel at its Kampala Headquarters as well as at various police academies or functional equivalents around the world. SBR personnel were selected from a few ethnic groups which the regime trusted, plus a limited number of people from suspected or distrusted tribes added for political purposes - and window-dressing.

In discussing how Idi Amin managed to stay in power, Avirgan and Honey (1982) state:

> Amin's security forces were also made up predominantly of Moslems and non-Ugandan mercenary recruits. The hub of the security system was the 3,000-member State Research Bureau dressed incognito in flowered shirts, bell-bottom trousers, sunglasses and platform shoes, and drove around in late-model cars with special licence plates. They were notorious for tossing their victims into the trunks of their cars and speeding off. Invariably the victims were never seen alive again.
> ... Thus from the foot soldier to the field marshall himself, this police state depended heavily on minority Moslems and non-Ugandan mercenaries ...[12]

Reliable evidence shows that SBR personnel received basic and advanced training in the USA and the UK.[13]

The functional brief of the SBR was not publicly announced, but it certainly must have been well known to its leadership and other operatives. For example, Lt. Col. Francis Itabuka, former Head of the SBR, while appearing as a reluctant witness before the Uganda Commission of Inquiry into Violations of Human Rights[14] conceded that his organization was to perform duties of a counter nature. To this the regime must have added, by design or default, the torture, terrorizing, intimidation and, indeed, liquidation of its supposed internal enemies. The SBR, through its top administrators, not only had direct access to the President but was directly under his control.

There was no published code of conduct for the SBR nor was its operational code published. It was, to all intents and purposes, above the ordinary law of the land. The SBR was accuser, judge and executioner all in one. Apparently, the SBR had unlimited access to resources for operations. It posted its personnel as and when it pleased - within government departments, institutions, the private sector and Uganda Embassies abroad. Money to lure victims to their death or to track them to any corner of the world seemed to be always available. So were fast cars to transport operatives and their victims; so were unlimited expense accounts.

So notorious was the SBR for its violations of human rights that the High Court of Uganda has had to rule that "to accuse anyone in Uganda of having been a member of the notorious and dreaded State Research Bureau was undoubtedly a very serious matter and highly defamatory". It also exposed such a person to vengeful feelings and actual risk to his life.[15]

National Security Agency (NASA)

Initially, NASA appears to have taken form during the period of the Uganda National Liberation Front (UNLF), which took over immediately after the forceful overthrow of the Amin regime in 1979. Some of the top personnel of NASA were former operatives of the General Service Department. Also the UNLF sent a number of Ugandans to Cuba for paramilitary training. The majority of these returned and were definitely deployed as NASA agents.

NASA became a force to reckon with during the second administration headed by Obote, 1980-85. The Minister of State in President's office, Chris Rwakasisi, took overall charge of the Agency, while its day-to-day running was the responsibility of its Director General.

The establishment of NASA cannot be traced to any specific law; apparently, it was established by administrative action. Some former NASA agents who have testified before the Commission of Inquiry into Violations of Human Rights have suggested that they were not systematically trained; they were told to read a few spy novels and then given common-sense advice on how to deal with security matters. This seems to have been an exercise in disinformation, however. Contrary evidence shows that new NASA agents are known to have been systematically trained at the Milton Obote Foundation. The Obote II regime set up a sophisticated NASA academy on the shores of Lake Victoria where agents were systematically trained. Agents were also sent outside Uganda for further training.

NASA did not recruit its agents through the normal channel of public service recruitment. Rather, it drew from members of supposedly trusted tribes who professed support and loyalty to the then ruling Uganda Peoples Congress (UPC), with recruitment through senior UPC members. NASA agents did not wear uniforms. But they carried arms and did not hesitate to use them. NASA's powers and operational code were never officially made public. However, the people soon learnt that these agents had enormous powers and were virtually above the law.

Uganda High Court Miscellaneous Cause No. 174 of 1979, In the Matter of Bob Musoke[16] reveals that on 9 November 1979, a writ of habeas corpus ad subjiciendum was directed to the Commissioner of Prisons, in response to which the applicant was produced before Court. At the hearing of the application, a letter was produced from President's office signed for the Director of Intelligence and reading as follows:

> In accordance with the powers conferred upon me by His Excellency the President of the Republic of Uganda and in the interest of national security, I hereby deliver to you 20 (twenty) men and two women for safe custody. They are former State Research personnel.
>
> In the interest of National Security, I should be pleased to receive your full cooperation in this matter.

It was sought to rely on the above letter as the authority for the imprisonment of the applicant. The court declared the applicant's detention illegal since it was not pursuant to any known law.

It is a fact testified to by many witness before the Commission of Inquiry into Violations of Human Rights that NASA agents killed, tortured, detained, robbed and looted Ugandans without hindrance. A former Chief Magistrate from Masaka told the Commission that several NASA agents operating within his jurisdiction countermanded court orders and harassed citizens, indeed, with the support of powerful people in the government. In addition to delivering people to the regular prison system for illegal detention, NASA had its own detention and torture centres where it tortured and killed with impunity. It also used military barracks for the same purpose. Amnesty International reported in 1985:

> Political detainees in Uganda fall into two categories: those detained in civil prisons or police stations, often under the provisions of the Public Order and Security Act, and those held "incommunicado in military barracks, intelligence headquarters or secret prisons run by the National Security Agency (NASA). "... it is reported that anyone detained unlawfully by the army or NASA is likely to be tortured.[17]

NASA agents played a key role during 1981-1985 in the three districts of Luwero, Mpigi, Mubende (the so-called "Luwero Triangle") where the National Resistance Army carried out guerrilla activities against government forces. NASA agents became as "computer men":

> They are called the "computer men", or just "computers". They come to wherever there has been trouble or anti-government feeling - Luwero, Karamoja, Mbarara or Kampala itself. They pick up the "bandits" or "dissidents" and take them away. Often these people are never seen again. There is nothing new

in the presence of security men, particularly in the troubled "Luwero Triangle". What makes the computer men different is their efficiency. They got their nickname from the bundles of computer printout that they carry with them - lists of opposition suspects and sympathizers. The computer men are agents controlled from President's office ...[18]

3. Some Conclusions on Paramilitarism in Uganda

From the above, we may offer a few conclusions as to the general tendencies which paramilitarism takes in Uganda:

(i) Until 1987, there was no legislation specifically dealing with paramilitarism. In theory, the paramilitary institutions were subject to the Constitution and the general law of the land. In fact, all the agencies were really a law unto themselves. They were instrumental in the perpetuation of state terror as well as anarchical terror in Uganda.[19]

(ii) Throughout the past 24 years of Uganda's independence, public announcements have been issued regularly inviting candidates to join the army and the police. I am not aware of a single public announcement inviting interested candidates to join any of the paramilitary organizations. Recruitment remained and still remains a secret and clandestine matter, based on criteria peculiarly known to the recruiters and the recruited. However, we may note that every regime has applied more or less sectarian recruitment criteria, selecting from "trusted" ethnic or political groups.

(iii) There are well known Police Training and Army Training Schools in Uganda, but not a single gazetted paramilitary training school. Many personnel of Ugandan paramilitary organizations have had police or army backgrounds. While some agents may want to play down their training, some effort is often made to train them in communications, intelligence, use of arms and indeed, techniques of torture. On the other hand, other operatives have had noting to recommend or qualify them besides their "safe" ethnic membership and presumed loyalty to the regime of the day.

(iv) Paramilitary institutions in Uganda seem to have had considerable resources for their operations: motor vehicles, sophisticated communication systems, weaponry of all convenience. Facilities for travel abroad for business or for pleasure have also been readily available.

(v) Paramilitary organizations in Uganda have been under the direct control of the President or of an officer especially trusted by the President. This served to reinforce the personality cult. It became increasingly and painfully clear that the paramilitary agencies were more concerned with the individual political survival of their bosses than with state security.

(vi) Functional briefs of the more sinister agencies have remained a secret within the agency. Very few ordinary Ugandans of the 1960s knew what the General Service Unit was supposed to do. Its personnel spied massively on citizens and others; it was instrumental in the harassment and arrest of thousands of alleged enemies of the government. In practice, the General Service Unit was an internal security agency. And yet, at its inception, the General Service Unit was meant to counter foreign espionage in Uganda.[20] Similarly, the State Research Bureau of the 1970s was, in practice, a ferocious instrument of internal state terror and repression. And yet the former Head of the State Research Bureau, Lt. Col. Francis Itabuka told the Uganda Commission of Inquiry into Violations of Human Rights that his agency was supposed to be a counter-intelligence organization. Such non-disclosure of functional briefs and decisively personalized control leads to diffuseness of functions and to more pervasive violation of human rights and undermining of the rule of law.

(vii) Not only have paramilitary organizations been above the law: they have also consistently enjoyed the prerogative of deploying non-standard methods in the course of their operations. Ordinary police had no power to torture people. Yet, the paramilitary could and can torture with impunity. To this one may add such methods like carrying suspects in car-boots, demanding ransoms, blackmail, extortion, murder, etc.

(viii) The foreign contacts of the paramilitary in Uganda have been considerable. The founder personnel of both the General Service Unit and the Public Safety Unit were Israeli-trained. Uganda paramilitary personnel have received training in the UK, the USSR, the USA, Ghana, India, North Korea, Tanzania, Cuba and Libya. Indeed the very dungeons of the State Research Bureau at Nakasero were designed and built by foreigners. The agencies have been beneficiaries of foreign systems of communications, supporting services and actual line personnel from outside Uganda.[21]

We must emphasize that Uganda's paramilitary agencies have not only been principal instrumentalities of violations of human rights in Uganda: they have also served to perpetuate regimes in power. Selective ethnic composition has tended to exacerbate sectarian conflicts within Ugandan society. They have thus undermined the development of national democratic institutions and the emergence of rules of fair play in Ugandan public life.

4. Future Perspectives

In attempting to envision the future, we must emphasize that paramilitarism is a universal principle of contemporary life. This is not to say that it is here to stay: but it will certainly remain a matter to reckon with for the foreseeable future. We also need to avoid the mistake of abstracting paramilitarism from the general body politic. Paramilitarism is a necessary complement of state power: thus it would be unrealistic to expect a paramilitary organization to be qualitatively better than the state it is meant to serve.

Let us note the following letter, which appeared in Africa Now in August 1983:

> The situation in Uganda
> I am an Acholi army officer situated at one of the barracks around Kampala. I have been forced to write this letter because of the numerous Ugandans of the Baganda ethnic group who are being killed by us soldiers on orders from our commanders. These unfortunate and innocent people (young and old, men and women, and even babies) are being killed by us every day at military barracks, in their homes, villages and streets in Buganda.
>
> Instructions to kill are passed on to us by Acholi and Lango officers, and a few trusted Itesots, in the Luo language so that other Bantu soldiers may not know the idea behind the killings. We are ordered to kill Baganda of all ages so that this province with 4 million will be depopulated before the next general elections. By reducing the Baganda to a minority group, it will enable us northerners to rule Uganda without any problems from the Baganda.
>
> Recently, we were sent to the Luwero area with instructions to kill everybody and destroy all the homes, cattle etc. Thousands of people of all ages were killed, houses bombed, women and girls raped and a lot of property looted. A good number of the soldiers, particularly the Acholis, did this against their will for they see no reason for killing innocent people. The majority of us Acholis now wish to leave the

army but are afraid of the consequences which will be brutal. We are told that after successfully depopulating Luwero and Mpigi Districts (which is currently being done) the next area will be Mukono and then Masaka. All this must be completed in 1985.

The purpose of this letter is to draw the attention of the world to the thousands of people who have been killed in government institutions, in villages, etc. and to the fate of innocent Baganda awaiting death. In fact more people have been killed in Buganda during the last two years than in eight years of Amin. History will show this.

I wish to end by appealing to all Uganda Army soldiers, especially the Acholis, to disobey the killing orders and save the lives of the Baganda - for humanity's sake and for the sake of our tribe's future.

(Worried Acholi Soldier - Kampala, Uganda.)

Whether this "Worried Acholi soldier" was for real or just a flag of convenience, the issues raised in the letter still cut deep in Ugandan society. One could easily have substituted any paramilitary organization then operating in Luwero for the Uganda Army. A progressive future perspective on paramilitarism in Uganda must address the attenuation of the maze of obvious primitive forces in which the military and paramilitary find themselves inextricably caught. This an absolute necessity if one is to reduce the temptation and attractions of paramilitarism-power, wealth, money, fame.

Even then paramilitarism would very much still be with us. However, Ugandan society might then collectively afford itself the opportunity to review its policy on paramilitarism and decide on the forms and character which it ought to take. Such review should concern the necessity for a multiplicity of paramilitary agencies over and above Army, Police, CID, Special Branch, Customs Police, Immigration, etc.; the functional brief of paramilitarism; which brief should necessarily determine the requisites of training, resources, recruitment criteria, operational codes etc.; collective control on paramilitarism; public accountability of paramilitarism, etc.

I contend that the relative absence of thorough-going scholarly work on paramilitarism is hypocritical, since paramilitarism is no temporary accident in human society.[22] A society like Uganda which has suffered and continues to suffer at the hands of paramilitary agencies cannot afford to push the subject under the carpet.

Since the National Resistance Movement assumed power in Uganda in January 1986, it has taken various significant steps affecting paramilitarism. The NRM government set up a Commission of Inquiry into Violations of Human Rights which may have occurred between 1962 and January 1986.[23] The commission is generally "to inquire into all aspects of violation of human rights, breaches of the rule of law and excessive abuses of power, committed against persons in Uganda by the regimes in government, their servants, agents of agencies whatsoever called, during the period from the 9th day of October, 1962 to the 25th day of January 1986 and possible ways of preventing the recurrence of the aforesaid matters"

The Commission has been taking evidence in Kampala, Mbarara and Luwero and is expected to take evidence from practically all over Uganda. Many people concerned with human rights are awaiting the Commission's final report with considerable interest. The revelations already made before the Commission on the nefarious activities of paramilitary agencies in Uganda have shocked many Ugandans and human rights watchers the world over. Indeed, the very public revelation of the wide range of gross violation of human rights by these paramilitary agencies will inevitably have a salutary effect on the future of the paramilitary phenomenon in Uganda, quite apart from any constructive recommendations which the Commission may deem fit to make.

The NRM government has also enacted the Security Organizations Statute, 1987 (Statute No. 10 of 1987). This Statute establishes two security organizations, the Internal Security Organization and the External Security Organization. Their functions are:

(a) to collect, receive and process internal and external intelligence data on the security of Uganda;

(b) to advise and recommend to the President or any other authority as the President may direct on what action should be taken in connection with such intelligence data.

One of the major themes of the Statute is to extract public accountability from paramilitary operatives. The Statute declares that "No officer or employee of either organization shall have power to arrest, detain or confine any person by virtue only of being an officer or employee of the organization". The enactment of this Statute is clearly a major step in the right direction. But it would be unrealistic to consider it sufficient in itself. Paramilitarism is a complex phenomenon in Uganda, so a good deal more will have to be done at the intellectual and practical technical level if Uganda is to be saved from future paramilitary operatives turning into murderers, rapists, sadists, and torturers. Above all, prescription must be backed up by enforcement.

Notes

1. Plate, T. & A. Darvi: Secret Police. London: Sphere Books, 1983.
2. Ibid., and Walter, E. V.: Terror and Resistance: A Study in Political Violence. London: Oxford University Press, 1969; and Bowden, T.: Beyond the Limits of the Law. Harmondsworth: Penguin Books, 1978.
3. Plate & Darvi, op.cit., have a comprehensive listing of countries and their paramilitary agencies throughout the world.
4. The details are minutely documented elsewhere, e.g., Martin, D.: General Amin. London: Faber and Faber, 1974; Melady, T. & M.: Idi Amin Hitler of Africa. Kansas, USA: Shead Andrews McMeel, 1977; Sempangi, K.: Reign of Terror, Reign of Love. London: Regal Books, 1979; Kyemba, H.: State of Blood. London: Paddington Press, 1977; Gwyn, D.: Idi Amin Deathlight of Africa. Boston, Toronto: Little Brown & Company, 1977; Mazrui, A. A.: Soldiers and Kinsmen in Uganda. Beverly Hills: Sage Publications, 1975; Listowell, J.: Amin. Dublin: Irish University Press Books, 1973; Mamdani, M.: Imperialism and Fascism in Uganda. Nairobi: Heineman Educational Books, 1983; The Minority Rights Group: Uganda and Sudan. London: Report No. 66, 1984; Amnesty International: Uganda Six Years After Amin. London, 1985.
5. I have explored this matter extensively elsewhere, see Khiddu-Makubuya, E.: The Rise of the Authoritarian State in Uganda. Paper presented at the Second Triennial Congress of the Organization for Social Science Research in Eastern Africa (OSSREA) held in Eldoret, Kenya, 28 - 31 July, 1986.
6. See e.g. Mudoola, D.: The Role of the Army in Society, Lessons from Uganda. Paper presented at the African Association of Political Science Regional Workshop on "Constitutionalism and Political Stability in the Eastern Africa Region" held in Nairobi, Kenya, 5-7 January 1987; and, Mujaju, A.: The Conquest Syndrome and Constitutional Development in Uganda. Paper presented at the same workshop.
7. Akena-Adoko: From Obote to Obote. New Delhi: Vikas Publishing House PVT Ltd., 1983.
8. Government of the Republic of Uganda: The Birth of the Second Republic. Entebbe: Government Printer, 1971.
9. Gingyera-Pinycwa, A.G.: Apolo Milton Obote and His Times. New York/-London/Lagos: NOK Publishers, 1978.
10. In Akena-Adoko, op.cit., the author forcefully defends himself and the General Service Department.
11. The origins of State Research Bureau are documented in detail in a Uganda High Court election petition which challenged the 1980 electoral victory of Mr. Abubakar Kakyama Mayanja, inter alia on the ground that since he had once been Acting President during the Amin regime he must have participated in the management of the SBR, which ipso facto disqualified him from being a member of the Uganda Parliament. See Christopher Sebuliba vs. Abubakar Kakyama Mayanja Uganda High Court Miscellaneous Cause No. 1 of 1981 (Matter of Election Petition/Mubende South East).
12. Avirgan, T. & M. Honey: War in Uganda. Dar-es-Salaam: Tanzania Publishing House Ltd., 1982.
13. Mamdani, op.cit.

14. The Commission was set up by the Minister of Justice by Legal Notice No. 5 of 1986 to inquire into all aspects of violation of human rights in Uganda 1962-1986.
15. Lt. Col. Bazalaki v. Ilakut in High Court Monthly Bulletin 36, 1980; and Matias Edul v. The Uganda Times Ltd in High Court Monthly Bulletin 45, 1982.
16. High Court Monthly Bulletin 22, 1979.
17. Amnesty International: Uganda Six Years After Amin. London, 1985.
18. Africa Now, July 1984.
19. See Afterword by A.A. Mazrui in Gwyn, op.cit.
20. Akena-Adoko, op.cit.
21. Mamdani, op.cit. and Avirgan & Honey, op.cit.
22. McDougal, M.S., H.D. Lasswell & W.M. Reisman: "The Intelligence Function and World Public Order" in (same authors) International Law Essays. Mineola, New York: The Foundation Press, 1981.
23. Legal Notice No. 5 of 1986.

Ijuka Kabumba

Ethnic Conflict within the Public Service

1. Introduction

The public service is, like other large and complex organizations, characterized by the potential for conflict. This paper concentrates on the ethnic form such conflicts may take, in the Ugandan Public Service. On the basis of information from in-depth interviews of or completed questionnaires by a number of Ugandan public servants, informal discussions with others, observations, review of some relevant literature and our own experience - we take up the following questions:[1]

- Is there ethnic conflict in the Uganda public service?

And if so:

- Where in the hierarchy does it occur?
- How is it manifested?
- What are its sources and causes?
- What are some ways of dealing with it?

Our major assumption is that total ethnic harmony in the public service is inconceivable when there is ethnic conflict in the social, economic and, especially, political environments in Uganda. For one thing, the public service of any country is one of the subsystems of the national system.[2] Consequently, what happens in the one affects the other. Thus, the public service is influenced by, and also tries to influence, the social, economic and political events of its country.

Developing countries seem especially prone to ethnic conflicts. We may briefly cite to neighbouring Kenya[3], where is obviously ethnic conflict which will reflect itself in the public service. Indeed, this conflict has been admitted reasonably frankly; and also, happily for the country and generally, it has not yet got out of hand. In Kenya, the conflict takes two forms. Sometimes it is the major tribes (Kikuyu, Luo, Luhya and Kamba) rivalling one another, with the Kikuyu/Luo-rivalry, especially during the 1960s and 1970s, bordering on open hatred. At other times, the major tribes are seen as posing a threat to the smaller ones like the Nandi and the Masai.

2. Definition of some Key Words

It is important at the very outset to specify what we understand by certain key words.

2.1. Ethnic and Associated Terms

According to Webster's, "ethnic" means "of or relating to races or large groups of people classed according to common traits and customs".[4]

There is a close relationship among the terms "ethnic", "ethnic group", "ethnicity", "tribe", "race", and "culture", so we need to make clear how they will be used here.

Morris defines "ethnic group" as "a distinct category of the population in a larger society whose culture is usually different from its own".[5] The members of such a category are, or feel themselves, or are thought to be, bound together by common ties of race or nationality or culture.

Ethnicity refers generally "to the perception of group differences and so to social boundaries between sections of a population".[6] In this sense, adds Wallman, ethnic difference is the recognition of a contrast between "us" and "them".

Writing about tribal society, Lewis gives two definitions of "tribe". First, in general use, "tribe" is taken to denote "a primary aggregate of peoples living in a primitive or barbarous condition under a headman or chief".[7] Second, as a technical term, it denotes "a territorially defined political unit", a usage which recalls the original Latin use of the word for the political divisions or patrician orders of the Roman State.

"Race" is defined more unambiguously by Webster's than by some of the writers consulted: it is "a family, tribe, people, or nation belonging to the same stock" (p 704). This definition corresponds to "social race" - rather than "biological race" - in which there is stress on descent and descent rule, and the decisive test of group membership involves the calculation of genealogical relationships.[8]

We now turn to "culture". As far back as 1871, Taylor defined it aptly as "that complex whole which includes knowledge, belief, art, morals, law, custom, and any other capabilities and habits acquired by man as a member of society."[9]

For our purposes, "tribe" will mean a territorially defined political unit, and be equated with "ethnic group". "Clan", "tribe" or "ethnic group" and "race" are directly and vertically linked.

The clan is the smallest, while race is the largest of them. For instance, in Uganda, the Basakuru, Basigi and Beinika are clans comprising the Bakiga tribe in Kabale district. The Bakiga are part of the Bantu peoples of Uganda and other black African countries like Tanzania and Zambia. In Uganda, the Bantu (such as the Bakiga, Baganda and Bagisu) are culturally very different from the Nilo-Hamites such as the Langi, Acholi and Iteso. The Baganda, being a large tribe, come nearer to being a nation or nationality.

Furthermore, except where the context clearly indicates otherwise, "ethnic" or "tribal" should be taken to refer also to "clan" (at a lower level) and "regional" (at a higher level). This interpretation is especially true where either there is one commonly used language (e.g. Luganda in the south) or two or more but very similar ones (as in the west).

2.2. Conflict

Generally defined, "conflict" can be taken to mean "a breakdown in the standard mechanisms of decision-making so that an individual or group experiences difficulty in selecting an action alternative."[10]

This definition is particularly helpful when looking at the individual and organizational forms of conflict. Viewing it from the social angle, Coser defines conflict as a "struggle ... in which the aims of the conflicting parties are not only to gain the desired values but also to neutralize, injure, or eliminate their rivals."[11]

Building on Coser's definition, Katz and Kahn conclude that conflict is "the direct interaction of two or more parties (persons, groups, organizations, nations) such that the actions of one tend to prevent or compel some outcome against the resistance of the other."[12]

2.3. Ethnic Conflict

"Ethnic conflict" is conflict involving tribes or ethnic groups. We shall define ethnic conflicts as

> the direct or indirect pursuit, by members of different ethnic/tribal groups, of incompatible objectives where the winner takes all that there is, or the bigger share, of what

> is available, in a situation involving interaction which consciously or unconsciously is characterized by overt or covert acts meant to neutralize, injure or eliminate the rival group(s) before, during or after the said pursuit.

This definition excludes that of March & Simon and is nearer to those of Coser and Katz & Kahn, on the other.

2.4. Public Service

In Uganda, the public service comprises the following: the Traditional Public Service, the Teaching Service, the Diplomatic Service, judges of the High Court, members of all other Courts of Law established by Parliament, the Uganda Police Force, the District Administrations, and Urban Authorities.[13]

Unless otherwise specified, our discussion will refer only to the above organizations. All the same, obviously, it may well be relevant to other areas of the public sector such as the Armed Forces, Makerere University or public corporations.

3. Ethnic Conflict in the Uganda Public Service?

Before asking our respondents, "On the basis of your experience, observations, etc., is there ethnic conflict in the Uganda public service?", we wanted to ascertain how the term "conflict" was interpreted. For this reason, we asked a prior question, "What do you understand by the term "conflict"?"

We were impressed by the responses. Of the 67 respondents, 62 (92.5%) gave extremely helpful definitions. Words/expressions recurring frequently in these definitions are given in Table 1 below.

Of the 67 respondents, only 4 denied that there was ethnic conflict in the public service or said simply that they did not know. The rest (93.5%) agreed that this form of conflict exists in our service. Thus, its existence as such is too self-evident to be disputed.

Table 1
Words/expressions Used Commonly in Respondent' Definitions

Word/expression	Respondents Number	Percentage
1. Disagreement	20	29.9
2. Differences (or "different", "differ", "divergence")	13	19.4
3. Misunderstanding	10	14.9
4. Interests	4	6.0
5. Struggle	3	4.5
6. Lack of harmony	3	4.5
7. Other relevant expressions	9	13.4
8. Irrelevant	3	4.5
9. No answer	2	3.0
Total	67	100.0

4. Levels in the Hierarchy where Ethnic Conflict Occurs

Responses concerning where in the public service hierarchy ethnic conflict is seen as occurring are summarized in Table 2. Top level positions include those of Permanent Secretary (Principal Secretary), Head of Department plus other U1 or equivalent posts. The very bottom level is that of unestablished employees ("Grouping Scheme").

Table 2
Levels in the Uganda Public Service where Ethnic Conflict Occurs

Level (in the hierarchy)	Respondents Number	Percentage
1. Throughout the hierarchy/services	35	52.2
2. Mostly at the top	26	38.8
3. Top and bottom levels	5	7.5
4. Middle ranks	0	0.0
5. Junior ranks	1	1.5
6. The very bottom	0	0.0
Total	67	100.0

The fact that there are no responses or only one from middle ranks downwards is explained, we believe, by the nature of the answers given in 1-2. Thus, "throughout the service" and "mostly at the top" could be seen as covering all levels.

The reader may rightly wonder why so many respondents believe that there is ethnic conflict at the top. The following two elaborations by respondents are illustrative. One said, "The top level is where the control of resources is greater". Another put it thus: "Ethnic conflict is related to political alignment. Now, politics tends to work mostly at the top. So, ethnic conflict also tends to manifest itself at the top."

Two other statements made in connection with alternative number 3 in the table we found very revealing. Both reinforce the possibility of ethnic conflict being sharpest at the top. One respondent said: "Basically, ethnic conflicts are found among the lower groups of employees where technical qualifications are not a prerequisite and among the occupants of the highly political posts where benefits look lavish."

Another, while maintaining that ethnic conflict takes place at all levels within the public service, added, "but most directly at the lowest levels, and most indirectly at the highest ones (Permanent Secretary and equivalent levels)."

Ethnic conflict seems to take place throughout the service, <u>especially</u>:

- in those cadres (like Foreign Service, Administrative Service, Personnel Management) which are by their very nature highly political, or in which professional/technical skills are not directly or obviously a prerequisite for initial entry;

- among all those employees who lack "exportable" skills. Here the "export" market could be inside the country (private sector or self-employment) or outside;

- in jobs requiring no or very limited skills (sweeper, garden worker, etc.), especially if incumbents have got them through nepotism or similar non-merit channels, and since appointment, disciplining, etc. are delegated to Heads of Departments;

- among employees who themselves have political ambitions or are opportunistic; and

- in those posts at the very top where incumbents exercise considerable political and economic power, such as those of Permanent Secretary.

Despite what some writers say about the need to separate politics and administration, today's reality is otherwise.[14] As other writers like Long[15] and Seidman[16] have ably pointed out, politics and administration are very much interlinked, especially at the higher levels. Most top public servants are political animals. So, whether they admit or realize it or not, the fact is that they arrive at their top posts, stay in them, and, finally, lose them, because of politics - and not purely on the basis of their technical competence, although the latter is usually a requirement. And, to the extent that in Uganda ethnic conflict is still part and parcel of politics, top civil servants will not be unaffected by that conflict - whether as its initiators, or manipulators, or victims.

We maintain this although it might sound an overstatement, especially compared with what the Uganda Constitution says. Some might argue that it is not generally true that top civil servants are politically appointed, deployed, disciplined or removed from their positions; the exceptions would be the posts of Permanent Secretary, District Administrator and officers on the personal staff of the President - in the sense that the Head of State does not have to seek anybody's advice, let alone have appointments, etc. follow the normal Public Service Commission machinery. They might add that even with these positions, appointments are usually made from public officers already serving in related fields and possessing the requisite qualifications, competence and experience.

Maintaining our position need not contradict such arguments. Here, space does not permit us to answer them fully or to go into details on, e.g., the theory and practice of the separation of powers. Suffice it to repeat that most top civil servants almost anywhere in the world are political animals. Furthermore, in Uganda, politics tends to pervade the entire public service, with varying degrees of intensity depending on several factors - such as one's level in the hierarchy, educational background, tribe, career ambitions and the current period of the country's history.

5. Symptoms

Different respondents mentioned a number of "symptoms" from which we have made the selection below. The number of respondents mentioning each is indicated in parentheses:

- Nepotism/favouritism (47)
- Unfair dismissals or suspensions (16)
- Corruption (6)
- Openly expressed mistrust (5)
- Lack of cooperation (5)
- Violent, physical or verbal, confrontation (5)

- Elimination/murder (3)
- Use of own (vernacular) language in the department/ministry which happens to be dominated by a particular tribe (3)
- Ethnic-based informal groups (2)
- Discrimination in the approval of financial requests or claims (2)
- Character assassination (2)
- Openly expressed hatred (2)

Most of these do not require further elaboration. But let us explain briefly the final one, and "lack of cooperation".

"Openly expressed hatred" is where an official may openly refuse to see or may criticize another or a client/visitor, for no other reason except the latter's tribe. This type of hatred seems to permeate the entire service. However, while more visible at the junior and middle levels, it is somehow suppressed but present at the top. We were told that political leaders also indulge in it, in their dealings with senior public servants.

Essentially, "lack of cooperation" involves withholding relevant information from officials of another tribe or other tribes, until too late for it to be acted upon; and sabotage by members of one ethnic group of the efforts of the members of other tribes. Such lack of cooperation extends to the uncommitted implementation of instructions and decisions and, according to one interviewee, is responsible for most of the administrative bottlenecks in the public service. It also makes inter-departmental and inter-ministerial coordination and cooperation difficult.

6. Sources and Causes

6.1. General Remarks

To understand the sources of ethnic conflict in the public service needs a full appreciation of at least two basic facts: conflict is part and parcel of the human condition, and it has multiple causes, some obvious, others less so. The first fact has been ably summarized by Katz and Kahn:

> The fact of conflict - of being somehow involved with opposing forces - must surely be among the most common of human experiences. We recognize conflict in the opposition of wishes within ourselves, in the clashes between others whom we observe, and in the full struggles against those we

> ourselves oppose. And, according to our temperament and experience, we seek it or avoid it, fear it or enjoy it, call it sickness or call it life. (p. 612)

Merloo argues that "every war is a dramatization of man's inner war, the externalization of his inner conflict."[17]

It may also be helpful to remember the behaviour, circumstances and actions of Shakespeare's Iago, and their consequences as we try to understand the sources of conflict inasfar as the Uganda public service is concerned. (One of the main reasons for Iago's hatred of Othello is failure to get promoted to the position of second in command to the Moor- which position was given to Michael Cassio, a Florentine, to whom Iago contemptuously refers as "a great arithmetician" and a theoretician with no practical experience of warfare.)

Sometimes, what appears as conflict over one factor - such as a desire to promote the interests of an official's tribe - might be no more than an effort on that official's part to punish another individual who has won in a contest to secure a prize from within or without the service. Or, it might be a case of an employee who has been dismissed purely on grounds of inefficiency, wishing to hide the fact by claiming to have been so treated because of his tribe, region, etc.

6.2. Responses

As with symptoms, different sources were cited by different respondents. We have grouped a number of these sources into six major ones below - with the number mentioning each shown in parentheses.

- Nepotism/favouritism (47)
- Political factors (19). These include thirst or greed for power; the fanning by politicians of ethnic differences; and conflict over goals between bureaucrats and politicians, usually concerning the siting of national assets.
- Historical circumstances (including colonial legacies) (14)
- Cultural differences (11)
- Prejudice (6)
- Economic inequalities (5)

Nepotism was seen as both a symptom and a source, which is why it appears under both headings. Regarded by most respondents as synonymous with favouritism, "nepotism" is defined in Webster's Seventh New Collegiate Dictionary as "favouritism shown to a relative (as by giving an appointive job) on a basis of relationship". In the Ugandan/African context, the term "relative" should be interpreted liberally to include a member of one's clan or tribe or region or even religion or political party, but especially the first three. While one's relatives might be comparatively few, members of one's clan or tribe or region will be many. They will, just like relatives, tend to be beneficiaries of an official's acts of nepotism. Nepotism is also reinforced by other factors or considerations like the old boy/girl network and professional ties and associations.

It is not possible to explain here all the sources listed above. We will elaborate on two - prejudice and cultural differences- since they are immediately relevant to ethnicity and because they tend to be pervasive in their influence, if in an indirect manner.

6.3. Prejudice

According to Klineberg, prejudice may be defined from a popular view or a social science one. From the former viewpoint, it means "a prejudgement or preconcept reached before the relevant information has been collected or examined and therefore based on inadequate or even imaginary evidence."

From the social science viewpoint, it is "an unsubstantiated prejudgement of an individual or group, favourable or unfavourable in character, tending to action in consonant direction."[18]

Below we give selected examples of some prejudice-oriented statements by some public officials about certain tribes within the public service.

Tribe A

- "Very hypocritical. Very proud. Very submissive";
- "Give A's money and they will be okay";
- "Very elusive. Very nice on the surface but inwardly very malicious. Very good diplomats because diplomats are liars. Will stay with you and then stab you in the back".

Tribe B

- "Arrogant as A's. They look at others as inferior creatures";
- "Very arrogant. They don't believe that other ethnic groups are also people".

Tribe C

- "Outright rude and violent";
- "Rude; have little respect for law, order and discipline";
- "Very aggressive, uncultured, undisciplined, ambitious"

Tribe D

- "Conmen and gamblers";
- "More opportunistic than arrogant";
- "Very opportunistic. Like chameleons; they will take on the colour of the political party in power at the time; will sing to the tune of any ruler, however cacophonous".

Tribe E

- "What the master says - so do I say";
- "Submissive. Always following the existing (political) order as though blown by the wind";
- "Non-aligned in political matters".

Tribe F

- "Crude, rough, highly united, industrious, no nonsense";
- "Generally hot-tempered, aggressive but at the same time very good people to associate with due to their openmindedness";
- "Open-minded, strong, hard-working but like fighting and drinking".

6.4. Cultural Differences

Three specific examples were given of cultural differences as a source of ethnic conflict:

- The tendency to use rude or arrogant language when addressing officials or people from other tribes;
- Poor communication or breakdown in communication; and
- Differences in values and attitudes such as those relating to defeat and victory.

Poor communication or breakdown in communication was associated with the manner in which some tribes speak or make approaches. Thus, some tribes are said to speak "as if giving orders" or "quarrelling" even when making requests. Others do so in a "soft" or "diplomatic" manner.

But here, as in beauty, the softness or harshness of the language is a relative thing. With some tribes, soft, diplomatic language is generally not appreciated. It is associated with weakness - both physical/literal and psychological/figurative.

What is appreciated is forceful language. With other tribes, there is a distinct preference for soft, diplomatic language; and the response is likely to be negative if a request or even order is made in a commanding tone.

The factor "differences in values and attitudes" covers many aspects including food and sex; it also goes very deep. As an example, we were told of a case where two Ugandan university professors (call them X and Y) were playing a game. The time was in the early 1980s. X won. Because of that, Y boxed him. Onlookers were greatly shocked that Y could not accept defeat even after a fair, friendly contest. Since X and Y were from distinctly different tribes, it seems, sadly, even very high education may not always help remove the more negative of ethnic/-cultural differences. For surely, in most contests, there are always losers and winners, and it is very important in life to learn to accept and bear defeat, however painful it may be.

Nevertheless we are inclined to believe that the issue of people accepting or refusing to accept defeat is profoundly human and personal, not tribal - although attitudes and intensity may differ from tribe to tribe. Uganda's tribes are different, and the ways in which they react to defeat are likely to differ. However, we do not know of any tribe that tolerates defeat so easily that none of its members will ever attempt to reverse it - whether immediately and openly or much later and secretively or indirectly.

Also, there can be two types of refusal to accept defeat. The first type is more direct and crude: however human, it is negative and dangerous. The second type is associated with determination in the pursuit of, hopefully, a worthy objective, and not being easily discouraged; and this is positive. But, just like the first, it is not the monopoly of one tribe.

7. Ways of Dealing with Ethnic Conflict

7.1. Responses

Well over 55 suggestions were made as to how ethnic conflict in the Uganda public service could be brought to an end or reduced. We have grouped these into 14 categories as follows, with the number mentioning each in parentheses.

(i) Educational reforms and efforts (16)

(ii) Reduction of (political) conflict outside the public service (10)

(iii) Clarification of the role of party politics in the public service (6)

(iv) Equitable distribution of national resources/sharing of the national cake (5)

(v) Streamlining of, and adherence to, procedures in the public service (5)

(vi) Good, honest, sensible and selfless political leadership (4)

(vii) Increased use of, and reliance on, committees rather than individuals in decision-making (3)

(viii) Introduction of a national language (Swahili or Luganda) (3)

(ix) Improvement of the terms and conditions of service of public servants (2)

(x) Increased use of the Inspector General of Government (2)

(xi) Inter-marriage (2)

(xii) Strengthening of Statutory Appointing Bodies like the Public Service Commission (2)

(xiii) Increasing the national cake so there is more to share (2)

(xiv) Clearer definition of the objectives, role and functions of departments/organizations, including systematic job evaluation, job descriptions and job specifications (2)

These 14 suggestions can be sub-grouped further into 4 broad categories - organizational, social, economic and political.

7.2. Organizational Measures

These relate to points (v), (vii) and (xiv) namely: strengthening of, and adherence to, procedures in the public service; increased use of, and reliance on, committees rather than individuals in decision-making; and a clearer definition of the objectives, role and functions of departments/organizations and their sub-units. Let us elaborate on the second point (response vii).

The use of committees was interpreted by one interviewee to include, broadly, consultations within the service including the "absolute" need for politicians to consult technical personnel on all decisions on which they intend to make pronouncements.

This should be the practice even if the politician may take a stand counter to the professional advice given. It was stressed that such consultation must take place before rather than after the politician has taken a final decision. The tendency for politicians to make statements about which public servants learn from the radio - just like other members of the public - was considered not only unfair but also likely to lead to non-implementation, or to the deliberately slow implementation, of policy pronouncements and decisions.

In this connection, it was stressed that what politicians call "sabotage" is not necessarily sabotage as such: it may merely be refusal to implement what public servants consider bad policies. We were reminded that Ugandan politicians tend to dictate or direct - with little or no prior consultations with the public servants concerned. Some of what they say is wrong. In such a situation, the public servant many times finds himself having to choose between implementing bad policies and ignoring them. Often he does the latter: and, depending on his tribe and that of his political master, conflict might not only arise but also take on ethnic colours.

Needless to say, in a multi-ethnic service like Uganda's and where political leaders have no clear and definite mandate from the people, confusion will arise. Anybody - politicians, public servants, the military, etc. - can claim to represent the "people's" interests, although these might be no more than one's own or those of one's tribe.

7.3. Social Measures

Purely social measures are mainly two - educational reforms and efforts; and inter-marriage.

Educational reforms and efforts are meant to encompass many aspects, such as:

- Actual reforms of the school education system;
- Introduction of universal, free and compulsory primary education;
- Politicization - in schools like Kyankwanzi; in places like the Uganda Institute of Public Administration; and at mass rallies;
- Literacy campaigns to help the mass of illiterates in the rural area and a few urban ones to learn how to read and write about the cultures of other tribes;
- Self- and other-people initiated education about the cultures of other tribes;
- Posting of especially the more senior officers to places other than their own or away from the capital so they can learn how other people live;
- The usual seminars and other training programmes with an

emphasis on human relations and team work in multi-ethnic organizations;

- Counselling by supervisors at all levels in the hierarchy;
- "Positive" reliance on religious organizations, especially churches and mosques, to preach unity - as was done by the Uganda Ministry of Health during 1986-87 when it successfully solicited their assistance in the child immunization programme;
- A systematic, properly executed national policy on adult education that goes beyond literacy campaigns.

While the actual reform of the education system should concentrate on the young, we should not forget that adults can and should be assisted to become fully conscious of the social, economic and political realities of Uganda. Respondents felt that the present system emphasizes differences rather than shared values among Ugandans. Children are not consciously and deliberately encouraged to grow up as Ugandans. The reforms should include making and assisting the young to study in different parts of the country, AND also to pursue practical rather than purely theoretical subjects so that they can become job creators rather than job seekers.

Such reforms are likely to be more effective if Uganda chooses and pursues a definite political ideology, as e.g. Tanzania has done.

7.4. Economic Measures

Measures of an economic nature are the equitable distribution of natural resources/sharing of the national cake on the basis of well worked out and generally accepted criteria; improvement of the terms and conditions of service of public servants; and increasing the national cake so that there is more to share.

According to one interviewee, "most of the problems associated with ethnic conflict within the public service and, indeed, in the entire country, are but symptoms of poverty". At any rate, there is no doubt that in a situation of persistent and prolonged scarcity of goods and services to share, what is "good behaviour" becomes difficult to define. Otherwise very decent people, including public servants, can be easily reduced to the state of scrambling for mere bones, and flimsiest excuse, including ethnic differences, will be seized upon to engage in barbaric and primitive acts.

By contrast, in a situation of relative plenty - with reserves and an assurance of future supplies and a well-worked out and generally accepted system of sharing the bounty - it is likely to be easier to reduce greed and its many attendant evils. Incurable thieves (and these are likely to be a minority found in all tribes) can be more easily separated from the vast majority (again to be found in all tribes) who might have become thieves due to negative environmental circumstances.

7.5. Political Measures

These constitute the largest number of measures mentioned-perhaps logical since most sources are also political in nature. We shall say a word on three of these - strengthening appointing bodies, provision or existence of good political leadership and the reduction of political conflict outside the public service.

The suggestion of strengthening the statutory appointing bodies must not be considered superficially. It is too often forgotten that these bodies, especially the Commissions, such as the Public Service Commission (PSC), have two distinct but closely related parts - the Commissioners and the Secretariat.

Now, while Commissioners tend to be persons of great integrity, expertise and experience - witness, for instance, the calibre of those appointed in June 1987 under John Bikangaga - officials comprising the Secretariat tend to be less qualified and experienced. This is most unfortunate. The two parts of the Commission need to be roughly equally experienced and, at any rate, equally competent. The criticisms sometimes levelled at the PSC may well refer, even if unknowingly (because of the tendency to confuse Secretariat staff with Commissioners), more to the Secretariat than to the Commissioners. As long as the Secretariats of the Commissions remain weak, the work of the latter, and hence the entire public service, will continue to suffer.

Lastly, let us consider briefly the provision of honest political leadership, and the reduction of political conflict outside the public service.

Respondents voiced the wide-spread feeling that when there is tension or conflict, ethnic or other, within the political atmosphere - and we would add, the social and economic atmosphere or environment - this is bound to spill over into the public service. (In this connection, we find it hard to believe the assertion - though an interesting one - by an interviewee, that whereas in the political atmosphere such tension/conflict tends to be "hostile" or "antipathetic", in the public service, it is "sympathetic".)

Since late 1965, Uganda's political leadership has lacked genuine, fundamental legitimacy. Vital national questions - who should rule Uganda, for how long, under what system of government, etc. - remain unanswered, and yet these answers directly affect the public service. Once satisfactorily answered - through free and fair elections, with leaders accountable to the people- then ethnic conflict is likely to be much less than it is now, at the time of this writing in 1987.

8. Conclusion

Yes: there is ethnic conflict in the Uganda public service. It exists throughout the hierarchy but mostly at the top. It has several symptoms - the three leading ones being nepotism, unfair dismissals or suspensions, and unfair transfers. Sources are multifarious but the leading categories are those of nepotism (both a symptom and a source) and political factors.

There are several ways in which ethnic conflict can be brought to an end or reduced - through a variety of organizational, social, economic and political means. Essentially and ultimately, however, total ethnic harmony in the public service is impossible without such harmony in the general social, economic and political environments.

In the past, these environments have been polluted by squabbles and even physical fighting among politicians - assisted, directly or indirectly, by some public servants, particularly those at the top. The squabbling and fighting still continue, if with much reduced intensity. Once these squabblers and combatants reach peace, and conflict among them ceases, much ethnic conflict in the public service will cease or remain negligible. What will remain will be individual and organizational forms of conflict; these are universal and can never be really completely got rid of.

Clearly, therefore, the onus of ending ethnic conflict in Uganda, including the public service, is on politicians, top public servants plus, to some extent, all educated citizens. All those interested in ending conflict based on ethnicity may wish to reflect on what Mazrui said in his Reith Lectures: "In the future people will quarrel over incomes, jobs and commodities. They will quarrel less over race and tribe."[19]

Personally, we believe otherwise, however. Ethnic ties and consciousness have been in the past, are today, and will in future continue to be very strong - throughout the world. What has changed and will continue changing is the manner in which we express consciousness of or loyalty to such ties. In general, the more "modern" or "civilized" a society is, the more subtle/-hidden will be that manner, and vice-versa. In organizations, junior employees are likely to be more open in expression while the "top people" will tend to hide their feelings in demagogic or diplomatic acts - only to let them loose when in private, sometimes with a ferocity and a viciousness that defies both genuine civilization and humanity.

We are not disputing the importance of class or class consciousness. Nevertheless, we believe that these two never have, and never will, really and fundamentally replace ethnic/tribal/-racial ties and consciousness, except at the levels of rhetoric and sentiment.

Indeed, there is nothing inherently wrong with attachment to one's tribe. What is wrong, and should therefore be resisted, is an attempt by one tribe or group of tribes to "swallow" or subjugate or undemocratically dominate another or others; or to deny other tribes their due share of the common cake or to deprive them of that "cake" which, through their own efforts and without harming others, they have baked for their own enjoyment.

Tribes may have aspects and practices that are or can be injurious to others, and this must be fought and/or discouraged. But tribes also have aspects and practices which are innocent or harmless or, indeed, which if copied/learnt by others, can prove generally beneficial. Such positive aspects and practices should be encouraged and permitted to flourish.

Let us then hope and pray that, in future, and against a background of total African unity and increased individual and collective prosperity, the more negative aspects of tribes will be a thing of the past.

Appendix: A Note on Methodology

As pointed out in the introduction, we got our information from several sources. We wish to elaborate on two of them - interviews and questionnaires.

We interviewed 11 mostly very senior officers for between 1 and 2 hours each. These were persons known to us. In addition, we distributed 141 questionnaires to participants on 9 different in-service programmes run at the Uganda

Institute of Public Administration. Of the 141 questionnaires, 56 (or 39.7%) were returned. All this took place during May-June 1987. This means that in addition to our own experience, observation, etc., our conclusions are based on information supplied by 67 public officers.

Regional distribution was as follows: Eastern (18), Western (17), Northern (10), Southern (13), and no region indicated (9). The types of public service represented were: traditional public service (48), public corporations (7), local authorities (i.e. District Administrations and Urban Authorities) (6), teaching service (3), and others (3). Religious affiliation: Protestants (Anglican or other) (31), Roman Catholics (28), Moslems (4), Orthodox (2) and others (2).

Ethnic distribution: Baganda (13), Basoga (8), Bakiga (7), Acholi (7), Banyankole ("cultivators"/"Bairu") (6), Iteso (6), Bahororo (4), Madi (3), Batooro (2), Langi (2), Lugbara (2), Bagisu (2), Samia (2), Jonam (1), Munyole (1), and Mugungu (1).

The officers fell into the following salary scales: U1-2 (11), U3 (8), U4-5 (45), and U6-8 (3). In this connection, it should be noted that in most of their public service, the scales applicable are U1 (highest) - U8 (the lowest) plus the Grouping Scheme.

We placed the officers' experience in years into seven categories or brackets as follows: 0-5 (12), 6-10 (36), 11-15 (8), 16-20 (6), 21-25 (zero), 21-25 (zero), 26-30 (4), and over 30 (1).

We would like to end this note by saying how deeply grateful we are to all these officers for their cooperation. We were touched and gratified by their willingness to discuss a fairly sensitive aspect of our country's political sociology in a frank manner. Their frankness and cooperation augur well for our country, including its public service, despite the many problems it is facing.

Notes

We are very grateful to the many officers who granted us interviews or completed our questionnaire and to the following for reading a draft of the paper and offering us very helpful criticisms: S.L.N. Serwanja and V.P.M. Ngwabe, respectively, Permanent Secretary/Special Duties, and Commissioner for Personnel Development, Ministry of Public Service and Cabinet Affairs; H.S. Opika Opoka, Permanent Secretary, Ministry of Energy; and Prof. J. Kwesiga, of the Centre for Continuing Education, Makerere University. We nevertheless accept full responsibility for the views expressed in the paper. These views do not reflect those of Uganda I.P.A.

1. For a detailed note on methodology, see the Appendix.
2. For a fuller discussion of the systems concept, see e.g. Katz, K. & R.L. Kahn: The Social Psychology of Organizations, 2 ed. New York and elsewhere: John Wiley and Sons, 1978; especially pp. 18-34.
3. Gertzel, C.J. et al. (eds.): Government and Politics in Kenya. Nairobi: East African Publishing House, 1969, especially pp. 35-70. This work is particularly useful because it contains specific references to the interaction between happenings in the public service and those in the social, economic and political world of Kenya. And it remains useful even today when it can be said that in addition to ethnic conflict in this country, there is ideological conflict between the left and the right.
4. Webster's Seventh New Collegiate Dictionary. Springfield, Mass.: G. & C. Merriam Company, 1970, p. 285.
5. Morris, H.S.: "Ethnic Groups", in Sills, D.L. (ed.): International Encyclopedia of the Social Sciences, vol. 5. New York & London: The Macmillan Company & The Free Press, 1968, p. 167.
6. Wallman, S.: "Foreword" in Wallam, S. (ed.): Ethnicity at Work. London: The Macmillan Press Ltd., 1979, p. ix.

7. Lewis, I.M.: "Tribal Society", in Sills, op.cit., vol. 15, p. 146.
8. Harris, M.: "Race", in Sills, op.cit., vol. 13, p. 264.
9. Quoted by Singer, M.: "The Concept of Culture", in Sills, op.cit., vol. 3, p. 527. See his entire discussion (pp. 527-541) concerning the works of writers like A.L. Kroeber and C. Kluchohn (on the pattern theory of culture) and Radcliffe-Brown (on the social structure as a theory of culture).
10. March, J.G. & H.A. Simon: Organizations. New York and elsewhere: John Wiley & Sons, Inc., 1967, p. 112.
11. Coser, L.: The Functions of Social Conflict. New York: The Free Press, 1958, pp. 232-236. Quoted by Katz & Kahn, op.cit., p. 615.
12. Katz & Kahn, op.cit., pp. 613 and 649-50.
13. Republic of Uganda:
(a) The Constitution of the Republic of Uganda. Entebbe: Government Printers, 1967, Article 130.
(b) Laws of Uganda, 1969: Statutes. Entebbe: Government Printers, 1969, pp. 187-197. (The Public Service Act, No. 18 of 1969).
(c) Legal Notice No. 3: Proclamation. Entebbe: Government Printers, 14 June 1985.
(d) Circular Standing Instruction No. 3 of 1985. Circular issued by the Ministry of Public Service and Cabinet Affairs, referenced EC 1121 of 21 June 1985. Both the notice and the circular were meant to guide public officers who intended to contest the ill-fated general elections of late 1985. Such officers had to resign their posts in the service, or retire, if they had reached retirement circumstances, by 13 June 1985 (according to the notice) and 30 June 1985 (according to the circular). The circular omits Urban Authorities but includes Makerere University, and all parastatal bodies.
14. See, for instance Barlow, C.H.M.: "The Public Service Crisis in Independent African Countries", in AAPAM: The African Public Services. New Delhi: Vikas Publishing House PVT Ltd., 1984, pp. 1-18.
15. Long, N.E.: "Power and Administration", in Rourke, F.E. (ed.): Bureaucratic Power in National Politics. Boston: Little, Brown and Company, 1965, pp. 14-23.
16. Seidman, H.: Politics, Position and Power. New York and elsewhere: Oxford University Press, 1970. The entire book is relevant.
17. Merloo, J.A.M.: That Difficult Peace. Great Neck, N.Y.: Channel Press, 1961, p. 16. Quoted in Bettelheim, B. and M. Janowitz: Social Change and Prejudice. New York and London: The Free Press & Collier-Macmillan Ltd., 1964, p. 51.
18. Klineberg, O.: "Prejudice: The Concept", in Sills, op.cit., vol. 12, p. 439.
19. Mazrui, A.A.: The African Condition. London and elsewhere: Heinemann, 1980, p. 44.

Ruth Mukama

The Linguistic Dimension of Ethnic Conflict

1. Introduction

For a multilingual country like Uganda, the language factor represents quite a problem in the face of the many varied priority requirements of a modern state, such as internal cohesion, accelerated development, effective communication systems, etc. No one would of course insist that language should be named the number one priority on the nation's programme for rapid advancement. But at the same time, no one would dispute the fact that no country has ever rocketed ahead without paying serious attention to the effectiveness and efficiency of linguistic communication. Language underlies and permeates all development programmes. Indeed, Ugandan governments are erecting their own formidable obstruction along the road to development by continuing to overlook the language variable in the planning process.

The major premise of the paper is that the vacillation surrounding the language question on the part of Ugandan governments is an epitome of the seething ethnic discord that continues to plague our nation. In section 2, we begin by discussing the national language question, which still awaits a definite solution. Section 3 examines the haphazard and ineffectual communication channels in use in the various government ministries and other institutions. In section 4, we go on to comment on the implications of the continued linguistic stalemate, noting that language policy deliberations are bound to remain on the emotive and irrational level. Reference is also made to the priority development programmes which require the mobilization of the good will and involvement of the people; these cannot be accomplished as expeditiously as they should. Possible language policy options for Uganda are analyzed in section 5, while in section 6 a proposal is made towards initiating and revitalizing existent communication avenues. The highlight of the design involves setting up a national communication centre to coordinate and preside over information dissemination. Finally, in section 7, we comment in broad terms on the advantages of this proposed communication design.

2. The Ethnic Curb to the Making of a National Language[1]

> A nation without a national language is a nation without a soul. A nation with a national language which is not very much cared for and respected is a crazy nation.[2]

2.1. Dilemma and Challenge

Well, Uganda has survived without "a soul" up to today; but with what consequences? This paper attempts to provide part of the answer to this question.

Tribalism and linguistic prejudice are subjects Ugandans would rather not talk about - except when imputing them to others, never to oneself. The truth, however, is that tribalism is unfortunately quite rampant, and it heavily prejudices even the most innocent of discussions about language, also among linguists at the University.

When governments are perpetually faced with sensibilities of this sort, selecting a relevant road to a viable linguistic solution for the future becomes both a dilemma and a challenge. As a dilemma, it might lead to considerable ambivalence or lack of a clear sense of direction among policy-makers with regard to goals and plans to be adopted. As a challenge, it might require of policy-makers a high degree of dexterity of mind (to enable them to consider all the options); clarity of vision (to enable them to arrive at the optimum option, discarding the irrelevant), and boldness of decision (a necessary condition for sticking only to what one believes right and in the public good).

So far, Ugandan governments have remained caught in the dilemma, unable to take up the challenge.[3] As a nation we appear to be running away from the reality of our linguistic situation, its complexity and the special considerations and handling that it requires.

2.2. The Period 1960-1971

Between 1960 and 1971, governments steered clear of formal discussion of the choice of a national language for Uganda.

Throughout that period, the only occasion on which we had a glimpse of near-coherent statements on government policy on language was when Milton Obote was opening a Seminar on Mass Media and Linguistic Communications in East Africa in Kampala. He explained:

> ... the Government and the people of Uganda do realize that there are certain advantages in our learning English. We could not, for instance, adopt Lugbara ... as our national language. ... the task of teaching Lugbara itself would be beyond our capacity and ability ... teaching Lugbara or adopting it would result in serious riots and instability. ... the same applies practically to every other language in Uganda.

and

> ... we find no alternative to English in Uganda's present position. We have, therefore, adopted English as our national language (actually meant: official language[4]); in fact it is the political language. (Obote 1967).

These statements clearly show a non-committal position on the subject, although later on in the same paper Obote hinted at the remote possibility of change of policy in the future.

As if to cudgel the Government into an earlier change of language policy, the public started a debate on a possible national and official language for Uganda which culminated in the Kyambogo Conference organized by the Uganda Language Society.[5] The conference reached some kind of consensus to

> recommend to the Government that Kiswahili be introduced as the national language, but that the Luo should be taught a Bantu language and the Bantu be taught a Luo language.[6]

Indeed, this debate seemed to have come very close to obtaining the desired results when, on being installed as Chancellor of the University in October 1970, Dr. Obote urged Makerere University "to establish a proper school for African languages" and said that "the Government would endeavour to introduce the teaching of Swahili in the schools".[7]

The University went far in fulfilling its own part of the undertaking, but the Government never did. So the 1960-71 period remained a non-committal one with regard to the national language debate.

2.3. The Period 1971-1979

On 7 August 1973, Kiswahili was declared the national language of Uganda, in characteristic Idi Amin style - by decree. But unlike other Amin decrees this particular one was not the result of an overnight dream; it was based on a recommendation by a representational body - every district who gathered at the International Conference Centre, Kampala, after weeks of deliberations. However, the swing in favour of Kiswahili was not by unanimous consensus: twelve districts voted for Kiswahili, while eight voted for Luganda.

The heated debate that preceded the vote is a clear testimony that the ultimate line-up of the voters was to some extent guided by ethnic differences. For instance, a delegate from the Armed Forces is quoted as arguing that if Luganda were chosen the national language it would create "tribal superiority". Another delegate, a "friend of Swahili" from Tororo, added that if Luganda were to be chosen the other "tribes would feel that it has been imposed on them"; adding that Swahili should be chosen because it "belongs to no particular tribe" in the country. And the West Nile delegation warned that if a local language was chosen, "rather than serve as a unifying factor, it was certain to create a cleavage". (Lulua 1976, ch. 17, pp. 12-13) The districts voting for Swahili were Bunyoro, Toro, Kigesi, East Acholi, West Acholi, Lango, North Karamoja, South Karamoja, Madi, Teso, Sebei and West Nile. And those which voted for Luganda were all the four districts of Buganda - East Buganda, West Buganda, Masaka and Mubende; the three districts in the Eastern region - Bugisu, Bukedi, and Busoga; and in the Western region, the district of Ankole. Thus the observation made by A. Mazrui in 1967 was confirmed in 1973: "Among the greatest friends of Swahili in Uganda are in fact, Nilotic peoples ... The greatest antagonists of Swahili within Uganda were in fact, fellow Bantu people - the Baganda." (Mazrui, 1967, p. 15)

The decree was, however, never implemented; and although it has never been repealed, it has received no attention whatsoever from successive governments. Indeed, many Ugandans swear that they have never heard of this decree.

Clearly, apart from the incident of the national language debate of 1973, also this period lacked a coherent government policy on language. Our divided population which continues to wrangle over language can hardly provide a firm base for a definite language policy.

2.4. The Period 1980-1985

The year 1980 started with a little hope for language policy, at least according to the UPC party manifesto:

> UPC will seek to promote an African language such as Kiswahili, to the status of a national, unifying language. At the same time UPC will encourage and foster the development and teaching of various indigenous languages as part of our heritage. English will remain the official language. (p. 4)

English remained the official language all right, but the other two resolutions on language development came to naught. There was no formal address to language development either in Parliament or in the Ministry of Education. The sole official reference to language in the period 1980-85 was made by the Minister of Education, I.N. Ojok, when opening the OAU Linguistic Experts Meeting held in the Conference Centre, Kampala, in June 1985. He showered praises upon the African languages and reaffirmed, in accord with the National Language Decree of 1973, that Swahili is the national language of Uganda and that English is only an official language. Apart from this polite mention to suit the occasion, no significant contribution was made to improve the language situation, despite the appeals of the Uganda Kiswahili Club for official reinstatement of Swahili as one of the languages to be taught in schools.

2.5. Since 1985

Renewed hopes for a decisive step forward, towards a coherent language policy for the nation, were rekindled by the ascendancy of the NRM government to power. On his first official visit to Mbarara in April 1986, President Museveni criticized previous governments for failing to foster and develop a national language, before he started to speak in Runyankole. And some months later, in September 1986, the Prime Minister, Dr. Kisekka, also repeated the criticism in Kampala, while opening a seminar of the Central Kampala Resistance Council. He finally decided to speak in Luganda on that occasion. As could be expected, these allusions to a national language aroused some public interest. Accordingly, the newspaper Weekly Topic urged:

> ... the (...) NRM government should stop lamenting over the absence of a "local" language. They should boldly take practical steps and give this country a common medium of communication. ... President Museveni and Prime Minister Kisekka should lead us, so as to translate their wishful laments into fruitful action. ... In a nutshell, the NRM government should consider designing the development of a national language as the eleventh point in its programme.[8]

If there is now an eleventh point on the programme, it is not language development as far as we know.

The only other reference to the language problem after the hints mentioned above was made by the Minister of Education, Mr. Mayanja Nkangi, in opening the language seminar organized by the Department of Languages, Makerere University, in conjunction with the Summer Institutes of Linguistics (SIL), 16-20 March 1987. On the question of media of instruction, he called upon the participants "to study and improve a group of local languages for use during the early part of school education". And concerning the national language question, his statements were tantamount to censoring the National Language Decree of 1973. He explained that we need not "import another language" for the purposes of inter-ethnic communication, adding that we should "preserve and enhance our national albeit multi-cultural Ugandan identity by improving and adapting one or two of the local languages or language groups so that they can be employed when Ugandans of different tribes meet". So far the Ministry has done nothing to provide the lead in responding to that challenge.

Understandably, all this inertia on language policy cannot be squarely blamed on ethnic antagonism alone. Nevertheless, it is also very true that many governments in multilingual states like Uganda resort to vacillation when, amid other formidable national problems, they fear to aggravate the emotive linguistic sensibilities by making a definite ruling on language choice. Be this as it may, Uganda still remains among those countries with no national language.

3. Reaching the People by Expediency

Almost all government ministries and agencies need to educate the masses on the value of priority programmes. And in the absence of a common forum for planning how to reach them, each ministry has had to define its own strategy.

In 1968 Radio Uganda was broadcasting in 16 Ugandan languages as well as English and Hindustani (Ladefoged et al. p. 21). Today the number of Ugandan languages on the radio has risen to 19, bringing the overall total to 21, with English and Swahili. However, in most cases, programmes consist mainly of recorded music presented under a title such as "Lumasaba Requests". Occasionally, programmes will be interspersed with short discussions; otherwise, they are largely devoid of any educational content.

In its literacy programmes, the Ministry of Culture, Youth and Sport seems guided by the same criteria used by the Ministry of Information, with regard to radio broadcasts. By 1968, literacy campaigns had been conducted in 20 different languages. Ladefoged et al. add that there is hardly any literature for further reading in most of these languages. This means that learners cannot go beyond the scope of the literacy campaign booklets; there is nothing more to enable them to strengthen and sustain their literacy acquisition. And yet the literacy seminar held at the IPA in Kampala, 7-14 July 1987 seems to have recommended the use of even more languages!

The Ministry of Agriculture, "primarily for economic reasons", print their "leaflets giving advice to farmers in English and only four Ugandan languages" (Ladefoged et al., p. 22). That is why communication between the agricultural officials and the farmers is mainly "by word of mouth" directly through interpreters. Ladefoged et al. continue:

> The policy of the Ministry of Education is to use six Ugandan languages in the primary schools and English in the secondary schools and higher education. These six languages are spoken by 61 percent of the population; but in practice only a little more than half of the children who are in school are being taught in their own language. (pp. 21-22)

The six languages are Luganda, Akarimojong/Ateso, Lugbara, Luo, Runyoro/Rutooro, and Runyankole/Rukiga. Except for Luganda, which is taught in schools in Buganda thanks to the availability of teaching materials produced by individual effort, there is no official effort to teach the Ugandan languages nor is there any drive to produce any teaching materials in them.

The Ministry of Health is operating very much like the Ministry of Agriculture, in producing leaflets and posters in only a few languages. These may then be translated and passed on to the other language groups "by word of mouth" by the local health workers.

Many other government ministries and parastatal organizations which are among the main sources of public services to the rural sector have no systematic language programmes outside the domain of English. Only the Coffee Marketing Board has started putting up radio programmes in several Ugandan languages. But as Ladefoged et al. have observed, "Uganda is a country where information travels primarily by word of mouth" (p. 22) rather than by radio or newspapers, so the masses will still be largely oblivious of the information provided by the Board, or even of the very existence of the Board itself. By thus keeping information among the elite, these ministries and parastatals fail to contribute to the development process. For, as L. Omondi puts it:

> There is planned development through which specific issues and ideas are considered worth selling to the people. Any aspect of planned development which is not communicated still-birth. Many of the people who need development most speak only the African languages. (Omondi 1986, p. 4)

But while some ministries and parastatals may survive only at the expense of development, politicians can keep to themselves only at their own peril.

Indeed, politicians cannot afford to remain uncommunicative; they continually find themselves before large audiences of different language backgrounds. That is why they feel the need for a common language more poignantly than other government employees, as evidenced by the remonstrations from President Museveni and Prime Minister Kisekka, as noted above. It is interesting to note that some of their predecessors also felt the problem equally keenly:

> When I move out of Kampala to talk to the people, I have to talk in English. Obviously, I have no alternative but I lose a lot especially as far as the Party is concerned. The Party welcomes everybody and some of the greatest and most dedicated workers are those who do not speak English and yet the Party Leader cannot call this great dedicated worker alone and say "Thank you" in a language the man will understand. It has to be translated. There must always be a third party, and that is why it is said there are no secrets in Africa." (Obote 1967)

Yet up to this day "tomorrow" has never come with regard to the language situation. If politicians are as concerned about the problem as expressed, why then the continued vacillation over language policy? Our main thesis is that they are immobilized by a foreboding of ethnic strife, imagined or real. This fear is largely hushed up, never expressed officially except in passing as it happened once; when Obote said that the adoption of language like Lugbara for a national language "could result in serious riots and instability" (Obote, 1967).

It is clear from this brief outline that the development effect and responsibility is dispersed among many parties all of which aspire to reaching the masses in disparate ways and to varying extents. No attempt at coordination of endeavours has ever been made.

4. Keeping Pressure off the Emotive Chord: Implications and Consequences

> We must keep our vernaculars in education. In my case, I used Luganda in my early schooling and things must remain that way. I am saying this with deep emotion ...

This was a share rejoinder from a Makerere University lecturer, a Ugandan, to a comment made by a University of Nairobi lecturer, a Kenyan, that Uganda should follow the other two East African states in using Kiswahili in schools. Such emotional outbursts are typical in the Ugandan language situation, and are particularly common among speakers who feel that their languages are rightful candidates for the role of a national language.

Two major camps of language choice have emerged on the emotive front. One camp is characterized by the inward-looking view: if there is to be a national language then it must be mine. The following argument is representative of the group:

> ... there <is> no useful purpose to be gained by introducing Swahili in this country ... Sir, may I appeal to all Africans in this House to forget our tribal differences and agree to a suggestion that we should try and have one language, say Luganda, which should be taken as our lingua franca. Why I say this, Sir, is not just because I happen to come from the Luganda speaking area ...[9]

It would have been interesting to see the reaction of the speaker if he were told soon after making that benevolent submission that Ngakarimojong was to be our lingua franca.

The second camp constitutes the more outward looking group; the one which holds the view that if it is not my language then no other Ugandan indigenous language. They argue that superimposing one "tribal" language over others would result in "tribal superiority" and would be bound "to create a cleavage" (Lulua, 1976). Only a firm but rational language policy can put an end to these otherwise endless emotionally charged conjectures.

Most Ugandans (93%) reside in rural areas; hence, if we are to develop as a nation, we must focus on the rural areas. If we genuinely want all groups in our society to experience progress in their well-being we have to ensure a real fundamental transformation in rural development. This will involve the acceleration of growth and change in such key sectors as agricultural production, education, health and nutrition, clean water supply and sanitation, housing and industry. And if this is to happen, the interest of the peasants has to be captured; they have to be mobilized to participate fully in decision-making and in implementing all the development programmes planned for their good. To date we have achieved very little in our rural development strategies precisely because we have repeatedly made the same costly mistake: the peasant sector has never been provided the foundation for decision-making or implementation of plans. The common practice is simply to take projects down to the villages, where the villagers are then expected to receive them gratefully, without question. Some people have already seen the futility of this type of approach, as indicated in the following observation:

> We have been taking resolution after resolution about immunization for all by the year 1990; clean water for all by the year 1990; health for all by the year 2000; but we are not at all anywhere near our goals. Now, why is this? We need to go down to the masses and educate them about the value of these programmes.[10]

Another development analyst also makes much the same comment:

> Uganda has the potential to develop. Yet the majority of the people are below the poverty line, many are unemployed and/or underemployed, a portion of the population go hungry because they have neither money nor access to food. The basic question then is "What happened? (Matovu 1983, p. 14)

In his view, the basic impediments of Uganda's development include the colonial factor, the geographical position of Uganda and the unmotivated public sector. Without minimizing the crucial importance of availability of funds in the development process, I wish to add that our failure to communicate with the peasants has also detracted greatly from our development efforts.

5. The Quest for a National Language

We do not wish to give a false impression by claiming that having a definite language policy, per se, will guarantee an efficient communication system. However, an established language policy would certainly be a good base from which to plan an efficient communication system. Has then Uganda in fact any language policy? This question could be answered in the affirmative in two ways. One, it could be argued that what passes for language policy in Uganda is an assemblage of disjointed statements that English is the official language; that six Ugandan languages (some of them paired), plus English are the media of instruction; that over 20 languages are broadcast on the radio; that since 1973, Swahili has been the national language by decree; that an MP has to be able to speak English, etc. Two, that Uganda's language policy is in fact to have no specific policy, such that language issues are left to sort themselves out in an evolutionary manner. Until some government comes out and gives serious attention to the language question, we shall never know the real answer to that question, however.

Even Ladefoged et al. were unable to determine Uganda's position on language policy. This is how they put it:

> Policy makers in Uganda appear to be torn in even more different directions. Almost no element of language policy can be regarded as fixed beyond challenge, and long-term plans for implementation must await basic decisions. (p. 10)

Nevertheless, it is our duty as linguists to offer our contribution towards possible language policy options in our situation. While it is healthy to have emotional reactions to language issues, we also note that emotionalism will have to be counter-balanced with a degree of rationality if we are to make wise decisions, as advised by Ladefoged:

> decisions on language questions are notoriously influenced by emotional issues such as tribal identifications, religious loyalties, national rivalries, racial prejudices, the desire to preserve elites, and so on. They may even run directly counter to all the evidence of feasibility.
>
> Policies will be efficacious only in so far as they succeed in reconciling national goals with actual possibilities. And if choices are made on emotional grounds alone, they cannot be expected to prove maximally productive. It is even desirable for the policy maker to have at his disposal as many facts as possible about the strength and nature of the emotional issues. (pp. 8-9)

With these observations in mind, let us now look at four possible language policy options:

1. A decision to leave the situation as it is.[11]

2. Three languages to be selected and modernized and promoted to the national level. These should represent the language groups/sub-families of Nilotic and both Eastern and Western Bantu. "A foreign language" is "unacceptable".[12]

3. "Kiswahili be introduced as the national language, but the Luo should be taught a Bantu language and the Bantu be taught a Luo language"[13], and "(In search for a national language) Our vote is cast for Swahili as the most agreeable choice".[14]

4. We have several language groups in this country, maybe four. Each of these, along with English, an international language, and Kiswahili, a regional language, must be declared as official languages. In the schools, we should teach the language of that area, say Luganda or Luo, and then both English and Kiswahili.[15]

The adoption of the first decision would confirm the cherished hope that English will eventually develop into a national language. That is, that there will come a time when the majority of Ugandans will be able to speak English. This would of course be a remarkable achievement. The case for the retention of English, an international language, is still strong. It would, therefore, be an ideal national language.

We have, however, to note that at present in Uganda English is a "trans-tribal language" only "at the level of the educated elite" (Mazrui 1970). After over half a century of teaching and learning English, all we have to show for it is that 21% of the population are able to hold a conversation in English. This rate of English acquisition may not necessarily improve even after the start of the programme of universal primary education, if the majority continue to leave school at the primary level. Many primary school leavers are unable to hold a reasonable conversation in English and even those who can, forget soon after leaving school for lack of reinforcement. There is also the issue of the relationship between the English language and our cultures. Speaking at the debate on the national language, A. Nsibambi pointed out that the political problem of using English is that it involves alienation from one's culture.[16] And what is more, even the most fluent Ugandan user of English will find it hard to express all aspects of our ways of life and other cultural nuances in the English language. To most of us, English is strictly a scholarly language with very little else to do with our typically social and family concerns.[17] This domain of language demarcation could be a serious impediment to the spread of English among the masses.

Further, states which adopt recommendation number (1) for a policy also tend to believe that their language situations are cases of multilingualism en route to monolingualism, i.e. that one language will eventually substitute for the other languages in all roles: formal or informal scholarly, professional or social. The supplanted languages will then simply die out through disuse. This is the most acceptable way of solving language problems since it involves no use of force which could lead to the flare-up of emotions. However, we have hardly any precedents to demonstrate that such a solution has actually ever aided any state in solving its multilingual problems. And in Uganda, where languages are more or less inalienably rooted in ethnic groupings, it is highly improbable that such a solution will ever be applicable as long as ethnic groupings still exist. The majority of Ugandans share Mr. Babiiha's sentiment when he says:

> It would be very destructive to the cultural background of this country to abolish our native languages. Nobody wishes to destroy his tribal language. They are our traditional institutions. If we destroy them today we would be completely detribalized and de-nationalized.[18]

Thus if we opt for recommendation (1), Uganda may never have a truly national language; English is bound to remain essentially an official language. At the same time, Ugandan languages are not threatened in any way by impending natural death.

And over and above the ethnic sentiments, there is also the growing Africanist feeling inherent in comments such as the following:

> It is very important for the black man to have a language with which he could identify himself. Africans are open to attack from within and without because they had no common language in which they could communicate. Because they had no such language, they could not keep their privacy."[19]

This attitude too could be a significant obstacle to the rise of English as a national language.

The choice of recommendation number (2) would be guided by the reasoning that Uganda needs to foster its own typically national culture as a basis for consolidating its national identity. However, proposers of this line of action do not agree on the number of languages to be upgraded to the role of "national" language. The Makerere Seminar report recommends a Nilotic language, an Eastern Bantu language and a Western Bantu language. But if, in all fairness we wish all language groups and subfamilies to be represented nationally, then we have to include a language from the Sudanic group as well. And if we are ready to recognize the distinction between Eastern and Western Bantu languages, we must do the same for the Western Nilotic (formerly "Nilotic"), and Eastern Nilotic (formerly "Nilohamitic"), for the later sub-groups are far more different from each other than are the Bantu sub-groups. Accordingly, for the selection based on the language family criterion to be fairly representative, at least five languages will have to be upgraded to national status.

The other aspect of proposition number (2) is that the selected languages are to be made compulsory "at primary and "0" levels" in all schools and that every school goer be "compelled to learn at least one language other than a language from his language group or sub-family". A committed implementation of this part of the programme will go a long way to end the present zoning[20] practice that only serves to entrench the languages into the ethnic groups immediately associated with them, thereby confirming the erroneous belief that languages are the exclusive properties of the respective ethnic communities. Decision (2) would, in that way, contribute significantly towards raising the level of multilingualism among the population and, consequently, the improvement of inter-tribal communication.

The main dark side to this type of policy is the risk of "linguistic isolation" for the nation as a whole, as has been pointed out before:

> The adoption of any one of our present languages in Uganda may just go to endorse our isolation; we cannot afford

> isolation. It is possible today for the people of Uganda to communicate with the people in the neighbouring countries in broken Swahili but it is not possible for the people of Uganda to communicate with the neighbouring countries in broken Luganda. If we cannot communicate with our neighbours in broken Luganda today, how much more difficult would it be to try to communicate in first class Luganda? (Obote 1967)

and

> There is a lot of nonsense that is usually argued against Swahili in this country. But if we attach any significance to regional unity and cooperation, leave alone our national unity, then we should not choose to remain a chaotic island of English and "tribal" languages surrounded by neighbours who opted for Swahili. (Weekly Topic, 1.10.86)

The other serious difficulty of the solution exclusively based on indigenous languages relates to its feasibility. Implementation is likely to face two set-backs, especially as it is advised that we also retain the English language. One set-back would be the problem of motivation for learners required to learn so many languages within the short span of their primary and secondary school life. For as Nsibambi rightly reiterates in all his reflections on the language question in Uganda, languages will only sell themselves to people through their "practical utility", as was the case among the members of the NRA when they were in the bush:

> Faced with a practical problem of communication and unity while in the bush, the NRA was bailed out by Swahili. This is a good historical lesson. (Weekly Topic, 1.10.86)

A Ugandan child who speaks Suk (or Pokot), one of the languages within the Karamoja area, would hardly be motivated to learn Luganda, a language which, in his view, has no practical use. The same problem would face a Luganda-speaking child forced to learn Luo or Lugbara, for example.

The other set-back concerns language choice and acceptability. As already observed, this subject always stirs up cultural and sub-nationalistic emotions among Ugandans.

This is what Nsibambi describes as "questions of political sensibilities and sensitivities of tribal groups" (Nsibambi 1969, p. 119). The policy of the Ministry of Education so far is to use six

Ugandan languages as media for instruction in addition to English. But among the six, three are paired, thus yielding nine. Concession is also made to Kumam in the Teso area, which brings the total number to ten. Despite this liberalism in the Ministry, there are many disgruntled pockets of ethnic groups who resent the fact that their children have to learn in the medium of another language. In the Luganda educational area, for example, the Jopadhola and Iteso of Tororo have never actually accepted Luganda.[21] The Sebei have also always resented the use of Luganda. And in the north-east, the trial marriage between Ateso and Ngakarimojong has never actually worked. An for the Ik (or Teso) people, Ngakarimojong is as different from their own language as English is, so the burden of language learning is much heavier for them than for others who find in school an "official" vernacular the same or similar to the home language. In the Western region the Banyarwanda have never accepted Runyankole/Ruhororo; just as the Bakonjo are visibly hostile to Rutooro.[22] All is not well in the West Nile region either. Thus, while demanding the use of Kakwa over Radio Uganda, the Kakwa "argued that the majority of them do not understand Lugbara and that they feel discriminated against whenever they have to listen to the programmes through Lugbara" (Nsibambi 1969, p. 196). We also learn from the same source that when the Kebu in the "official" Alur language zone demanded a separate country, they "felt that they were "despised", "insulted" and "looked down upon by the Alur"." Now, if with ten languages accommodated in education we still have these wrangles, what will the situation be like if we reduce the number to only three? The situation of Radio Uganda and in the Literary Programmes shows that nearly 26 ethnic groupings are demanding recognition and representation of their languages. This should indicate that once you choose to go purely indigenous it is difficult to do so only in part.

Policy recommendation (3) favours promoting Kiswahili to national language status but also advises that considerable attention be paid to some indigenous languages. The enemies of Kiswahili in Uganda always make it appear as though its "friends" are pleading for it to be introduced into the country for the first time. But Kiswahili is not new to Uganda; it has been spoken for a long time, since its introduction as a trade language before 1900. During 1900-1912 it was the Official Local Language. Until 1952 it as one of the recognized vernaculars in Ugandan schools. And for a long time it was the official language in the police force and in the army. Since Independence many analysts of the

Uganda language situation have catalogued a list of points which favour the adoption of policy (3):

(a) Kiswahili is a popular language and easy to learn as attested in the following observations: "When I first went to school round about 1928 and 1929, I and all my class and school-mates started with Swahili. We were all happy to start with Swahili, but nobody knows why the teaching of Swahili was abolished."[23] or "It takes six months for an African of Bantu tribe here to learn Swahili of a high standard. From the early days up to the year 1935, Swahili was being taught in Makerere College in a class which was known as the general vocational class. In one year a man could attain a high Swahili standard ..."[24]

(b) It is now spoken by the educated as well as those who never went to school.

(c) It is an African language (unlike English) and is thus able to preserve African cultures and feelings.[25]

(d) It is akin to the vernaculars of two-thirds of Uganda which consists of Bantu, and is agreeable to the other one-third (Nilotic and Sudanic).

(e) It is in itself a neutral language, relatively free from tribal sensibilities.

(f) It has a considerably large and rich literature.

(g) It is widely studied in various universities all over the world, and is broadcast daily over East African and foreign radio stations.

(h) It will be relatively cheaper to promote than any of the indigenous languages, because the task of its further development is now shared internationally.

(i) It will act as a unifying force by facilitating uni-lingual inter-tribal communications.

(j) It will help Ugandan businessmen throughout East and Central Africa.

(k) As a regional language, it will promote closer cooperation and understanding in East and Central Africa.[26]

With all these good points to the credit of Kiswahili, why then the continued vacillation of the State over the formulation of a clear official policy concerning the language? Why is it still officially banned from Ugandan schools, although the decree which declared it the national language 15 years ago is still among the statues of the country?

Related questions on the subject of Kiswahili have been posed by other scholars who have previously paid serious attention to the Uganda language situation. As already quoted in part, A. Mazrui lays the blame for the official ban on Kiswahili from

Uganda's schools squarely on the Baganda. The quotation continues as follows:

> Swahili was taught in Uganda schools for some time before World War II. It disappeared from Uganda schools mainly because it was regarded as a serious rival to Luganda. (Mazrui 1976, p. 15)

Nsibambi has argued very persuasively that there is no evidence to substantiate this claim, and to some extent he has a point. However, there is some truth in Mazrui's observation as well. The only overt written evidence we have managed to obtain so far is the memorandum written by Daudi Chwa.[27] His main objective was to oppose the introduction of Kiswahili as an official language in Buganda. But he disclosed other unfortunate traits of ethnic/linguistic arrogance objectionable to many other ethnic groups. For instance, his memorandum included, inter alia, clauses of the following nature:

> Buganda Kingdom forms the most important Province within the Uganda Protectorate; My ancestors have always kept up the supremacy of Buganda Kingdom among the surrounding native tribes of East Africa. It is therefore not unnatural that I and my people should feel that the compulsory use of another native language is derogatory to the prestige of the natives of Buganda Kingdom.
>
> ... the Luganda language has now developed
>
> ... I fail to see why the Kiswahili should be considered to take precedence over the Luganda language ...
>
> ... the Baganda ... consider this language as ... without literary value.

If Mazrui had access to publications of this kind, then he had a point in making the statement quoted above. Daudi Chwa's memorandum went far beyond being an innocent policy objection. And as the British rulers were then depending on Baganda agents to administer other parts of the country, such a scathing attack on Kiswahili from their administrative partners might have greatly prejudiced their further plans for Kiswahili in Uganda.

Further, as Nsibambi explains, historically, "the economic and educational opportunities were concentrated in Buganda". Uganda's representation on all the important inter-territorial committees and commissions was manned solely by Baganda, which means that they could easily veto any propositions favourable to Kiswahili.

An example is in fact given of how such a veto was exercised in 1931:

> In 1929, Governor Cowers of Uganda, discussing the multilingual nature of the country, recommended the adoption of Swahili as the educational and administrative language of the Uganda Protectorate instead of Luganda, but the unpopular nature of the decision can be seen in the reacting of the Joint Parliamentary Commission on Closer Union which met in May 1931. The commission recorded that "it would be desirable to encourage a gradual change from Swahili to English" after hearing African witnesses (all of whom were Luganda speakers). (Ladefoged et al. 1971, p. 88)

Even "the important language policy decisions of 1952 ... that Swahili was no longer a recognized vernacular in Uganda schools" (ibid., p. 91) could have come about under similar circumstances.

A more recent demonstration of Buganda's consistent opposition to Kiswahili as demonstrated in 1973 when Idi Amin, who always sardonically enjoyed presiding over discord, initiated a countrywide national language debate involving the choice between Kiswahili and Luganda. He himself whimsically set the ball rolling by casting his vote for Luganda. As already noted above, 12 districts voted in favour of Kiswahili while 8 districts voted for Luganda. This line-up is very significant because, much as we wish to desist from attributing all conflicts and differences between peoples to old and traditional animosities between tribes, it marked a persisting cleavage between two ethnic blocs with regard to Kiswahili. One bloc, which favoured Luganda, was led by Buganda, supported by four of her historical vassals, among them Busoga:

> For a long time past, Busoga was a tributary state of Buganda Kingdom, and Basoga used to pay tribute to the Kabaka (Mwanga). Since then the Basoga, with no written vernacular of their own, have tended to look to Buganda for guidance. (Lulua 1976)

The other three were Bugisu and Bukedi in the Eastern region and Ankole in the Western region. It has been explained that the history of the Luganda language in these districts "may be traced to the domination of Baganda evangelists and government agents during the early years of this century". (Lulua 1976) The other bloc, which preferred Kiswahili, comprised the rest of the districts which constituted themselves into some kind of recalcitrant front to prevent Luganda from being "imposed on them". (Lulua 1976)

Thus the Luganda/Kiswahili opposition has threatened to carve this nation into two major ethnic blocs: Bantu versus non-Bantu, the latter being the chief supporters of Kiswahili, as noted by Mazrui. We note that Sebei, which is historically in the Luganda zone, voted against Luganda, together with the rest of the non-Bantu. The only distinctive exception came among the Western Bantu, which are among the chief historical protagonists in resisting Buganda rule. In their case, political sentiments cut across ethnic allegiance. Their dissent is vital in the Luganda/-Kiswahili opposition because then Kiswahili is put decisively in the lead, supported by about 54% of the country, while Luganda has 41%, the rest of the population being non-Ugandan.

Such Luganda/Kiswahili opposition is still keenly alive today as well. In section 4, we noted the emotional outburst of the University lecturer, a Luganda speaker, in response to a view that Uganda should reinstate Kiswahili in schools. Then recommendation number (2), to upgrade Uganda languages to the exclusion of a "foreign language", was made by the writer of the Report of the Makerere Language Seminar, another Luganda speaker, who, against all rules governing report-writing, was then to formulate far-reaching recommendations on a subject never discussed at the seminar itself.

However, I agree entirely with Nsibambi that the Luganda/-Kiswahili opposition in itself would not have continued to bar Kiswahili from official circles if the successive governments had wished to keep it there. "In view of the fact that Luganda's political hegemony and special position were abolished under the 1967 revolution", Kiswahili's upward swing would have been boundless. As stated by Ladefoged,

> If the government wished to change its language policy, there is no doubt that language attitudes would also change. (Ladefoged et al. 1971, p. 30)

One other observation to be made concerning the Luganda/Kiswahili opposition at the national level is that it epitomizes the ethnic/linguistic conflicts at the sub-regional level. These were noted under policy number (2) above, and they include dissensions like Kakwa versus Lugbara, Kebu versus Alur, Lukonjo versus Rutooro, Runyarwanda versus Ruhororo/Runyankole, Ateso/-Dhopadhola versus Luganda (Tororo District), Kupsabiny versus

Luganda (Sebei district), etc. The added advantage of Kiswahili is that it cuts across all this sub-regional linguistic discord, as most ethnic groupings already accept it as lingua franca. Further, many listen to Kiswahili programmes from Kenya, Tanzania, Rwanda and Zaire and know that Kiswahili would be an asset if they wished to visit those countries; thus, they would be more motivated to learn it.

However, the general trend of reasoning seems to be that in the event of the adoption of Kiswahili as an official/national language, we should "not throw English out of the window or the vernaculars overboard".[28]

Language policy recommendation number (4) incorporates all the requirements specified by Musisi. Policy (4) seeks to resolve the conflicts pertaining to the selection and acceptance of Ugandan indigenous languages in the field of education by advising the use of the language of the area in schools. This would effectively reinforce the inculcation of traditional cultures in most parts of the country. Problems would come only in areas where either a school is shared by children from widely divergent ethnic/linguistic backgrounds, or where some tiny ethnic/linguistic group has no school in the vicinity. Considering the complexity of our linguistic situation, complications of this nature cannot be avoided. However, policy recommendation (4) does offer three possible ways of resolving the problem. One would be to use the official indigenous language representative of a language group. Option two would be to use Kiswahili, and the third alternative would be to use English. Thus policy advice number (4) effectively caters for inter-tribal, inter-regional national communication, as well as incorporating a mechanism for narrowing the disparity between home and school domains of language use for the majority.

Another problem likely to arise with proposition (4) is the choice and acceptability of the languages to represent the respective language groups officially. Whatever criteria we may use for the purpose, the dissensions discussed under proposition (2) are bound to continue. However, if Kiswahili were among the official languages, ethnic groupings averse to the official indigenous languages of their areas would be free to use it instead.

The cost factor is often invoked to render the proposition to utilize all indigenous languages inconceivable. However, as argued elsewhere (Mukama 1986), despite the cost, the price of using the indigenous languages in education is worth paying.

As a general comment on the national language issue, my personal view is that we need to retain the indigenous languages in the early levels of school; and we may also develop some of them for inter-tribal communication. But as noted in the preceding discussion, due to old and traditional feuds in cultural/-political parochialism, indigenous languages tend to perpetuate separatism. We therefore still need lingua francas with the potential to transcend ethnic dissension: we already have English among the educated, but we also need Kiswahili, which is non-sectarian, for mass utility. In essence then, policy proposition number (4) may well be the answer for Uganda. And while deciding on what course to take, we may reflect on the observations made by R.B. Le Page, for they are still highly pertinent to today:

> If one out of a number of local languages is chosen, national unity may or may not be fostered through it; it is possible that the privileged position given to that language-group will arouse violent hostility from other groups. If several local languages are given equal status, separatism will tend to continue. The adoption of a trade language or lingua franca already spoken at a low level of efficiency by members of all groups can unify without arousing hostility, and can provide a natural linguistic response to the local environment and the multi-lingual context (as in Indonesia). (Le Page 1964, p. 79)

6. Towards a Design of National Communication

Linguistic communication is basically the "transmission of information to elicit a response". (Hamelink 1973, p. 40) But in totality it is a multi-faceted activity involving a "source" (or "sender"), a "receiver", a message, and a medium through which the information is transmitted. Traditionally, communication is perceived as a one-sided process originating from a sender and going to a receiver. According to C. Hamelink, this view of communication gives us a pyramidal type of communication:

> ... pyramidal communication models have been created in which the few talk to the many. And even if the few send to the many messages which are completely irrelevant to their situation, they still receive them, because they have internalized the conviction that they have nothing to contribute, that they are not equal partners in the communication process. (Hamelink 1973)

A more progressive view of communication which seeks to break through this pyramidal situation sees communication as an activity in which all those involved have a share. This view leads us to a communication model comprising three elements: participation, equality and potentiality. Anyone has the potential to participate in a communication activity as an initiator or receiver and vice versa, in accordance with equalitarian laws.

Uganda, like most developing countries, operates within the pyramidal type of communication framework. Policy-makers and implementors continue to talk down to the masses instead of talking with them. Government officials and agencies are permanently the senders of information, while the masses remain ingrained in the role of receivers. In this sort of situation, the communication act is never complete because no contributory response is ever elicited. Thus, communication is reduced to a process of continuous imparting of information, with no provision for the exchange of ideas. In the case of Uganda, two factors are responsible for the continued recurrence of incomplete communication acts, and the subsequent failure to reach the masses: lack of regular medium, and absence of a well planned and adequately implemented communication system.

At this stage we may well ask what, generally speaking, the medium of communication in Uganda is. So far in this paper we have endeavoured to develop the thesis that old and traditional ethnic feuds, coupled with cultural and sub-nationalistic arrogance or parochialism, have contributed greatly to the failure to develop a language of mass communication. In other words, our near-chaotic language situation mirrors our surging ethnic antagonisms which we endeavour to disguise, in vain. There is, therefore, no simple straight-forward answer to the foregoing question. Also the Language Survey conducted in 1967-1971 by Ladefoged et al. came to the same conclusion:

> Our general task was to discover the pattern of communication within Uganda. .. As long as all the people can speak, read, and write the same language, information can flow freely in all directions - from the government to the people, throughout religious, social and economic institutions such as churches, political parties, and nation-wide businesses and among the people themselves. But in a country such as Uganda communications are not so simple. The nine million people are divided by more than 30 languages, so that the average person knows about events outside his own group only through a foreign language. In a country such as this

> there are numerous language problems. (Ladefoged et al. 1971, p. 16)

As already explained, the elite continue to communicate among themselves in English, and government agencies maintain the use of English and aspire to reach the people solely through interpreters. No wonder they find it difficult to reach them, and they may never reach them at all if the approach is not changed. Because of the haphazard nature of our communication channels, political policies and other government programmes remain largely unknown to the people: and they may become unknowable if no deliberate change is made. For instance, the 1980 general elections showed that the masses continue to cast their votes not on the basis of rational political analysis but in terms of prosaic comparisons of party symbols. One hears naive logic of an incredible kind: a hand is more indispensable to a human being than a hoe; a hand-shake symbolizes friendliness and good-will; while a fist is indicative of hostility, antagonism or provocation, etc. A variation of the same stock interpretation relates to religious differences: Party A is Catholic while party B is Protestant, etc.

In that vein the masses continue to be cheated. There is no way of educating them on the realities of the situation because efficient linguistic communication, which lies at the very heart of education, is not available to us. Interpreters/translators are also renowned for unwitting or deliberate misrepresentation of information. An illustration of this type of distortion is what happened when Amin held a farmers' forum in 1971. It is reported that from the meeting there ensued an impressive assortment of recommendations duly attributed to the farmers who attended. But later on, when a team of researchers from the University interviewed some of the farmers concerning the recommendations attributed to them, it turned out that the recommendations which the farmers themselves had made were in fact never recorded; officials from the Ministry of Agriculture had merely proceeded to list what in their opinion were the needs of the farmers. (Byarugaba 1983, p. 11)

Clearly, then, we need to pay serious attention to language policy. We are hardly communicating with the masses in the English medium, so the sooner we start cultivating a language which will enable us to reach the masses and elicit constructive responses, the better. Mamdani has noted rightly that "only from a position of state power can you have the arrogance to speak to people in a language they don't understand." (Mamdami 1986)

But is this to continue? Something must be done about it. Assuming that Uganda will finally settle its language policy problem, the decision taken will have to be planned and implemented systematically. For even countries like Tanzania - which has largely sorted out the "medium" aspect of communication- also still have the problem of inability to reach the people; apparently, government officials and agencies there are also still merely talking down to the masses and not with them.[29] In other words, they also still operate within the pyramidal framework which hardly leaves room to elicit responses from the receivers.

As the Tanzanian experience shows, even through a straightforward medium, government officials and agencies can still maintain the tendency to go to the rural areas on token official visits rather than with a view to communicating with the people. And even the officials of the service ministries who go to or reside in the areas may maintain strictly administrative roles (i.e. routine operations). Thus, within the pyramidal type of communication, while leaders preach rural development with growth and change, none of them actually work to achieve it. Real growth and change can be brought about only by a complete change of the communication model, from pyramidal to equal participation. And to effect this type of change, the administrative structure will have to be re-organized: "There is a need for a re-organization of Uganda's administrative systems if an effective and viable organizational structure for rural development is to be established." (Bibangambah 1981, p. 30)

Uganda has already made a good start towards the necessary structural reorganization by the inception of village, trans-village (miluka), and sub-country (gombolola) councils. We further propose the creation of a National Communication Centre to coordinate the inter-ministerial and other communication undertakings pertaining to rural development. The structure shown in Fig. 1 maps some of the recommended activities of the Centre.

The chief concern of the Centre would then be to preside over and oversee the two-way communication network between the leadership and other service agencies, and the rural masses. As Ladefoged et al. have noted, "Uganda is a country where information travels primarily by word of mouth". The mass media serve mainly the population in the capital city.

Even the radio and newspapers, which might have been expected to reach the rural population much more readily than television, hardly get there. Even the small proportion of rural dwellers who have radios either cannot afford the batteries, or rarely listen to most of the programmes, due to ignorance of the timetable or lack of time. Sponsoring rural visiting teams would, therefore, be more rewarding than funding expensive programmes on television and radio. The Communication Centre could even set up regional branches to facilitate increased accessibility. This proposed communication system would be additional to the channels already in operation: radio, newspapers, etc. The latter should also be extended to have more relevance to the rural masses.

Serve as a Resource Bank
on any other types of
inter-communication

Liaise with
village councils
to disseminate
information and
obtain feed-back

Co-ordinate
govt. ministries/
rural areas
inter-communication

NATIONAL
COMMUNICATION
CENTRE

Co-ordinate
NGOs/
rural areas
inter-communication

Co-ordinate
parastatal bodies/
rural areas
inter-communication

Organize and/or co-ordinate
the activities of
information-imparting/eliciting
visiting teams to rural areas

7. Pay-off of the Proposed Communication Design

Beside establishing well-organized means of reaching and involving the rural masses into national affairs and activities, the formulated communication network would be useful in three other ways.

First, by organizing and co-ordinating the activities of visiting teams and theatre groups in rural areas, the network would foster and enhance the dynamics of personal interaction. This will in turn promote mutual understanding and the subsequent lessening of suspicion and distrust which have served to perpetuate old ethnic animosities.

Secondly, as outlined above, the various ministries and other government bodies have adopted separate home-made language policies in their efforts to reach the masses. A co-ordinative body will certainly bring in some consistency in language use. For instance, it might be suggested that the Ministry of Education, Radio Uganda and the Literacy Programmes adopt one pattern of language use: the utilization of nearly all the languages. The rest of the service ministries and agencies would then adopt another pattern.

Third, once the necessary element of uniformity and consistency is present, joint material production, presided over by the Centre, should be possible. Such co-operative undertakings are bound to eliminate piece-meal ventures and expensive duplications of programmes in different ministries. Thus, one tour of a specified rural area of the country could cover programmes from a group of ministries; this will reduce the costs of sponsoring individual ministry visits for the same purpose.

All this and even more can be attained - provided we resolve to free ourselves from the old fetters of ethnic prejudices and animosities, and adopt a language policy that will duly take into account our national identity without flouting or minimizing the importance of regional and international co-operation.

Notes

1. According to Mosha, 1971, p. 105, "A national language, as opposed to an official one, is the common language of a political and socio-cultural unit. It is the language of daily intercourse between, at least, the majority of the nationals of a given state".
2. The Nationalist, Dar-es-Salaam, 5 January 1967.
3. Only Idi Amin toyed with the idea of taking up the challenge. But then Amin was never serious on positive matters so his national language decree of 1973 never went beyond the pages on which it was printed.
4. An official language is the language (or languages) selected, and very often prescribed, by the government for use in certain specified situations, e.g. education, broadcasting, parliamentary debates, administration, commerce and industry, etc. In short, an official language is the language of government business: legislative, executive, judicial, administrative, commercial and industrial.
5. Held on 16 April 1970 and reported in Uganda Argus on 17 April 1970 by David Musoke.
6. Ibid.
7. Reported in Sunday Nation, Nairobi, October 1970.
8. Editorial comment in Weekly Topic, Kampala, 1 October 1986.
9. S.E. Kulubya in a parliamentary debate, 8 June 1960.

10. Dr. Kigenya, in a discussion on Uganda Television on 13 July 1987 by the Uganda Medical Association.
11. Cf. Obote, 1967.
12. "Report of the Language Seminar" held at Makerere University, 16-20 March 1987, p. 7.
13. Kyambogo Conference; cf. note 5 above.
14. Weekly Topic, 1 October 1986.
15. M. Mamdani in Weekly Topic, Kampala, 22 October 1986.
16. Cf. note 5 above.
17. As pointed out by the editors, this is possibly an overstatement as an increasing number of educated people now use English outside the scholarly and official situations, despite their expository limitations in the language.
18. J.K. Babiiha in a parliamentary debate, 8 June 1960.
19. Okello-Oculi; cf note 5 above.
20. The term "zoning" is employed here to mean the restriction of languages to specific areas or zones.
21. My father, who was a proper "vernacular" primary teacher, failed to teach in Kwapa-using Luganda and had to go back to the Lugwere area, although both places are in Tororo District which is part of the Luganda educational area.
22. Bakonjo women refused to fill in a questionnaire which Action for Development (a women's organization) wrote in Rutooro; they swore that they could not understand Rutooro.
23. G. Oda in a parliamentary debate, 8 June 1960.
24. Cf. note 18 above.
25. Supporters of Swahili view it as a unifying language which could be used to consolidate and bring out the universal aspects of African cultures, thereby contributing to the fostering of what we might refer to as the overall "African culture".
26. Adapted from Lulua, 1976, pp. 14-15.
27. Published in Uganda News on 22 February 1929, edited by Mr. Stirman.
28. Musisi, C.; cf. note 5 above.
29. W. Mlay makes comments to this effect in the following extracts:

The problem was not only lack of funds but how the government (and donors) had gone about implementing projects. There was little participation by the villagers.

Despite policy statements intended to safeguard the democratic participation of peasants, the government and party increasingly adopted a top-down posture in its decision-making and in implementation ... and this is the underlying cause for the poor performance in both agricultural production and service provision in rural Tanzania. (1983, p. 16)

References

Atiku, J.: "Population Planning for Social-economic Development in Uganda". Paper presented at the Administrative Secretaries Seminar/Workshop on Population and Socio-economic Development, Mweya Lodge, Uganda, 24-30 June 1984.

Bibangambah, F.: "An Analytical Overview of the Rural Development Problem in Uganda", in Nsibambi, A. & J. Katorobo (eds.): Proceedings of the Conference on Rural Rehabilitation and Development, vol. 1. Kampala: Makerere University, September 1981.

Byarugaba, F.: "Food as Alternative Development Policy in Uganda". Paper presented at the OSSREA Congress, Addis Ababa, 13-17 June 1983.

Department of Languages: "Report on Language Seminar" held at Makerere University, 16-20 March 1987.

Hamelink, G.: "Women and Communication", in Zabolai-Osekme, E. (ed.): Leadership Development for Women, 1973, pp. 39-41.

Ladefoged, P., R. Glick & C. Criper: Language in Uganda. Dar-es-Salaam: Oxford University Press, 1971.

Le Page, R.B.: The National Language Question. London: Oxford University Press, 1964.

Lulua, A.: "Origins and Development of Kiswahili in Uganda: With Reference to the Question of National Language". Kampala: Makerere University Library, 1976. Unpublished manuscript.

Mamdani, M.: "Language and Democracy", in Weekly Topic, Kampala, 22 October 1986.

Matovu, N.G.W.: "The Development Deadlock in Eastern Africa: The case of Uganda." Paper presented at the OSSREA Congress, Addis Ababa, 13-17 June 1983.

Mazrui, A.: "The National Language Question in East Africa", in East Africa Journal, June 1967.

Mazrui, A.: "Democracy and the Future of Swahili", in Uganda Argus, 12 August 1970.

Mlay, W.: "Pitfalls in Rural Development: The Case of Tanzania". Paper presented at the OSSREA Congress, Addis Ababa, 13-17 June 1983.

Mosha, M.: "The Role of Language in Nation Building", in Journal of the Language Association of Eastern Africa, vol. 2, no. 2, 1971.

Mukama, R.: "The Viability of the Indigenous Languages in the Ugandan Context", in Mawazo, Kampala, vol. 6, no. 3, 1986.

Musoke, D.: "The Kyambogo Conference: A Plan for a National Language", in Uganda Argus, 17 April 1970.

Ngugi wa Thiong'o: Decolonizing the Mind: The Politics of Language in African Literature. Nairobi: Heinemann, 1986.

Nsibambi, A.: "Some Political Problems of Linguistic Communication in Uganda", in Communications in East Africa, by Ouma (ed.), J.P.B.M., 1969.

Nsibambi, A.: "Language Policy in Uganda: An Investigation into Cost Problems", in Journal of African Affairs, vol. 70, no. 278, January 1971.

Obote, M.: "Language and National identification", in East African Journal, April 1967.

Omondi, L.N.: "The Role and Status of African Languages in the East African Context". Paper presented at the Linguistics Subject Conference for East African Universities, Arusha, 19-20 December 1986.

Rubadiri, D.: "The Importance of Language", in the Uganda Teacher, vol. IV, no. 1, February 1966, pp. 59-61

Uganda Government: Proceedings of the Uganda Legislative Council, Part III, 40th Session, June 1960, pp. 1211 and 1225-9.

Uganda Peoples Congress: Manifesto. Kampala, 1980.

Firimooni R. Banugire

Uneven and Unbalanced Development: Development Strategies and Conflict

1. Introduction: Basic Issues and some Viewpoints

The economic elements underlying social conflict centre around barriers to the social mobility of individuals or social groups. Uganda has been characterized by a relatively high degree of horizontal social mobility, in the various regions of the country and between the rural and urban areas. This mobility is highly dependent on differences in the distribution of natural resources, the level of exploitation of these resources and general levels of development - all of which have been significant to varying degrees. Vertical mobility between the hierarchy of social groups has been more restricted upwards than downwards, due to the rise of a regressive magendo economy since the mid-1970s.

The main purpose of this essay is to raise more questions than it can answer concerning the relationships between uneven regional development, unbalanced development strategy, and social conflicts in Uganda.

The first question is whether or not Uganda's God-given resource endowments (mainly agricultural land) are fairly evenly distributed and whether dwellers in every region have adequate resource frontiers to occupy their energies. Here we may conclude without much ado, that Uganda's 11 agro-ecological zones are, in general, adequately endowed in terms of potential food and non-food cash crops, with very minor exceptions.

The second question is whether the current levels of development (or the levels achieved by 1975) reveal inequalities capable of generating conflicts among regions. Here we should note that, true, there is a substantial uneven development, but that this has not been a major factor in creating those inter-regional or inter-tribe conflicts that exist. This, however, is not to say that they will not generate conflicts in the near future if existing trends should continue towards even greater inequalities. More important, the existence of this unevenness, despite the more even distribution of natural resources, is a telling manifestation of the unbalanced nature of past development strategies.

The third question is whether the various social groups in either rural or urban areas have substantially unequal access to wealth or income-generating opportunities. We may conclude that in general the institutional framework (legal, economic and political) has been such that the majority of the working population, especially peasants but also workers, have in relative terms been excluded from reasonable access to "productive" and "self-improvement" resources. Most of the "capitalist" classes (those capable of living on property incomes and accumulated wealth), have been excessively rewarded beyond their social worth, so that they have little incentive to engage in productive agricultural and industrial activity. These two opposite imbalances in resource allocation constitute a vicious trap in the rehabilitation and transformation of Uganda's economy. They represent a barrier to the creation of an independent, integrated and self-sustaining economy. Without any corrective strategy this trend is likely to worsen at the expense of both accelerated economic growth and the satisfaction of basic needs, thereby laying a basis for future social conflicts.[1]

Fourthly, we shall consider to what extent past strategies have contributed to both regional imbalances, and barriers to vertical social mobility and self-improvement of the working population. These four questions are taken up in sections 2 and 3. Section 4 argues that a comprehensive strategy to resolve the economic imbalances and social conflicts must be geared to the rapid attainment of a progressive economy, as a precondition for a progressive society. It also outlines the key elements of a progressive economy in the present Ugandan context.

2. Uneven Development and Unbalanced Strategy:

2.1. Regional Inequalities in Development Potential

The development potential of Uganda, at both national and regional levels, is determined largely by its natural resource base, particularly agricultural resources (arable and pasture land, plus forestry and fishing). Of the 11 agro-ecological zones (Table 1), 6 are found in the North and East and are generally known as the cotton-cereal zones, with the exception of Karamoja and Elgon mountain slopes. They are also among the least exploited (most underutilized) agro-resources, with very favourable landman ratios. In terms of nutrition, they are more dependent on cereals (50% and above) than on rootcrops and matoke, and are capable of generating a food surplus in cereals, pulses, and certain rootcrops. They have the potential to act as the granary of Uganda, but this has hardly been developed - even up to 25%.

Although they have a cash problem because of poor performance in the cotton industry, these arcas have adequate cash-generating agricultural opportunities including food, cash crops, livestock, cotton, tobacco, as well as agro-industry centred on oil-seed processing, food processing, starch, textiles, etc. However, none of these is yet well developed, except perhaps textiles.

The remaining 5 agro-ecological zones cover the Southern and Western region. They are largely grouped under the coffee-banana zones, with the exception of Kigezi and Rwenzori highland regions.

Table 1
Patterns of surplus/deficit for staple cereals per agro-ecological zone, 1981 and 1986 ('000 tons)

Agro-ecological zone	Trade surplus 1981	Projected surplus 1986	Projected surplus 1991	Nutritional importance %	Population in zone %
Busoga/Bukedi	-24	14	12	50	10
Bugisu/Sebei	33	56	76	40	7
Teso	233	265	257	70	4
Karamoja	-42	-50	-60	45	3
Lango/Acholi	180	195	170	50	10
West Nile/Madi	-32	-13	-14	45	6
Bunyoro/Toro	37	75	125	30	11
Ankole	-78	-65	-87	40	10
Kigezi	-72	-68	-80	60	6
Lake Victoria Crescent	-211	-248	-299	15	23
North Buganda	-	-	-	20	10
Total	-	-	-	39	100

Source: Royal Tropical Institute (Amsterdam): Towards a National Food Strategy: Main Strategy Report, vol. 1, Kampala: Uganda Government, July 1984.

In food terms, the Buganda area is dependent on the banana (60%) rather than cereals (15%), although the share of cereals is bound to increase. Bunyoro/Toro zone is biased towards rootcrops (55%) and cereals (30%) rather than matoke; whereas Ankole depends on matoke (50%) and cereals (40%); and Kigezi depends more on cereals (60%) and rootcrops (20%).

In general, the coffee-banana zones are grain-deficient areas, while more or less self-sufficient otherwise. They have better cash opportunities than the North because of both food and non-food (coffee, tea, cocoa, tobacco, etc.) crops. However, some of these areas have minor food problems - which can be easily resolved.

In general, Uganda's agricultural potential is fairly evenly distributed, all regions having adequate access to all the major food and non-food cash crops. Even the poorest districts among them have adequate but underdeveloped resource potential. For example, relatively over-populated Kigezi, with limited cash crops, can become a major producer of dairy products, wheat, barley, vegetables, honey, forestry products, etc. Similarly, Karamoja is a major supplier of cattle. Both areas also have unexploited mineral wealth.

2.2. Regional Inequalities in Development Level

Whereas development potentials are thus fairly evenly distributed, we may note marked regional differences in development. These are largely explained by access to cash crops, as developed by the Colonial government and continued by post-Independence regimes. To a smaller extent, such differences are also explained by the pattern of urbanization and industrialization.

In general, the richest areas are in (a) the Lake Victoria Crescent, where urbanization is most developed and where there is coffee concentration; (b) Western Ankole and Bunyoro/Toro (coffee, tea, cereals, pulses, bananas, industries); (c) Bugisu-/Sebei (coffee, bananas). Access to both agricultural and non-agricultural employment combines with dominance of major cash crops to yield relatively high incomes. Uganda's poorest areas include: (a) Kigesi (lack of non-food cash crops, plus over-population); (b) parts of West Nile (relative over-population and limited non-food and food cash crops); (c) Karamoja, due to aridity and entrenched traditionalism. The income gap between the richest and the poorest districts is probably around 41. But we should note that the richest areas have their pockets of poverty, and the poorest regions pockets of plenty.

These inequalities can largely be explained by the development strategies pursued during the Colonial period and simply continued after Independence, with minor exceptions. First was the emphasis on non-food export cash crops (coffee, cotton, tea, tobacco) which determined intra-rural migration from areas poor in cash crops to the rich ones. This led to the neglect of potential traditional food cash crops which could have found export markets (e.g. maize, oil-seeds, beans/peas). Second was the failure to introduce marketable food cash crops not originally grown in Uganda (especially rice, wheat, soyabeans, etc.), which would have extended the cash alternatives further through import substitution and exports. Thirdly, there has been <u>lack of regional development planning</u> geared to maximizing resource utilization, and this has led to limited access to cash opportunities in some areas.

While these policies were a deliberate Colonial strategy, their continuation by post-Independence governments was a grave error, since the nation's development potentials are in fact evenly distributed. Perhaps the only exception is the attempt to develop cassava into a major cash crop in the North through the establishment of a starch factory - which failed, however, due to lack of appropriate supportive programmes. These examples will suffice to illustrate the importance of having an appropriate agricultural development strategy based on decentralized regional planning.

It is often said that the poverty of the North relative to the affluence of the South underlies the past and present political crisis in Uganda. Further, that the Acholi and Langi dominated the Army because of their unemployment problem back home. Rather, it should be the other way round: because they found easy access to the Army and police, they thereby deprived their areas of the necessary labour force and entrepreneurial incentives. By continuing the colonial strategy of underdeveloping the North relative to the South, Obote and Amin betrayed both the North in particular and Uganda in general.

The disparity between the richest areas in the South and the poorest areas in the North, has been, indeed, very significant. However, this has not been a conflict-generating situation, since until recently the North controlled the instruments of state power and the North had been neglected by the Northerners themselves.

2.3. Rural-Urban Inequalities

With development, the incomes and social welfare of urban areas tend to grow faster than those of rural areas, giving rise to a rural-urban welfare gap. In Uganda, however, this rural-urban gap and any tendency to widen it have been minimal; indeed the gap seems to have narrowed with the regressive trend in the economy. That this gap has been so low is explained largely by the widespread cash-crop opportunities arising out of the natural resource base.

That the gap has in fact narrowed we can see in the fall in the rate of growth of urban population, from about 7% in the early 1970s to about 3% by the early 1980s. The increasing deterioration of urban incomes since then is likely to have lowered this trend yet further. Such narrowing of income differentials between the rural and urban areas cannot, however, be interpreted as a positive trend, since it has been propelled by urban poverty increasing faster than rural poverty.

The main policy implication to be drawn here is the need to raise the relative importance of poverty alleviation as a goal of national development policy. We need a goal-balanced development strategy focused on accelerated, self-sustaining economic growth and poverty alleviation through direct basic needs policy. This higher degree of social engineering is required so as to ensure the satisfaction of basic needs for the majority of the working population. However, such social engineering can be forthcoming only if the ruling regime is controlled by the working population, through democratic political and economic institutions. A political revolution is thus a precondition for the social reforms which Uganda needs. Let us hope that the present NRM regime can implement the minimum conditions for such a political revolution to enable social reforms to evolve.

2.4. Class Formation in Rural Areas and Self-Sustaining Growth

On average, about 70% of Uganda's rural population are "poor peasants" cultivating their own plots or labouring for others, while about 20% are "middle peasants" more or less above the poverty line, and only 8% may be called "rich peasants" capable of significant capital accumulation. Further, only about 2% may be called "capitalist farmers".[2] Therefore, if agricultural production is to be stepped up drastically over extended periods of time, development strategies will have to focus on the poor peasants, so as to increase their land and labour productivity as well as provide them with adequate access to health and education services. Otherwise they will stagnate in poverty and low productivity, thus constituting a drag on economic development-not least given the current high rate of population growth (3.3%).

Obviously, the proportions of poor and rich peasants vary widely among the rich and poor areas. For example, the proportion of poor peasants in a Buganda village (not among the very richest) was as low as 50%, and middle peasants as high as 37%, as compared to one in the North where these ratios were 83% and 3% respectively.[3] This is further evidence of regional imbalances in social and economic development which have arisen out of differences in exploiting development potentials.

Self-sustaining growth in rural areas is largely a matter of technological change and capital accumulation. Rural poverty is largely determined by access to cash crops, implements, credits, and markets. Technological change and central accumulation include the acquisition of high-yielding seeds of the right crops together with the necessary funds for implements and inputs. These, however, require supportive government services including know-how, transport and communication as well as infrastructure, moral support, and the necessary organizational element. In general, poverty is linked with lack of such mechanisms of technological change and capital accumulation. In the strong competition for these mechanisms between the poor and the rich, the former are bound to lose. Hence the need for democratic political and economic institutions to ensure that each social group receives its share of these mechanisms so as to maximize its contribution to economic development. Unfortunately, we may note a widespread lack of such institutions, as well as the presence of regressive tendencies in existing institutions both private and public. This is amply demonstrated by the failure of Uganda's Cooperative Unions to make an impact on the rural economy and their tendency to act as exploitative mechanisms for enhancing the fortunes of rural and urban capitalists. The persistent crisis in crop-finance whereby funds from financial institutions are paid 20-30% less than government producer prices, is ample proof of the regressive nature of such institutions today.

2.5. Class Formation in Urban Areas and Poverty

In urban areas the picture is similar to the one just sketched for rural areas, and probably substantially worse, as illustrated by the grave plight of the wage-earners and the rising pool of workers in the "informal sector".[4] The characteristics of urban poverty and its impact may be summarized as follows:

(a) The poorest wage-earners of the formal sector cannot meet more than 2% of their needs from their wages, and thus resort to all sorts of magendo activities to survive; still they do not succeed in covering more than about one-third of their needs.

(b) The most privileged group of professional wage earners in the civil service and in teaching professions cannot meet 5% of their needs, and so resort to magendo activities as well.

(c) The magendo activities imply minimum levels of labour productivity as well as systematic disinvestment in the social overhead capital, which has deteriorated to minimum levels.

(d) Attempts to fill up these wage-gaps through conventional wage policy cannot succeed, so reforms in the payment system are necessary to ensure that workers will share in the operating surplus of productive enterprises and to compensate those in non-productive services.

(e) Attempts to rehabilitate the capital stock without adequate machinery to eliminate misappropriation of resources by the powerful few, and to uplift the real wage of the worker, are likely to fail. The end-result will often be a transfer of these resources to personal coffers. Here too we note the need for fundamental institutional and leadership reforms in politics and in financial institutions.

Therefore, the urban situation, like the rural situation, requires democratic reforms to ensure systematic poverty alleviation and rising worker productivity. The political preconditions for their generation are therefore at issue; these must be addressed if the economic crisis is to be resolved and social tensions reduced.

3. Unbalanced Development Strategies

3.1. Types of Imbalances

Uganda's development strategies right from Colonial times to the present have been typically unbalanced in almost all major aspects. We shall consider the following types of imbalances in order to point out their potential impact on social conflicts:

(a) goal imbalances;

(b) biases in exploitation of natural resource frontiers;

(c) biases in development of human resources;
(d) sectoral imbalances;
(e) social group imbalances;
(f) imbalances in financial institutions;
(g) imbalances on resource allocation mechanisms.

3.2. Economic Growth versus Basic Needs

During the post-war Colonial period in Uganda, significant attempts were made at formulating nation-wide strategies to transform society and economy into a dynamic process of socio-economic development. The focus was on rapid expansion of non-food cash crops and accelerated economic growth, largely by transforming peasants into "progressive farmers".

Since the population was starting from more or less the same subsistence level, there was no need to pay special attention to the basic needs of the majority. These premises have been continued up to the present, even though since 1975 there has arisen a basic needs problem due to the deterioration of most people's real incomes to well over one-half of 1970 levels. The rise of this poverty problem has been ignored by the policy strategies of the 1980s, which has further contributed to the worsening of the problem.[5]

Yet it is clear that the promotion of economic recovery and accelerated, self-sustaining growth is necessarily closely related to the issue of poverty alleviation.

3.3. Natural Resource Frontier

That the exploitation of natural resources has been biased to non-food export cash crops has generated the following imbalances:

(a) Failure to create exportable food surplus and to eliminate certain imported foodstuffs (e.g. rice, wheat, barley) has persisted for decades up to the present, when the NRM regime initiated the barter trade strategy as a fundamental economic reform for resolving the problem. This failure has contributed to regional imbalances in levels of development.

(b) Failure to exploit the agricultural resource base as a primary tap root of accelerated industrialization has led to the relative neglect of the cotton-grain agro-ecological zones of the North and encouraged neglect of the resource frontier everywhere. This problem has yet to be resolved through a comprehensive resource-based industrialization strategy.

(c) Uganda's mineral resource potential has been relatively neglected, to the detriment of accelerated industrialization especially with respect to building materials and chemical-based industries. This also contributes to regional imbalances insofar as such agriculturally poor but mineral-rich areas like Karamoja and Kigezi have been neglected.

3.4. Human Resource Development

The education system in Uganda was relatively well developed in the 1960s, compared to other African countries. However, several imbalances with major impacts on both economic growth and basic needs have already emerged. First, there is the question of relatively too little spending on social services (health and education), to the detriment of the development of manpower resources. Second, there is the problem of rapidly increasing inequalities with respect to access to educational facilities. Rural areas are falling behind urban areas, and the poor are increasingly being left behind. This creates a basic needs problem for the poor, which at the same time has long-term negative effects on economic growth. Third is the question of neglecting technical and vocational training at all levels of the education ladder, thereby creating serious imbalances between future manpower requirements and supply. There is also a question of wasting scarce resources on an inappropriate educational menu at the expense of human resource productivity in the economy.

Clearly, if these imbalances persist, they will have negative impacts on regional and rural-urban inequalities in development levels, as well as vertical social mobility in society. Such increasing barriers in access to development may well generate social conflicts. Hence the need for comprehensive reforms in the educational system to ensure that these barriers will be progressively eliminated.

3.5. Sectoral Imbalances

Sectoral imbalances in terms of excessive emphasis on one sector at the expense of other sectors do not seem to constitute a major problem. We cannot say that there has been an excessively active industrialization strategy at the expense of agricultural transformation or vice-versa, throughout the first, second and third Five Year Development Plans as well as the rehabilitation programmes of the 1970s (Action Programme) and the 1980s (Recovery Programme, 1982-85; and Investment Plan 1987/8-1990/1). In the development plans, attempts were made to ensure balanced growth-oriented programmes. In the rehabilitation plan, emphasis was put on restoring previous production capacities and rehabilitating the necessary social infrastructure.

What Uganda needs is a comprehensive industrialization strategy based on maximum exploitation of the natural resource base (both agricultural and mineral) for national and regional export markets. An industrialization-based strategy is more likely to address the problem of regional inequalities than an agriculturally based one. This does not mean that agriculture will be neglected, but that the emphasis will be on agriculture for agro-industry. Whereas export-based agricultural development will tend to neglect industrialization, agro-industrially biased agricultural development will automatically feed the export markets, partly because it generates greater modernization efforts.

The human resource development strategy will need an upward shift in priority, to come in line with the comprehensive industrialization strategy. Hence greater emphasis on social infrastructure as an instrument of both social transformation as well as regional and social development.

3.6. Social Imbalance and Economic Reforms

Uganda's is essentially a regressive economy. Upward social mobility has been reduced: middle class professionals and civil servants have fallen into the poverty traps while the lower-income groups have been thrown out of formal employment into informal unproductive magendo activities. This social retrogression has taken place without any adjustments in formal payment systems, so that these activities have become dominant survival mechanisms. Such survival mechanisms cannot be relied upon to promote economic recovery and reconstruction; indeed most of them are inconsistent with social transformation. This inconsistency lies at the core of the institutional and political traps which are propelling Uganda's economy towards regression and stagnation.

A strategy for fundamental institutional economic reforms is therefore needed to initiate a reversal of this regressive trend and propel the economy towards self-sustaining progress.

One type of reform concerns the balance between public sector and private sector in social infrastructure; public sector and private sector business enterprises; and peasants and commercial farmers.

A second type concerns the balance among the various resource allocation mechanisms, namely, the invisible hand of the market (price mechanism); the visible hand of the state (planning mechanism); and the visible hand of the community (popular participation through collective community action). The degradation of the working classes has actuated the need for communal mechanisms of resource allocation, as currently being institutionalized in the form of National Resistance Committees (NRCs), as a key corrective and/or defence mechanism against further misery and exploitation.

4. Towards a Progressive Economy in a Progressive Society

4.1. Need for a Progressive Economy

We have noted that the Ugandan economy is essentially a regressive one in which the working population has been degraded below the poverty line, caught in a price-wage trap as well as in numerous institutional traps. Hence the failure to generate a process of self-sustaining growth and to alleviate the poverty of the working population. Therefore, there is a strong need for institutional, economic and political reforms to extricate the economy from these traps and create a progressive economy capable of accelerated social progress.

A progressive economy is a necessary precondition for a progressive society. But without progressive political reforms, such a progressive economy cannot be realized. The NRM regime, therefore, has dual tasks: to create progressive democratic, political reforms, and to establish progressive economic reforms. Without such a comprehensive approach to the current economic and social crisis, the underlying potential social conflicts are likely to surface.

In general, we may say that the present political crisis originates from the political process, and not from economic contradictions. These must be resolved first, to create a progressive political system in which the working population has an effective voice, a voice necessary to reverse the regressive economic trends through genuine fundamental economic reforms. These reforms will have to revolve around the following issues.

4.2. Property Rights and the Appropriate Economic Mix

The Ugandan economy is a mixed one with three principal ingredients: the public sector, the private business sector, and the peasant sector. With the rise of the regressive economy these sectors have been plagued by several regressive tendencies: a tendency towards systematic privatization of the public sector (bias against the public interest); a tendency towards personalization of the private business sector (bias against corporate interest); and a tendency towards exploitation of the peasants by the state bureaucracy and business interests (bias against peasant self-determination).

The privatization syndrome has weakened the social services and public sector enterprises, reducing them to private estates of politicians, bureaucrats and managers. Corrective mechanisms needed in the political sphere include progressive revolutionary politics with forward-thinking leadership, integrated political process in the form of a national progressive democratic front as the vanguard political organ, democratic checks and balances between the executive, legislature, and judiciary; and systematic politicization of the bureaucracy. In the economic sphere, there is a need to create an effective planning mechanism in the government bureaucracy, to establish politically responsible boards and management of state-owned enterprises, and to enforce effective accounting systems as performance criteria for management and boards. Management and boards should be appointed on a contractual basis, conditional on specific performance. Such performance conditionality should be supervised by autonomous institutions responsible to the executive arm of government (e.g. to the newly created Inspector of Government).

The tendency towards personalizing private enterprise militates against the establishment and consolidation of the corporate mode of management so necessary for a dynamic, vibrant and responsible private enterprise sector. Much has been said about the mismanagement of the public sector through the privatization tendency; now it is necessary to address the question of irresponsible, disorganized, and mismanaged private sectors, which is no less important. This requires a legal framework for economic activity to enforce proper management procedures and the effective administration of justice in these respects. Such a reformed legal institutional framework should embrace all the three sectors (parastatal, private business and peasants) so as to eliminate the rampant abuse of property rights at all levels of the economy.

As Mamdani (1986) has noted, the peasant has been subject to a host of compulsions and manipulations from above, including forced labour, forced contributions, forced enclosures, forced crops and forced sales.[6] Further, only rarely has the peasant received the declared producer prices for export crops - receiving on average 20-30% less. This systematic mismanagement and exploitation of the peasant sector has taken place through Cooperative unions, Government bureaucracy, and the local administrations. Reversing this state of affairs requires democratic political and social institutions at these levels.

It is hoped that the National Resistance Committees (NRCs) will address themselves to these questions. But more is required, especially in the form of a reformed cooperative movement and an institutionalized system of regional development planning.

4.3. Reformed Cooperative Sector

As mentioned, the present cooperative sector is both regressive in terms of exploiting the peasants and inefficient in terms of resource allocation and utilization as well as producer incentives. The sector needs to be re-organized into an instrument for diversifying economic power (economic democratization), for social transformation of the present sector into small-scale commercial farming, and for rural industrialization. One pertinent proposal is the establishment of a system of rural, peoples', cooperative development banks as the appropriate financial intermediate technology for the rural sector. Another strategy involves transforming marketing cooperatives into producer cooperatives, with marketing activities playing a secondary role. This marketing role has also to be re-organized and consolidated to ensure that farmers reap a larger share of the market value of their produce.

4.4. A System of Regional Development Planning

The call for an independent, integrated self-sustaining economy implies a development strategy geared to rapid transformation of the rural peasant economy, maximizing the utilization of natural and human resources. Without a regional focus in decision-making and planning, very little progress can be made in this direction. Regional development planning is required to resolve the regional imbalances in exploiting the national resource base and to reduce regional inequalities; and this is bound to have positive impacts on the structural transformation of the economy. The barter trade strategy is a major element in this transformation; it needs to be managed at local levels through regional planning.

4.5. Basic Needs Infrastructure

One cannot reverse the impact of economic retrogression on the satisfaction of the basic needs of the working population without building new delivery systems for basic needs services for health care, education, shelter, and sanitary environment. Nevertheless, the policies which the International Monetary Fund are forcing on African governments tend to erode people-oriented delivery systems, or their creation where these do not exist.

Such policies are part and parcel of the regressive mechanisms which have to be re-organized and reversed in building new progressive delivery systems. The detailed characteristics of such systems are yet to be identified and promoted as an integral part of the national development planning process.

4.6. Central Planning Agency

It must be noted that economy-wide reforms such as egalitarian cooperativism, basic needs infrastructure and effective regional planning, cannot be realized as long as there is a vacuum at the centre. The current economic management is characterized by a monetarist approach dominated by external agencies, especially the IMF and the World Bank (Banugire 1987). This militates against effective real resource planning, demonstrated by the absence of an effective central planning agency. Neither the Ministry of Planning nor the Ministry of Finance, nor the Presidential Economic Council can act as an effective national economic planning mechanism. A National Planning Commission with adequate technocratic competence and political authority is required to resolve this question.

5. Conclusion

This brief review of Uganda's economy with respect to past development strategies suggests several conclusions. First and foremost, there has developed a regressive economy in which workers and peasants in rural and urban areas are trapped in a web of exploitation and alienation. Progress in economic growth and in basic needs requires a reversal of this trend and movement towards a progressive economy in which all social groups have the opportunities and support to enable them to maximize self-improvement development efforts.

Secondly, past development strategies have neglected maximum exploitation of Uganda's natural resource base, being biased primarily to the promotion of non-food cash crops for export. The present regional imbalances in development levels are largely explained by this continuation of the colonial development policy and the failure to promote an appropriate effective system of national economic planning. Correction of these policy imbalances and areas of neglect is a precondition for accelerated social progress.

Thirdly, we note the urgent need for fundamental economic and institutional reforms to reverse the above negative tendencies. Institutional reforms of the decision-making process (planning system reforms) and of the mechanisms for resource mobilization and utilization in private sectors are called for, to enable correct economic and social strategies to be formulated and implemented for structural transformation of the economy and of society. Key institutional reforms to promote the rise of the progressive economy include:

(a) legal and administrative reforms to recognize and protect the property rights of all social groups, including the public sector;

(b) reform of the cooperative movement;

(c) a system of decentralized regional development planning;

(d) progressive social service delivery systems; and

(e) an effective central planning agency in the form of a Planning Commission.

Notes

1. Banugire, F.R.: "Employment, Incomes, Basic Needs and Structural Adjustment Policy in Uganda, 1980-87". Paper presented to the international conference of the Institute for African Alternatives on The Impact of the IMF/World Bank Policies on Africa, London, 7-10 September 1987.
2. Banugire, 1987, op.cit.
3. Mamdani, M.: "Forms of Labour and Accumulation of Capital: Analysis of a Village in Lango Northern Uganda", in Mawazo, vol. 4, no. 2, December 1984.
4. Banugire, F.R.: "The Impact of the Economic Crisis on Fixed Income Earners", in Dodge, C.P. & P.D. Wiebe: Beyond Crisis: Development Issues in Uganda. Kampala: Makerere Institute of Social Research, Makerere University and African Studies Association, 1986, pp. 137-151.
5. Banugire, 1987, op.cit.
6. Mamdani, M.: "The Agrarian Question and the Democratic Struggle with Special Reference to Uganda". Kampala: Makerere University, Political Science Papers, 1986.

Apolo Nsibambi

The Land Question and Conflict

1. Introductory Remarks

This paper seeks to identify the major causes of conflict in land ownership and utilization in Uganda. We shall suggest ways of minimizing conflict and of ensuring that land is used for developmental purposes which can benefit at least the majority of the people of Uganda.[1]

First, it is essential to describe briefly the existing land tenure system. In 1900, the British introduced in Buganda the Mailo tenure system, which is a modified form of freehold. Under the 1900 Agreement, land was divided between the Kabaka (King), notables and the Protectorate Government. About 1,000 chiefs and private people received land amounting to 8,000 square miles. The remaining land, roughly 9,000 square miles in area, was vested in the Queen as Crown Land.[2] The Buganda Land Law of 1908 disallowed a mailo owner to transfer his land to a person not of the Protectorate without the consent of the Governor and the Lukiiko (Buganda's Parliament).

The 1928 Bussuulu and Envujjo Law fixed the rent and tribute payable to the mailo owner by a plot holder, limiting the freedom of the mailo owner to evict tenants. The mailo land system created a landowning class and a land market, because land was henceforth a commodity which could be sold or mortgaged.

Outside Buganda, freehold titles were granted to Africans who had been holding land under customary tenure pursuant to the Crown Lands (Adjudication) Rules of 1958.[3] There were also native freeholds peculiar to Ankole and Toro Kingdoms.

Customary tenure, the predominant form of landownership in Uganda, enjoyed statutory protection under the Public Lands Act of 1969. For example, it was lawful for a person to occupy customary tenure in rural lands not alienated in leasehold or freehold. Furthermore, a controlling authority had no power to grant a freehold or leasehold of any land occupied by customary tenure, without the consent of the customary occupiers.[4]

Leaseholds estates also existed, both private lease and public or statutory lease. Private lease was granted by an individual landowner to an individual or organization under terms agreed on by the respective parties. Statutory leases were provided for under the Public Lands Act of 1969.

President Amin introduced the Land Reform Decree of 1975, making all land in Uganda public land to be administered by the Uganda Land Commission in accordance with the Public Lands Act. Freeholds in land and any absolute ownership, including mailo ownership, were converted into leaseholds.[5] Such leaseholds on conversion were for 199 years in case of public bodies or religious organizations and 99 years in case of individuals.[6]

The security of the customary tenant was reduced: according to section 7 of the Decree, a lessee on conversion was authorized to terminate customary tenure on his leasehold, provided he give the holder of the tenure not less than six months' notice, with a copy to the Commission.

It must be made clear that the Decree did not abolish private ownership of land and the right to sell land; moreover, many parts of the Decree were not implemented. For example, former mailo land owners do not pay ground rent to the Government. Many parts of the Decree were not implemented because Amin's regime was too often anarchic. Furthermore, once the Decree enabled Amin to grab the land which he wanted at Bombo, he did not care about the subsequent land tangles and niceties. We must also mention that under Amin's regime, there were no attempts to flirt with socialist slogans. Capitalism was allowed to flourish, so the "socialistic" aspects of the Decree were simply ignored.

2. Six Causes of Conflict

Conflict in land is caused inter alia by extreme scarcity of fertile land which gives rise to landlessness, especially as the population increases. This problem is aggravated when new techniques of increasing land fertility are not adopted. Uganda, like many developing areas, had not yet acquired the appropriate technology and skills to maximize land utilization.

The author has, however, shown elsewhere that Uganda does have enough fertile land and that landlessness has not yet become a critical issue in Uganda.[7] There are six causes of conflict: The first is ideological, the second is absence of a clear land policy, the third is that of eviction, the fourth is concerned with protecting indigenous people against the exploitation of foreigners, the fifth is related to corruption, while the last one is concerned with the high cost of surveying, registration and administration of titles.[8]

2.1. Ideological Conflict

There is a conflict between hard core capitalists and a group of people who range from Marxists to socialists. The hard core capitalists, believing in private ownership of land, assert that if a person can use land productively, he should not be limited in the amount of land he may possess. As early as 1961, the World Bank Mission observed that private ownership in Buganda had created a land market, and that the right to own land and conversion of land into a negotiable asset had assisted in the emergence of a group of producers commercially oriented and specialized in production for the market.[9] The East African Royal Commission argued that the individual tenure gives an individual a sense of security in possession, as well as facilitating purchase and sale of land.[10] It must be added that individual ownership of land per se cannot enable a landowner to perform miracles. The landowner must have credit possibilities, business acumen and other facilities. The "capitalists" are not a homogeneous group except for the factors which unite them. Some are opportunists, whereas others are persons genuinely interested in uplifting society largely through individual initiative. So far they form the majority of the Ugandans who for generations have grown up under a capitalistic system.

The "Marxists-Socialists" are also a varied group: the most vocal ones include "oral-documentary" radicals and those whom Nabudere has called "left wing opportunists".[11] He argues that these persons are teaching a hotch-potch of neo-Marxist, neo-Trotskyist fabrications while trying to hide the militaristic character of the Ugandan situation.[12] The "oral-documentary" radicals give public lectures and write at length in newspapers concerning the plight of the peasants, without, however, necessarily practicing what they preach. They are opposed to the individual ownership of land and argue that land should be fully nationalized and re-distributed to the tillers of land. For example, the Minister of Water and Mineral Resources, Chango Machyo has argued:

> the individualization of land tenure develops socio-economic relations in the rural areas which become obstacles to genuine development in the countryside: hence the development of the class struggle in that sector.[13]

He advocates communal ownership of land:

> The African land tenure concept of communal ownership with the individuals enjoying the right of use only is more relevant to developmental philosophy and needs than individual tenure.[14]

Professor Mamdani attributes what he calls the "wretched condition" of the peasantry in Buganda to exploitation by the landlords.[15] He asserts that the average landholding of the landlord in Kitende Village is 2560 acres or 4 square miles while the poor peasant averages 0.66 acres. However, information which this author gathered from the Land Office of Kampala on 16 August 1986, was that there were 204 landowners in Kitende Village and that the biggest landlord owns only 84 acres of land. Since Kitende is only 8 miles out on the Entebbe road, it is easy to establish that the peasants whom he describes as leading a wretched life are in fact more prosperous than those in areas where private ownership of land does not exist.

What are the consequences of the ideological conflict between the two groups? Basically, this conflict complicates the task of the NRM (National Resistance Movement) Government in formulating a comprehensive and clear land policy. We now turn to this problem.

2.2. Absence of a Clear Land Policy

The ideological conflict is also represented within the NRM Government. We must make it clear that this is not a "communist" government, as some foreign papers have represented it. It is a broad-based government which has embraced the various ideological shades. A government grappling with a weak economy mismanaged since 1966 cannot afford to antagonize "landlords", because they are economically and politically well organized. At the same time, it cannot "ignore" peasants who are sometimes irresponsibly evicted by the ruthless lessees. Worse still, the ideological conflict complicates the task of ascertaining what is really happening, because the government tends to get exaggerated accounts from the two antagonistic camps. The government is also reluctant to endorse the Land Reform Decree so arbitrarily imposed by President Amin. Under these circumstances, some ministers have made pronouncements suspending the eviction of tenants, and yet the existing Decree allows lessees to evict tenants. This situation has caused conflicts and confusion. For example, on 20 January 1987, the Minister of Lands declared in a press release:

> The Government would like to state that it has learnt with dismay that some former Mailo Land owners are engaged in an act of evicting customary tenants (bibanja owners) from their bibanja "plots". Government would like to inform these landlords that under the 1975 Land Reform Decree, any such eviction is illegal unless approved by the Minister of Lands and Surveys. No Bibanja owner should therefore agree to such forceful eviction unless the landlord can prove through the Office of the District Administrator that the Minister gave consent to such eviction.
>
> (Source: Ministry of Lands and Surveys).

This statement was legally faulty because according to Section 7 of the Land Reform Decree, the lessee does not require the Minister's consent in order to evict a tenant. When the author interviewed Mr. Ben. Akello Luwum, Minister of Lands and Surveys, on 7 September 1987, he admitted that this statement was legally questionable. However, he added that it had been politically necessary, to protect customary peasants who are a source of the Government's power. His January 1987 statement provoked a sharp reaction from the landowners (lessees).[16] It was also alleged that the Minister had said that most of the people of the District of Mpigi and Mubende are no longer interested in private ownership of the land.[17] The Minister was challenged to disclose the names of those people not interested in private ownership of the land. Mr. E. Mulira, the Chairman of the Namirembe/Bakuli Parish Resistance Council II, Rubaga Division, District of Kampala, asserted that the "Baganda and land are interwoven and that the Government should not rush to tamper with the established land system".[18] The sub-county of Kira in Kyadondo passed a resolution requesting the Government to handle land matters most carefully.[19] The Minister conceded that his tours of Buganda had alerted him to the fact that the land question is very sensitive. It should be pointed out that there are many non-Baganda who have acquired private ownership of land in Buganda. Likewise, other groups have acquired land outside Buganda. Thus the issue is much larger than Buganda, which the Minister toured.

We should note that absence of a clear land policy has caused considerable friction between lessees and tenants. Some tenants, with the support of the Resistance Councils, behave as if they were the actual owners of the land. And yet according to the Land Reform Decree, which has not been amended, customary tenants can be evicted by the lessees. This paralysis must be resolved soon, lest the situation explode.

2.3. Conflict and Eviction

Eviction causes conflicts, for several reasons: It entails uprooting people from a familiar environment where in some cases they may have ancestral burial places. It also poses problems of adequate compensation, especially for peasants who may have lost the capacity to construct or buy new houses. Yet eviction is sometimes required in order to make a plot more economically viable for large-scale production. Eviction may also be necessary in order to consolidate fragmented land, a problem in Kigezi.[20] For whose development should people be evicted? Marxists might argue that since land is a gift of nature, people should not be evicted in order to satisfy the needs of a few individuals. Capitalists will answer that it is sometimes necessary for a few enterprising individuals to evict peasants so that one enterprising person may produce enough food to feed even the evicted peasants, who should be assisted to find work in urban areas. Industrialization therefore becomes essential to create urban job opportunities. Ultimately, the method of eviction and the objective behind it will assist us in determining whether or not eviction should be sanctioned.

As noted, the Decree made it possible to evict customary tenants. We must, however, remark that the safeguards in the Decree tended to be ignored. For example, according to the L.R.D. (sect. 7(4)), the Commission is expected, as far as possible, to resettle the evicted tenant. The Commission is expected to settle any dispute regarding the sufficiency of the notice to quit the land (L.R.D. sect. 7(2)). Dissatisfied parties are allowed to appeal to the Lands Tribunal, which consists of a Magistrate or other Advocate and two other persons, all of whom should be appointed by the Attorney-General in consultation with the Chief

Justice (L.D.R. sect. 12(2)). However, peasants lack the money and the knowledge to appeal when they are illegally evicted.

Let us turn more specifically to two important cases of eviction.

a. Mbale Peasants vs. Bugisu Co-operative Union (B.C.U. Ltd.)

The B.C.U. Ltd. bought 800 acres of land from Miss Nakibuka of the Kakungulu family for 200 million shillings and the title deed passed to B.C.U. Ltd.[21] Miss Nakibuka is a descendant of General Kakungulu, a Muganda warrior who helped the British to incorporate other areas in the East into Uganda and also spread the Kiganda system of administration in the Eastern region. He came to Mbale around 1903; in reward for his effective administrative and military acumen in the East, he was granted 20 square miles of land by the British. Subsequently, the Baganda who assisted the British in pacifying other areas of Uganda and placing them under British control, were resented and regarded as "sub-imperialist".[22]

The Baganda were held responsible for the harsh colonial measures because some of them had assisted the British in the administrative penetration of Uganda. The British then started acting as "impartial arbiters" by removing Baganda from the areas when they had acted as colonial agents. The indigenous people were thus diverted from identifying their fundamental political adversary, for the Baganda were made to act as the "political shock-absorbers" of the British. This was a system of divide and rule. It must be noted that even after Independence, there is a residual anti-Kiganda feeling attributable to the spread of the Kiganda culture and forms of administration to other areas of Uganda. Such anti-Kakungulu sentiments can be discerned from the Weekly Topic, which describes Kakungulu as "a mercenary" of the British, a thief and a traitorous man.[23]

It is against this bitter political background that the people of Mbale learnt on 3 October 1986, from Mr. Nagimesi, the Secretary Manager of CU, that the union was now their new landlord. The BCU, which is at least potentially a people's organization of Mbale, had plans of evicting some peasants, especially those not staying on the land, so that it could inter alia establish large-scale mixed farming in the area.[24] Those to be evicted were to be compensated in accordance with Section 7 of the Land Reform Decree. The author has information that some peasants suspected that the BCU scheme was intended to benefit the elites, not the peasants.[25] There were also opportunistic politicians who misrepresented the facts to the peasants. It was also widely known from statements made by politicians in power that some sections of the NRM Government were against eviction of the peasants. Clearly the politicians and peasants were here taking advantage of the "fuzzy" land policy. Furthermore, Miss Nakibuka was resented for having received so much money as a result of having inherited land which had allegedly been "stolen" by her relative, General Kakungulu.

The peasants, through their Resistance Councils, made the following resolutions:

- the colonialists had grabbed their land from them and given it to Kakungulu. Both of them had no legal right whatsoever over this land.
- this was a colonial error which must be remedied.
- the people will not leave that land, no matter what.[26]

The peasants formed a Land Defence Committee of 12 people to "direct" and "deepen" their struggle. Resolving to work outside the state structures, which it claimed were manned by opportunistic tendencies, the Committee mobilized all the people on the estate in both Bungokho and Nakaloke sub-counties to fight together. It issued a leaflet calling for all-round support for the Musotokoko people. The leaflet linked the "grabbing" of the peoples' land by the British colonialists to their exploitation through coffee and to their impending dispossession by the BCU, backed by foreign capital through the "infamous" World Bank.

The District Administrator appealed to the people to work by means of the Resistance Councils, who would present the issue to him so that he might send it to higher authorities for settlement, but his advice was not accepted. The BCU was physically blocked from taking possession of the land in question. The matter reached the Minister of Lands and Surveys, where there is a deadlock which has not yet been solved. Meanwhile, the peasants are utilizing the land.

This case reveals that there is no clear land policy. Consequently, the peasants who know that they have political support from an important section of the NRM Government have successfully used force to prevent landlords from evicting them regardless of the merits involved. Conflicts have thus entered the realm of using force. The Courts of Law and the political bureaucrats such as the District Administrator have been politically paralyzed.

Second, behind these "peasants" is a group of political economists, agitating that land should be fully nationalized and redistributed to the peasants, described by the Weekly Topic as the "tillers of land". These people have representatives in important newspapers such as the Weekly Topic, and in the Cabinet. For example, in a leading article of the Weekly Topic, the following assertions were made:

> Politically, the landless rural dwellers and peasants who form a sizeable percentage of the population can never really play an important role in national politics until they are given ownership of the land they work on, particularly their bondage to landlords must be broken. Squatters, these modern serfs, must be "liberated" by giving them land. A move should be started towards letting bibanja owners who till the land or those who pay grazing fees to absentee ranch owners, to legally "take-over" and possess the same land ... (Weekly Topic, 29 April 1987, p. 3)

These words are self-explanatory, and are meant to inspire the use of force to change land relations.

Third, the BCU has been denied the opportunity to utilize the land which is bought at such expense. The issues are no longer legal ones, because legally the BCU has the title; but politically its rights are being frozen. The Ministry of Lands has attempted to set aside some acres of land for peasants and to allow the BCU to develop the remaining acres, but the agitated peasants have rejected this offer.

Fourth, the resolution of the peasants - which amounted to dispossessing Kakungulu's descendants of the land which their grandfather had acquired - might have ugly ethnic consequences, especially when it is remembered that many people from Mbale have also acquired land in Buganda and other parts of Uganda.

Fifth, the notion of private ownership has been undermined by a situation under which it is not clear whether or not the landlord has authority over the customary tenant.

b. Ezekiel S.M.S. Mulondo vs. Fenekansi Semakula

The second important case of eviction involved Mr. Mulondo, the General Manager of the East African General Insurance Company Ltd., and his younger brother, Mr. Fenekansi Semakula. On 20 April 1980, Mr. Mulondo received permission from the Uganda Land Commission to develop his land at Namugongo and to evict his brother, a customary tenant. Mr. Mulondo had initially negotiated with his brother to find another place which Mr.

Mulondo would pay for. Mr. Semakula's land lay between two plots of Mr. Mulondo's and it was thus not possible for Mr. Mulondo to develop his dairy farm. His move was aimed at consolidating his fragmented land and having a viable piece of land for dairy farming. When his brother refused to accept his proposal, Mr. Mulondo served him with 6 months' notice to quit the land. Two independent firms of valuers agreed that shs. 117,599/- be paid to Mr. Semakula was also given a disturbance allowance and a value for one grave.[27] The money was taken to the Gombolola Chief where Mr. Semakula was requested to collect it. After expiration of the notice, Mr. Semakula refused to quit, alleging that his property had been undervalued. He also claimed that Mr. Mulondo had orally withdrawn the notice.[28] Mr. Mulondo filed an action in the Magistrates' Court at Mengo for eviction. On appeal by Mr. Mulondo, the High Court ruled that the Magistrate had no jurisdiction to entertain the action. The matter went to the Land Commission, which decided that the notice had been adequate and the amount of compensation fair and adequate. Mr. Semakula then appealed to the High Court, which dismissed the appeal. Again he filed the suit in the High Court and lost. He then appealed to the Court of Appeal at Kampala, where he also lost the case (Civil Appeal No. 4 of 1982). It was held in the various courts that a document under Section 91 of the Evidence Act could not be contradicted, varied or added to, or subtracted from its terms by oral evidence. It would thus not be accepted that Mr. Mulondo should have withdrawn his notice orally. The submission that the compensation was inadequate was also dismissed. Subsequently Mr. Mulondo established a successful mixed farm and now supplies milk to educational institutions. However, initially, he received a setback, because some of his cows had been poisoned.

This case is significant in the following respects: first, it showed conflict between the Kiganda traditional norms and development. Under traditional Kiganda norms, it was taboo to evict a brother from his land, especially when he had a grave on it. Mr. Semakula was paid shs. 80/- to exhume the remains and bury them at another place. A traditional Muganda would have been frightened of being revisited by the spirits of the departed, but Western values of development demanded that such fears be cast aside so that Mr. Mulondo could consolidate his land and produce food and milk on a larger scale. Social disapproval of Mr. Mulondo's actions was thus expressed when his cows were poisoned.

Second, this socio-legal conflict was protracted and expensive. In the long run, however, it was solved in an exemplary manner.

There was no political paralysis because the Government was known not to be vacillating about issues of eviction but was fully committed to the capitalist mode of development.

Third, this case shows an example where eviction was necessary and was accompanied by proper compensation, as upheld by the courts. Eventually Mr. Mulondo's economic venture benefited the larger society which buys his food and milk.

2.4. Protection of the Indigenous People against the Exploitation of Foreigners

Colonial and post-Independence governments have sought to protect indigenous people against exploitation by more skilled and more wealthy foreigners, in land and other matters. However, such protection measures cause conflict because they entail legislation which contains racial discrimination. Furthermore, protection measures may be so paternalistic that they prevent the indigenous Africans from bargaining successfully in the open market. It is also argued that ruthless indigenous Africans may be more of a danger to their fellow Africans than are foreigners. However, if poor countries become mortgaged by rich foreigners, this can of course lead to considerable friction.

When President Nyerere of Tanzania was arguing against individualization of the land, he observed,

> In a country such as ours, where generally speaking the Africans are poor and foreigners are rich, it is quite possible that within eighty or a hundred years, if poor Africans were allowed to sell their land, all the land in Tanganyika would belong to the wealthy immigrants, and the local people would be tenants. But even if there were no rich foreigners in this country, there would emerge rich and clever Tanganyikans. If we allow land to be sold like a robe, within a short period, there would be only a few Africans possessing land in Tanganyika when all others would be tenants.[29]

Nyerere was thus raising the twin problem of protecting the poor indigenous Africans against exploitation by rich and skilled foreigners <u>and</u> Africans. His solution, of nationalizing the land, raises the problem of lack of incentives where there is absence of private ownership of property. When he later retired from the Presidency, Nyerere admitted that his socialist experiment faced problems, from failing to ensure that incentives existed in

Tanzania. We should also add that those who allocate such nationalized land often tend to favour the elites by allocating to them fertile areas.

Two cases will be discussed to illustrate the conflict which has arisen in an attempt to protect the indigenous Africans.

a. Olive Amelia Kawalya-Kaggwa vs. Joanita Nyanzi Kaggwa[30]

Mr. Michael Hamilton Kawalya-Kaggwa died on 9 September 1971. He had made a will dated 2 June 1969, appointing his wife as his sole executrix and trustee of his will. On 11 February 1972, a petition was lodged in the High Court on behalf of the widow applying that she be granted probate, but on 25 February 1972, Mrs. Joanita Nyanzi Kawalya-Kaggwa, sister of the deceased, lodged a caveat. The caveator opposed the probate on the grounds that clause 7 of the will was void, in that it purported to bequeath land to a non-African in contravention of S.2 of the Land Transfer Act. (Mrs. Olive Kaggwa's father was a Gaa of Ghana and her mother was British.) Justice Fuad granted Mrs. Olive Kaggwa the probate, arguing that there could not be successful objection to the grant of probate on the sole grounds that some of the wishes of the testator were, by reason of some enactment, incapable of fulfillment. He further observed that Mrs. Joanita Kaggwa, the caveator, had disclosed no interest.[31] She applied for a stay of execution,[32] but Justice Saldanha argued that such a stay of execution would prejudice the estate of the deceased since it would prevent the estate from being developed. The stay was thus refused.[33]

This was a very important case because Mr. Binaisa, Counsel for Mrs. Joanita Nyanzi-Kaggwa, wanted a ruling from the highest tribunal in order to ascertain once and for all whether a non-African could be registered as proprietor of mailo land. He wanted this established not only in the interests of the widow but in the interests of the many European women married to Africans. There was also the issue of claiming the mailo land, should the widow fail to be registered as executrix.

When the widow applied to the Registrar of Titles to be registered as the proprietor of the mailo land, the application was rejected because she was not African and she had not received the Minister's consent, as required by the provisions of the Land Transfer Act. She filed the case to the High Court at Kampala (civil suit no. 627 of 1974). She argued through her lawyer that she wished to sell part of the land in order to settle outstanding debts and to vest the remaining land in her two sons: Daniel Kaggwa and Michael Kaggwa. (ibid., p. 3) She also pointed out that she was a citizen of Uganda and that she was of indigenous African descent because her father was of the Gaa tribe in Ghana. She added that her mother was British. Chief Justice Wambuzi held that the word "African" as it exists in the Interpretation (Special Provisions) Act, must mean a person of whose parents are or were members of an indigenous African tribe or community. He added, "it must be a combination of two Africans to produce an African" (ibid., p. 13). He also ruled that accordingly, the Registrar of Titles had acted properly in not registering the widow as the proprietor of the mailo land, and added that he hoped that the Minister of Lands would give the widow the necessary consent.

The widow appealed to the Court of Appeal for East Africa (civil appeal no. 38 of 1974). Mr. Wilkinson, who appeared for the widow, argued that while the widow was not a Muganda she had become a member of the Buganda community by virtue of marriage to the late Michael Kaggwa. He referred to her having borne his children, living in a house on his ancestral lands and mingling freely with her Baganda neighbours (ibid., p. 8). Mr. Matovu, who appeared for the Respondent, replied that this claim had never been advanced in the High Court. Justice Spry, the President of the Court of Appeal, accepted Mr. Matovu's objection and dismissed the appeal with great regret, observing:

> if proper evidence had been adduced to establish the facts, particularly the way of life of the applicant (the widow) and her acceptance, if she is accepted as a member of the Baganda community, it might well have been held that she is an African for the purposes of Land Transfer Act and Possession of Land Law. Such evidence might well have come partly from the applicant herself and partly from some Muganda occupying a position of respect and responsibility. It is not open to us to hold that the applicant is an African without any evidence on which to rely (ibid., p. 8)

Subsequently, the Minister of Lands and Surveys declined to give consent to the widow, as a result of which she and her children lost the mailo land. She left the country with her children in disgust.

According to the Kiganda culture, however, a non-Muganda widow who had been married to a Muganda could not have been excluded from the community of the Baganda. Her children were also Baganda. It was therefore very sad when the Land Transfer Act, which should have protected her and the children, was used to deprive them of their property. Clearly, the application of this Land Transfer Act caused a lot of conflict in this case.

Second, it is intriguing to note that Mrs. Joanita Kaggwa played a key role in preventing the sons of her deceased brother and her sister-in-law from acquiring their mailo land. The Court observed rightly that her interest in this matter had not been disclosed. It would be unfair to suggest that she wished to reclaim part of the property which her father had bequeathed to her brother. In this traditional Kiganda setting, the eldest son would inherit most of the property, an approach which minimized fragmenting the land and other types of property. But the heir was expected to fend for the entire family of the deceased. The late Kawalya-Kaggwa, who had been educated abroad and who married a person of part-British descent, did not accept the traditional heavy clan responsibilities. It is possible that this conflict between Western culture and Kiganda culture strained relations between the widow and her in-laws.

Third, this case worried and frustrated many Europeans married to Ugandans. They felt culturally and materially rejected in Uganda.

b. Mistry Amar Singh vs. Serwano Kulubya

We must pose the question, "Is the Land Transfer Act still necessary?" Such protection of the indigenous Africans shields them from taking necessary commercial risks, therefore delaying the realization of their economic entrepreneurship. Indeed, Mr. Serwano Kulubya, an enterprising indigenous businessman, leased his land to a Mr. Singh, an Asian, without getting the permission from the Governor and the Lukiiko. (After Independence, the Governor's consent was replaced by the Minister's consent.) He was thus able to enjoy the benefits of his business deal until a disagreement occurred between him and Mr. Singh. However, when Mr. Kulubya tried to evict Mr. Singh at the end of the lease and to obtain the land, there was protracted litigation in the High Court of Uganda. The case ended with the Privy Council of Britain, which ruled that Mr. Singh was in unlawful occupation of the plot.[34] Interestingly, the High Court of Uganda had ruled that both Mr. Kulubya and Mr. Singh had entered into an illegal agreement and that as a result, Mr. Kulubya as not entitled to recover possession of his land. It took the Privy Council to reverse the decision and to allow Mr. Kulubya to re-enter his land.

This case shows that some Africans find such "protection" cumbersome and that they try to avoid it. However, when they do so, they confront legal tangles, and these are costly and time-consuming.

It is also important to note that if foreigners bought most of the land in Uganda, it would create racial tensions like those existing in Fiji between indigenous Melanesian Fijians and Indians imported to work on the sugar cane fields 100 years ago.[35] The major cause of the conflict is that Asians today control the backbone of the economy. Indeed, a recent military coup was centred on removing the economic dominance of the Asians in Fiji.

From what we have discussed, it should be clear that indigenous Ugandans, who have not yet even attained national integration, do require some protection.[36] However, after attaining national integration, the Ugandans should cease being protected. A country like Britain has a functioning national economy and has attained a high degree of national integration. It also has highly skilled people. Consequently, it is difficult for foreigners to take advantage of it. If the national economy is in danger, the British adopt "national" measures and tactics, some of which remain confidential. This is possible because the "national question" has been largely settled in Britain.

We must affirm that once people have acquired citizenship, they should enjoy equal rights of access to land. Since Mrs. Olive Kaggwa was a Ugandan, she should have had the right to acquire mailo land. The Land Transfer Act should be amended to give equal opportunities to all Ugandans to acquire land.

c. The Expulsion of Asians and the Expropriation of their Property

Our discussion of the fear of being swamped by foreigners would be incomplete if we did not briefly deal with the expulsion of Asians. In August 1972, Amin expelled over 45,000 non-Ugandan Asians from Uganda. Some of these Asians owned land under leasehold agreements, and Asians had dominated the retail and wholesale trade. Amin's move was popular because he was dealing with people who were resented for dominating the economy of Uganda while often investing their profits outside Uganda.

However, Amin did not realize what Mamdani has expressed in these words:

> The fact was that the Indian commercial bourgeoisie was still a dependent class. Functionally it lubricated the export-import economy; financially, it was heavily reliant on and subordinate to British banking capital.[37]

The property of these Asians was taken by Ugandans, and soon property became a major source of conflict between Uganda and Britain, and between Ugandans! The British demanded compensation, while the Ugandans disagreed about distribution of the property. This disagreement led to murders. Since 1972, there have been several changes in Government in Uganda, and each has proposed a different formula for allocating former Asian property. When Obote regained power in 1980, he promised to return the property to the former owners under the Expropriated Properties Act 1982, thus nullifying Amin's allocation of the property. When the NRM came into power, it discovered many anomalies which were committed under Obote. For example, they came across certificates of re-possessing the property which were irregular, granted unilaterally by Obote who was both President and Minister of Finance. Thus the NRM has set up Verification and Negotiating Committees to work out a formula to ease transfer of the property to the rightful owners.[38]

This is a very complicated subject, fraught with many tangles. For example, some shops and the adjoining land have gone through many owners and it is now difficult to determine the rightful owner. There is also pressure that Amin's "economic war" against non-Ugandans should not be reversed. It should be remembered that Obote faced the same pressure and he was acting in such a way that he was not fully encouraging the departed Asians to return and re-possess their property, some of which was grabbed by Obote's political supporters. Recently, the Speke Hotel, which is being contested, was damaged through fire. The matter is being investigated. The international community, which has vested interest in the property, is also re-claiming its share of the property. Many owners of the land which had been leased by the former owners have not received ground rent since 1972! Clearly this issue is full of multi-faceted domestic and international conflicts.

d. Possible Solutions

In order to avoid having a different solution being proposed whenever there is change of Government, the current Government should consider buying some of the buildings so that it may let them out at commercial rates and thus raise revenue. Since there has been an acute shortage of accommodation in the Civil Service and parastatal bodies, the Government should also buy some of the buildings in order to solve this problem. The remaining property which is difficult to manage, like tea estates, should be sold to individuals at commercial rates. The non-Ugandan Asians should be compensated through a loan which can be negotiated with the British Government, whereas Ugandan Asians should regain their property.

2.5. Corruption Causes Conflict

A major source of conflict has been corruption between sellers of land and officials, so that people are sold "air" instead of land. One piece of land may be sold to four people, and as each discovers the fraud, either prolonged litigation goes on or naked violence take place. The matter is made more complex because the original title has been destroyed by the Land Office official involved in the racket. Ever since 1966, corruption has been rampant in Uganda. The rulers privatized the state and treated it as private hunting ground.[39] In turn, parastatal bodies and Ministries also privatized the public institutions, as a result of which there was absence of accountability. The NRM Government is now struggling to restore accountability to remove corruption. Forms of malpractice include the following:

(1) Forging signatures of officials responsible for land and administration, so that one certificate of title is illegally granted to more than one person;

(2) Issues of lease offers unauthorized by the controlling authorities

(3) Alteration of terms recommended by the Chief Registrar of Titles;

(4) Filing fictitious land inspection reports, so that leases are extended to full term without the land being developed;

(5) Destruction or removal of relevant records from land office files;

(6) Ministerial orders which violate existing laws.

We shall give a few cases of conflict which arose out of such malpractices.

a. The Dispute between former President Binaisa vs. Chief Justice Wambuzi, Sebalu and Lule Advocates

Mr. Godfrey Binaisa, former President of Uganda, claims that on 22 April 1970, he bought land at Kisugu and he acquired a certificate of title, Kyadondo block 244 plot 524 on Kisugu, where there is a quarry. He bought it from Mr. Ibrahim Ndawula. The Binaisa Government was overthrown in a military coup, as a result of which he left the country. On returning from Europe in 1985, Mr. Binaisa found that the land had been taken over by Mr. John William Charles Kabangala, who had in turn sold it to Waluse Ltd.[40] This company is jointly owned by the Chief Justice, S.W. Wambuzi; G. Lule, former Attorney General in Amin's government; and Paul Sebalu, former Legal Advisor to the defunct East African Community. It was the Busirike Stone Quarry Ltd. and as already stated, it claimed to have bought Mr. Binaisa's land. When Mr. Binaisa tried to get from the Ministry of Lands and Surveys a duplicate land title, he was informed that the originals were missing.

According to Sebalu and Lule advocates, when Mr. Yokana Kabangala died, Mr. Charles Kabangala acquired letters of administration of his father's estate, including the disputed land. Busirike Quarry, in which Lule, Sebalu and Wambuzi are partners, were authorized by Mr. Kabalanga to operate on his disputed land. They were about to buy the land from Mr. Charles Kabangala when Mr. Binaisa claimed that he had bought it from Mr. Ndawula. They sought from the Chief Registrar of Titles to establish the rightful owner of the land situated on block 244, plot 524, Kisugu, which is 2 hectares. The Chief Registrar instructed them to submit Kabangala's title for cancellation, on the grounds that she was satisfied that there was a valid prior title made in the names of Binaisa. Sebalu and Lule Advocates disputed the right of Binaisa to the property.[41] They argued inter alia that Mr. Binaisa's certificate of title (viz., No. KLA 57267 of 3.6.1970) shows only him and does not show from whom he bought it. Furthermore, the Transaction's Register in the Land Office which showed Kabangala's and not Binaisa's title was curiously missing. As I write this paper, the dispute is unresolved but has not been filed to the court.

Here we have a case of two people with two certificates of titles with respect to one plot 524, Kyadondo, block 244. The original title is missing from the Land Office. Furthermore, the Transaction's Register which shows details of land being sold, given etc., is missing. Either a fraud was committed or a genuine mistake occurred. Whatever happened, the case has caused an important conflict involving a lot of money and eminent personalities.[42]

b. An Example of a False Inspection Report

A false land inspection report was given about land in Namanve, as a result of which the lease was extended to Mr. Y[43] without any development. The Assistant Land Officer did not go to inspect, on the pretext that there were security problems in the area. Asked to explain the basis of his inspection report, he admitted that it was fictitious. Thus the requirement of extending the lease being based on development was violated.

The Uganda Land Commission has also been granting leases initially for five years after which they have been extended, provided the lessee can show evidence that he has developed his estate. When some Ugandans have been forced to go into exile because of the brutal regimes which existed since 1966, the Commission has been granting the leases to other people.[44] However, those later returning have wished to re-claim their leases. This has created conflict between "stayees" and "returnees"; in some cases, the practice has been abused by some returnees who wield political and military power.

2.6. Surveying and Registration of Titles

Conflict has been caused by dishonest and inaccurate surveyors. Some surveyors survey more land than was originally approved, and some survey land which they know is a subject of dispute. Cases have arisen where surveys have not been carried out but where cartographers have made out fictitious deed plans by mere tracing. Other cases have arisen where private surveyors have used pickets instead of markstones in order to save money. Such survey boundaries may disappear at a later stage, leading to dispute. Surveying instruments are scare and costly, indeed, even cement for making stones is not readily available. Consequently, surveying has become very expensive and out of reach of the ordinary people. The process of registering titles is also expensive, and the system of maintaining the main and transactions registers is unreliable and outmoded. Indeed, the practices of keeping registers in one Ministry is risky. If they should disappear, either through fire or wanton destruction, the records system would be crippled

3. Recommendations

3.1. Some Developmental Issues

What should be the basis of security of tenure? Khiddu-Makubuya has suggested that there should be a positive requirement that whoever owns land is duty-bound to effect improvements thereon and develop the same, or else forfeit it to the Government. The improvement and development of the land will then be the owner's sole guarantee of security of tenure.[45] We must point out that this requirement already exists especially with regard to urban land. Furthermore, according to the Land Reform Decree, underdeveloped land or unused land within a period of 8 years from 1975 could be forfeited. (Section 8 (i) and 9 (i)) However, this provision was not implemented, inter alia because land is very expensive to develop. And thus before one can consider Mr. Makubuya's recommendation, the following conditions must be fulfilled:

Credit must be more readily available to ordinary people, provided they have reasonable collateral. Agricultural chemicals must be provided cheaply to the farmers because hand labour is very expensive. Antidotes should also be available to deal with cases of poisoning. Oxen and ploughs should be made available at reasonable prices. Tractors should also be made available on a limited scale to individuals and to the Village Resistance Councils.[46] Many parts of Uganda have suffered heavily during the "liberation wars". Land owners and customary tenants will thus require at least 15 years to recover from the ravages of the war.

Forfeiting the land of people who have failed to develop it would undermine the cherished notion of proprietorship. Instead, we propose that after a period of 15 years in which security, rural credit, intermediate mechanization and the supply of agricultural chemical will be enjoyed, underdeveloped land should be liable to a special "developmental" tax.

Another urgent requirement is industrialization. For example, processing of agricultural products would boost employment opportunities and also create functional and symbiotic linkages between industry and agriculture.

Turning to the ideological conflict, we may note that most of the "Marxist-Socialist radicals" in Uganda are in fact oral-documentarists. They talk and write about radical issues, while in practice, they pursue capitalist ventures with vigour. Equally, many of the hard core capitalists lack capital. The two groups should concentrate on building a national economy which has functional, horizontal and vertical linkages. At a political level, our emphasis should be to create national integration. Tanzania has already taught us that if a country has a weak economic base, it weakens itself further by flirting with socialistic rituals which stifle the incentives of the people. The national economy must be buttressed by a democratic ethos and practices.

We must have a clear land policy with an unambiguous ideological focus. Private ownership of land must be affirmed. Eviction of customary tenants must be safeguarded by ensuring that tenants are represented on Eviction Committees, and landlords must also be represented on these committees. Evicted people must be compensated at market prices. They should also be given one year's notice instead of six months', and a disturbance allowance also be given to them.

Cases arise where a landlord (lessee) wishes to sell his land but his tenants lack the money to buy it. The state should encourage the tenants to form co-operatives which can borrow the money and buy the land. Customary tenants should thus be encouraged to acquire land titles. Initially they could do so through co-operatives. However, as soon as the tenants acquire enough money, they should negotiate with the landlord in order to get certificates of title. Meanwhile, customary tenures should be registered by the Resistance Councils. In the past, some dishonest peasants have by-passed landlords and acquired holdings through the agents of the landlords, creating conflicts between the landlord and customary tenants. In future, the new Land Law should require a customary tenant to have written evidence from the landlord stating that he bought the plot from the landlord. The Resistance Councils should have a copy of this letter which should state the dates on which the plot was bought.

The state should "reinstate"[47] the system of having active Government Surveyors equipped with the necessary tools and transport. Poor people should be assisted in getting their land surveyed by Government Surveyors at reasonable prices fixed by the Government.

The Ministry of Lands and Surveys should have an Inspectorate Division to keep the Ministry informed of what is happening in the field. It should report malpractices and also educate the peasants and landlords about the provisions of the existing Land Act or Decree.

It is essential to encourage land consolidation in order to reduce working time spent in moving between scattered fragments. This will also increase the possibility of controlling pests and diseases. Land consolidation will inevitably entail eviction of people and resettling them in other areas. However, we should avoid using force as much as possible. This should be a last resort only. Since fragmentation is partly caused by traditional inheritance procedures, it is essential to mount an educational programme to change people's attitudes. The teachers should include sociologists, political scientists, Church leaders and Resistance Council leaders.[48]

The Government should encourage those faced with a land shortage to move to places where land is abundant, through providing information. We lack information concerning people wishing to sell land and those who wish to buy. This makes it difficult for people from, say, Karamoja to buy land in Bunyoro. It is gratifying to note that already many Bakiga who are facing land shortage have bought land in Buganda and Kasese. This trend should be encouraged. It is, however, important to note that people who move from their area to a new one, should not form special enclaves where they may become targets of envy and suspicion. They should mix freely with the people of their new area.

The Land Transfer Act should be amended to enable all Ugandan citizens to enjoy equal access to the land regardless of race. However, to protect Uganda from being mortgaged by people with no stake in it, citizens wishing to acquire land should be resident in Uganda.

As long as a person can use land productively, there should not be a limit regarding the amount of land he can possess. Indeed, as we mechanize our agriculture, a few people will feed the country while many peasants will be released to work in industry.

Microfilming the records of the Land Office is long overdue. Three copies of the microfilm should be kept, as follows: One copy should be kept in the Land Office for daily use; another copy should be kept in the Land Office for occasional use; and a third copy should be kept in another place outside the Ministry of Lands and Surveys. This must be a very secure place, and there should be rigorous rules to ensure that it is not damaged or tampered with. The filing system should be computerized, and a Senior Officer familiar with computers should take charge of the records. The Inspectorate Section should look into the problem of selling "air" instead of land.

How can we eliminate corruption, which has caused so much conflict? This problem has particularly afflicted Uganda, not least because many of our leaders from 1966 to 1986 were irresponsible. Furthermore, the hyperinflation which has hit Uganda deprived people of a living wage. Leadership which is accountable to the people will go a long way to minimize corruption, and indeed it is gratifying to note that the NRM Government contains some persons who have shown exemplary leadership. The setting up of the Office of Inspector of Government Business has also assisted in disclosing sources and forms of corruption to the public. It is essential to give civil servants and other public servants a living wage. The recent salary increases point in the right direction; however, the increases are small especially when seen in terms of the rise in the price of fuel which has affected transport and other items. Obviously, as we restore our economy and institutions, Ugandans will have to accept sacrifices. In the past, people were not willing to accept sacrifices because they observed those in high office looting the state with impunity. We need exemplary leadership to go as a meaningful example to urge people to accept sacrifices at this critical time.

3.2. Conflict and National Integration

Conflict does not necessarily disrupt society. On the contrary, it can assist the realization of national integration. For example, political conflict provides an outlet for underlying tensions and thus forestalls violent explosions.[49] Social and political conflict makes it possible to adjust norms appropriate for new conditions to occur. Conflict thus helps to revitalize existing norms and it contributes to the emergence of new ones. When, for instance, through the process of conflict, people question norms otherwise taken for granted, a well-considered case is made to justify either retaining, amending or replacing them.

However, conflicts which contradict the basic assumptions upon which a society is founded, have a high propensity for destroying the unity of society.

4. Conclusion

In this paper, we have discussed six causes of conflict concerning land ownership and utilization as these affect Uganda. Since the conflicts concern land, and land is a fundamental source of livelihood and shelter, they can disrupt our society. Indeed, our society is vulnerable because many features of the modern state, such as courts and political parties, which can assist in the resolution of conflict have not yet been fully or adequately institutionalized.[50]

The suggestions we have made should be supplemented by creating virile political institutions. Furthermore, the process of reforming land tenure must take place within a clear ideological framework. We have suggested that the predominant ideology in Uganda cherishes private ownership of property, and that this should be taken in consideration in dealing with these vital issues.

Notes

1. This work is based on several interviews which included the following people: Mr. Okello Luwum, the Minister of Lands and Surveys, the Chief Land Officer, the Secretary of the Uganda Land Commission, the Deputy Registrar of Titles, the Permanent Secretary, Ministry of Lands and Surveys, Mr. N. Batungi, Surveyor and Senior Lecturer at Makerere University, Professor Kakooza, Dean, Faculty of Law, Professor A. Kiapi, the Acting Chief Valuer, and Mr. Mugenyi, a lawyer. Other people requested to remain anonymous. I have gained a lot of information as a farmer and a "landlord" who became a lessee in 1975.
2. For details, read Mukwaya, 1953, and Low & Pratt, 1960.
3. Khiddu-Makubuya, 1981, p. 310.
4. Ibid., p. 309.
5. The Land Reform Decree (L.R.D.), 1975, Section 2 (3).
6. For more information on the consequences of the Decree, read Nsibambi, 1981, pp. 287-300.
7. Nsibambi, 1987, pp. 2-9.
8. The pastoral Karamojong compete for land with the game parks and sedentary farmers. However, here shortage of space has made it impossible for us to discuss this matter. Cf. Nsibambi & Byarugaba, 1982.
9. The Economic Development of Uganda. Entebbe: Government Printer, 1961, p. 187.
10. East African Royal Commission, 1953-1966. HMSO, London CWD, 1955, p. 323.
11. Nabudere, 1986/87, p. 64. Cf. Nabudere, 1980, pp. 204-210.
12. Ibid., pp. 64-65.
13. Chango-Machyo, 1984, p. 8.
14. Idem.
15. Mamdani, 1984, p. 24
16. Technically, the landowner now is the Commission, but for the sake of convenience we shall refer to the lessee as the "landlord".

17. Ngabo, a Luganda newspaper, 4 May 1987, p. 1.
18. Personal interview with E. Mulira, 10 September 1987.
19. Ngabo, 4 May 1987, p. 1.
20. Kanyeihamba, 1969, pp. 137-48.
21. Weekly Topic, Uganda, 25 February 1987, pp. 5-8. See also Weekly Topic, 15 April 1987, p. 1.
22. Ingham, 1958, pp. 116-19.
23. Weekly Topic, 25 February 1987, p. 5.
24. We have deliberately said that the Union was potentially a people's organization because some Unions have been misused by their leaders.
25. Interview with an official of the Land Office who handled the matter but who requested to remain anonymous, for obvious reasons.
26. Weekly Topic, 25 February 1987, p. 8.
27. The firms included Katuramy & Co.
28. F. Semakula vs. E. Mulondo, in the High Court, Civil Suit no. 834 of 1981, p. 1.
29. Nyerere, 1967, pp. 55-56.
30. Olive Amelia Kawalya-Kaggwa vs. Joanita Nyanzi-Kaggwa, Administration case no. 21 of 1972, before Justice Fuad. See Uganda Land Reports, 1972, pp. 126-32.
31. Uganda Law Reports, 1972, Part 1, p. 128.
32. Joanita Kaggwa vs. Olive Amelia Kawalya-Kaggwa, Administrative case no. 21 of 1972.
33. Uganda Law Reports, p. 130.
34. Mistry Amar Singh vs. Serwano Wofunira Kulubya, in East African Law Reports, 1963, pp. 408-09.
35. For details, read Weekly Topic, 3 June 1987.
36. For details, read Nsibambi, 1969.
37. Mamdani, 1976, pp. 307-308.
38. The Star, 6 July 1987, p. 1.
39. For details, read Nsibambi, 1986/87.
40. This information is based on interviewing the following people: Mr. A. Kasirye of Binaisa and Company, Advocates (Mr. Binaisa was out of the country) and Sebalu and Lule, Advocates and Legal Consultants. See also The New Vision, 16 April 1987.
41. Interview with Sebalu and Lule Advocates on 18 September 1987.
42. It has been estimated that an acre of land at Kisugu cost not less than 5 million shillings in 1970.
43. Name withheld in order to avoid prejudicing the investigations.
44. Source: Ministry of Lands and Surveys.
45. Khiddu-Makubuya, 1981, p. 322.
46. It is gratifying to note that the Government has already embarked on making tractors available. Past mistakes of misusing them must be guarded against. We must also import tractors which can cope with deep-rooted growths.
47. Reinstate because it has almost collapsed.
48. Cf. Okoth-Ogendo, 1975, p. 172.
49. For details, read Coser, 1956, pp. 150-53
50. Mudoola, 1987.

References

Chango-Machyo, B.: "Communal Land Tenura and Rural Development". Paper presented at the Second Mawazo Workshop on "The Agrarian Question in Developing Countries", Makerere University, 10-12 February 1984.

Coser, L.: The Function of Social Conflict. Glencoe. Ill.: The Free Press, 1956.

Court of Appeal for Uganda, Civil Appeal no. 4 of 1982.

East Africa Law Reports, 1963.

East Africa Royal Commission, 1953-1955, HMSO, London CWD, 1955.

Economic Development of Uganda. Entebbe: Government Printer, 1961.

High Court of Uganda at Kampala, Civil Suit no. 627 of 1974 and no. 834 of 1981.

High Court of Appeal for East Africa, Civil Appeal no. 38 of 1974.

Ingham, K.: The Making of Modern Uganda. London: George Allen & Unwin Ltd., 1958

Kanyeihamba, G.: "Land Fragmentation", in Obol-Ochola, J.: Land Law Reform in East Africa. Kampala: Uganda Press Trust Ltd., 1969.

Khiddu-Makubuya, E.: "Land Law Reform and Rural Development in Uganda", in Nsibambi, A. and J. Katorobo (eds.): Proceedings of the Conference on Rural Rehabilitation and Development. Kampala: Makerere University, September 1981.

The Land Reform Decree (L.R.D.), 1975.

Low, D.A. & Pratt, C.: Buganda and British Overrule 1900-1955. London: Oxford University Press, 1960.

Mamdani, M.: Politics and Class Formation in Uganda. London: Heinemann, 1976.

Mamdani, M.: "Analyzing the Agrarian Question: The Case of a Buganda Village". Paper presented at the Second Mawazo Workshop on "The Agrarian Question in Developing Countries", Makerere University, 10-12 February 1984.

Mudoola, D.: "The Problems of Institution Building: The Uganda Case", in Dodge, C. & P.D. Wiebe (eds.): Beyond Crisis: Development Issues in Uganda. Kampala: Makerere Institute of Social Research, Makerere University and African Studies Association, 1987.

Mukwaya, A.B.: Land Tenure in Uganda. London: Kegan and Paul, 1953.

Nabudere, W.D.: Imperialism and Revolution in Uganda. London: ONYX Press, 1980.

Nabudere, W.D.: "The Uganda Crisis: What Next?", in UFAHAMU, vol. XV, no. 3, 1986/87.

Nsibambi, A.: "Some Problems of Political Integration in Uganda", in East African Journal, February 1969.

Nsibambi, A.: "From Symbiosis to Antagonism: The Case of the Relationship Between the Landlord and the Tenant in the Rural Development of Uganda", in Nsibambi, A. & J. Katorobo (eds.): Proceedings of the Conference on Rural Rehabilitation and Development. Kampala: Makerere University, September 1981.

Nsibambi, A. & F. Byarugaba: "Problems of Political and Administrative Participation in a Semi-Arid Area of Uganda: a Case Study of Karamoja", in The African Review, vol. 9, no. 2, 1982.

Nsibambi, A.: "Corruption in Uganda, 1971-1986", in UFAHAMU, vol. XV, no. 3, Winter 1986/87, pp. 109-18.

Nsibambi, A.: "Dimensions of Rural Poverty in Uganda". Paper presented to a Workshop on "Integrated Rural Development in Uganda", 25-29 August 1987, held at Mukono District Farm Institute, Uganda.

Nyerere, J.K.: Freedom and Unity. Nairobi: Oxford University Press, 1967.

Okoth-Ogendo, H.W.O.: "African Land Tenure Reform", in Heyer, J., J.K. Maitha & W. Denga: Agricultural Development in Kenya. Nairobi: Oxford University Press, 1975.

The Uganda Land Reports, 1972; Administrative Cause no. 21 before Justice Fuad.

Uganda Law Reports, 1972.

Akiki Bomera Mujaju

Internal Conflict and its International Context

1. Introduction

The "African crisis" is generally appreciated these days both within international fora, particularly those within the United Nations system and its associates, and within academia with a Third World outlook. This term has come to encompass phenomena such as repeated food shortages which frequently degenerate into famine situations for which emergency food "relief" measures have had to be resorted to. Even more well known and perhaps broader in scope are the problematic economies of Third World countries, particularly those in our continent which seem to be incapable of taking off, with the downward drift towards greater dependency on external aid. What is "crisis" about both these is that the African continent is very well endowed with resources to produce food for internal consumption and indeed a surplus for export - but instead of this coming about, emergency food aid has become the norm and surplus food produced inside the continent the exception. Instead of massive external funds enabling Africa to tap its vast natural and human resources to achieve an economic breakthrough, the continent is having to require more and more aid, not to advance but to pay interest on previously acquired loans which can only worsen the debt-repayment burden. How these apparent anomalies come about is obviously a matter of great international interest; equally important is that this cannot escape the critical analysis of academia.

Less frequent in international fora, even those of the United Nations whose principal objective was to be to spare the world of the <u>scourge of war</u>, is the phenomenon of international politico-military convulsions. Geneva has been busy talking about controlling strategic weapons; disarmament discussions hesitantly take place in the UN system, but these do not seem to focus seriously on the flow of conventional weapons into Africa and the rest of the Third World. Both the UN and the superpowers in Geneva, as well as the allied summits, seem to be busy thinking of avoiding a World War III - as if war is "war" only when it involves Northern Hemisphere countries generally and directly. In the Far East, in the Middle East, in Southern Africa, in Chad, in South-west Sahara, in Central and South America - in all these areas what is remarkably constant are the pounding guns, the downing or launching of MIGs, the movement of tanks and impressive military parades, although in few of them is any of this equipment manufactured. And, the same countries which tolerate these apparently inexplicable absurdities are those characterized by the crisis discussed above.

Underneath these crossfires - not among or between nations but within our countries themselves - are irritations between ethnic communities, religious identities, political affiliations, which very soon turn into open hostilities. In Uganda, in Ethiopia, in Angola, in Mozambique, in the Sudan, and in Chad, and beyond Africa in Sri Lanka, these form the bleak but prominent profiles of their respective national lives. Yet, research as an international effort on these matters is more conspicuous for its paucity. This monotonous barrenness of international indifference, in both scholarly and policy fora, has only intermittently been disturbed by the establishment in recent years of an International Centre for Ethnic Studies in Sri Lanka and the Research Programme on Ethnic Conflicts and Conflict Resolution at the International Peace Research Institute, Oslo, Norway.

Is there a relationship between the "crisis" previously presented and "internal conflict" now under reference? A broader posing of the question would clearly be useful because it is time that we start to identify problems in their entirety. Convenience, however, dictate a partial focus only. To probe the international implications of internal conflict and to suggest possible remedies for them form the underlying objectives of this paper. However, we cannot attain these two goals without first disposing of the question of <u>what really constitutes internal conflict</u>: how this phenomenon manifests itself, as well as its deeper effects on our political systems. Crucially important also is the need to conceptualize properly the relationship between the <u>domestic situation</u> and the <u>international situation</u>, which is why the paper bears its present title. I propose to deal with these, each in turn.

Here the view will be advanced that, given the nature of contemporary international forces, given the character of the state in Africa and throughout the Third World, the cracks which internal conflicts betray in our domestic situations pose the greatest risk to our development as viable entities and prosperous communities; further, that a great need, therefore, now exists to manage the international diversities of our states in a manner that can relegate inevitable domestic disputes and disagreement to inconsequence. Let us now turn to internal conflict as a phenomenon.

2. Internal Conflict

There is hardly any need for a full-scale entry into banalities over defining "conflict". Conflict is simply conflict; it is internal, meaning within a country, if the protagonists are internally located, or when externally domiciled, if they are internally rooted and the cause of conflict can be identified as domestic. Here there does arise a complication, as shall be demonstrated later. The conflict may range from inability to communicate because of the depth of feeling and the gulf created by disagreements among the parties involved, to full-blown military hostilities among the same.

These are two poles, separating two extreme positions of ill-feeling. They nevertheless constitute a continuum along which may be placed a variety of conflict situations. In the first, there are tensions between the parties involved, but without any demonstrable offensive action from either side. In military terms this may be a situation when arms are secretly stockpiled in anticipation of a future conflict. This may also be period for covert infiltration for espionage to determine the true extent of each other's intentions. These are under-surface tensions between actors whose interests and intentions are suspect, without involving any moves of open hostility.

Pressure may build on one side, because of hypersensitivity or misreading signals from the other side, or because of intra-group complications. This may lead to directly offensive action: the movement of troops, their positioning, increasing the quantity of arms and their sophistication, possibly also an intensification in the propaganda war. This is the period of mobilization. At this stage hostilities are open but still short of direct physical confrontation. This may, if mediating efforts do not assert themselves, escalate into a situation where pre-emptive and retaliatory military action is resorted to, and where a war is thus in earnest.

These terms are more frequently used to describe relations among conflicting states, but internal conflict also tends to pass through the same phases although the scale of their action may be smaller. The spectrum also tends to be longer in terms of time: unlike the international environment, which despite every good intention remains anarchic (R. Aron 1959), internal situations do have territorial authorities whose order or legitimacy may take longer to dislodge so as to create the conditions necessary for open military hostilities among or between internal belligerents. Needless to say, these circumstances need not make healing the wounds of internal conflict any easier, as Professor Wandira has so clearly pointed out. (Wandira 1987)

The contestants or belligerents may be classes, one in power controlling the state and its economy, the other(s) suffering under the subjection of the former which they seek to supplant. The hostility may be between communities, such as ethnic or tribal ones, or sometimes religious ones - especially if they predominate in a region part of a country in which they are politically, perhaps also economically, disadvantaged. They thus explain their disadvantaged status in terms of their religious identity.

Often also the conflict may be between undisciplined political parties, one in control of state power, the other(s) in opposition in conditions of zero-sum politics where tolerance is the exception. The conflict may be directly between rival armies, conventional or guerrilla, sponsored by the established disagreeing parties.

Whatever the case, conditions of internal conflict tend to be, either directly or potentially, ones of turmoil which can be ruinous to the economy. Particularly those of a military nature leave major scars on the bodies of the polity because mutual animosity and bitterness may be long-lasting, disrupting the process of developing stable, acceptable political relations. Moreover, because the contestants are members of the same country, this legacy of bitterness is highly disruptive: unless breaking away succeeds, creating two new sovereign units, the conflicting compatriots must learn to live together. To this extent, internal conflict is far more painful than international conflict. When it occurs, the consequent irritations must be eased, and this is certainly no easier than in inter-state conflicts. (Wandira 1987)

3. Causes of Internal Conflicts

Before addressing the causes of internal conflicts, let me stress that the natural condition among human beings seems to be one of conflict. There will be conflict over valued resources because people have different appetites for them; such resources are frequently economic and political. There will be conflict over food when it is in short supply, and conflict over jobs. Also possible are conflicts generated by egos, psychological needs for status, recognition, sometimes also adventure. Conflicts may also be generational. Hobbes may have a point in the way he describes the state of nature, because stripped of the veil of civility, human beings are indeed capable of the excesses of other beasts. Hobbes may have been vulgar and extravagant in the way he presented the state of nature and particularly in the solutions he advocated, but certainly conflict is its predominant quality.

3.1. Amoeba-type Political System

One condition conducive to frequent hostilities and to turning hitherto under-surface tensions into open hostilities in Africa are the amoeba-type political systems existing in our continent. These, like an amoeba, are small, internally fluid, constantly changing. However, unlike amoebae, when they change, establishing a new balance of stable relations becomes difficult. In addition, we need to apply another image: the one of being brittle, inconsistent as this may appear. To be fluid and changing and yet brittle at the same time sounds impossible, but impossible things happen in our systems. To this extent we can call them Bwegege political systems, because, in the attempt to establish a new balance, breaking is a real possibility.

This condition of fluidity, of possibilities of breaking and the elusive search for a new balance provides fertile ground for minor disagreements to develop into active conflicts which can escalate into open hostilities. In abundance are mutual suspicions on the part of persons and groups, political and otherwise, as is the absence of shared values and norms for attaining valued goals. Political leaders respect nobody and honour no pledges; economic actors act without regard for the social good; professionals forget their oaths as soon as they have uttered the final words of the same; armies define those who finance their barracks and pay for their uniforms and their weapons as objects for manipulation, even slaughter.

Governments are not governments of countries or nations, but of partialities serving particular interests. There has to be a party government, a movement government, an army government which in conditions of the zero-sum-game must take all. (Ake 1969; Riker 1962) This anomic situation heightens the conflict potential in Africa and beyond.

3.2. Poverty

There are many ways of looking at poverty. The term generally denotes meagreness of economic resources for sustaining life: clothing, shelter, transport, diet are all affected. To be poor is to be in the red, or near so, as far as these are concerned. But poverty can also denote deficiency of valuable but intangible things: self-respect, civility, respect and consideration for others. This is a matter which R.W. Wilson (Wilson, 1983) has dealt with in some detail in touching on three vital elements of moral development: reciprocity, empathy and individual responsibility.

Our countries are gripped by this condition. We may note the ruthless search for accumulation; or regarding public office as a licence for building up personal economic power and holding society to ransom. People live their lives and do things if there should be no moral inhibitions. In the case of post-Independence Uganda, these attributes have their clearest manifestations. No wonder that in a space of 20 years our country has had 3 civil wars. Poverty of this kind can be a true burden, exacerbating internal tensions.

3.3. Ineptitude in the Management of Diversity

Nothing is perhaps more generally dangerous than believing that only one's own side has a monopoly on virtue and has any real justification for existing; or believing that one can impose uniformity and thereby achieve unanimity.

This point we touched upon earlier, and it must be reiterated. Political science applies two terms to this tendency: intolerance, and the zero-sum game. One finds it difficult to accept and live with another person, another idea, another group (tribe, party, religion). Those who win in political competitions or struggles find it difficult to see that the other side has any contribution to make and therefore has any claim to authority. (Mujaju 1987/88; Riker 1968) This leads to a serious deficiency in managing differences. It leads to believing that differences can be shouted down; cultural diversity is frowned upon; and wholism is pursued to the exclusion of peculiarities.

Open hostilities among tribes, among religions, among political parties can arise from the sheer fact that one's own peculiarities are not appreciated. Minor irritations become the beginnings of national disasters. This is particularly so in modern circumstances when the world is more aware, where even the most illiterate and poor will yearn for freedoms and self-assertion. And yet, the age of democratic ideas, when people talk of human rights, surely cannot mean very much unless states can learn to manage diversities. The times we live in thus add to the difficulties of reducing internal hostilities unless serious thinking takes place on our part. (Mujaju 1987/88)

3.4. Psychological Variables

Not losing face, protecting one's ego, viewing oneself as beyond question because of unjustifiable confidence, sheer arrogance-these are psychological traits. Far too many countries have suffered when they have been led by leaders and governments whose actions can be described in these terms. Africa has had leaders who would rather destroy their parties, their armies and even their countries than have themselves lose power. Far too many of our countries have governments which think that statesmanship and glory come only from continuing in power, even when this leads to a bleeding nation and suffering people. People have not yet acquired the modesty to accept failure and voluntarily give their countries a chance to try someone else. The history of post-Independence Africa is replete with instances of leaders who have had to be forcefully removed in coups d'etat long after it should have been obvious that their countries were ripe for new political directions. These are obviously psychological and cultural problems, because at their root lie questions of how one judges one's role in history, whether one considers the country more important than its leader or its ruling party, army or government.

These are instances of psychological pathology, living side by side, in a mutually reinforcing way, with what one Ugandan scholar has termed "institutional pathology". (Mudoola 1985) They are part of the crisis environment which leads to such internal convulsions as those to which we refer in this paper.

3.5. Institutional/structural Variables

So far, we have touched on systemic, economic, psychological and moral variables which have contributed to the condition of recurrent internal conflicts in Africa and beyond. It remains for us to point to the internal structures and institutions as things which can constrain or facilitate leaders and allied elites to engage in acts which make a difference to internal tensions. Here we need to identify the relationship between what we have already discussed and possibilities as well as opportunities arising from structures and institutions.

First, it is important to note that groups, be they political or economic or both, are in contention, and that their contention may be intemperate. (Wriggins 1969) Further, that leaders both in government and in opposition are psychologically somewhat unrestrained in the political and economic sense, for which reason they become tolerant of others. On the basis of mankind's accumulated experience in politics, it is reasonable to assume that one way to maximize freedom is to impose institutional and structural constraints to the power of leaders. This is simply because no cultural checks or strongly internalized normality exist against excesses of leaders. Thus constitutional and political contrivances have to be instituted to restrain leaders.

Looking at Africa generally, what we see is a dire absence of strong checks on the executive leader. Power is strongly concentrated at the centre; one man at the top will normally have the free will to make and unmake anybody in the land. Ministers and Permanent Secretaries at the top; county and sub-county chiefs in the remotest regions; compositions of legislatures at the centre and of simple local councils in the districts; bosses of security organs in the centre; in the regions, chief justices and judges in the judiciary - all are subject to the whims of the central authority. Appointment organs in the civil service, the army and other security agencies in the judiciary and in parastatals - are all easily manipulated by the central authority. There are no checks and balances among various institutions of the state, since institutional autonomy is viewed with suspicion. There are no strong structures mediating between the centre and the periphery. One-party systems are frequently preferred, because the existence of other parties is considered a threat to "national unity" - which in reality means the unity of the central command which regards difference as subversive.

Even more remarkable is that the one-party state, in a vast majority of cases, degenerates into no-party state, and what appears as the one party is a lifeless shell (Wallerstein 1966; Bienen 1970) with no political control, frequently even as a vehicle of central command since the security and administrative agencies are used to circumvent the party. (Mujaju 1976; Gertzel 1970) The party becomes a semblance or an appearance that can be convened to give His Excellency a platform to pronounce, not to consult. Beyond this it is a limbo. (Mujaju 1976)

In short, missing in many of our countries is an element of self-government at the local level ensuring meaningful autonomy. This should be facilitated by greater devolution of powers to the regions in the case of unitary constitutions, or constitutional entrenchments in the case of federal states. Nor are there popular political institutions such as political parties which could mediate between centre and periphery. Even interest groups such as trade unions and professional or occupational associations are viewed askance. (Shivji 1983) Society is a mass of individuals on whom the power of the state descends directly without restraint. (Kornhauser 1960) Even the institutions of government at the centre may lack autonomy since, in some cases, presidents view themselves as ministers of every ministry, and verbal presidential statements are viewed as statutory instructions for immediate application to whom it may concern. In short, governments really talk to themselves, whereas the people are mere objects.

This situation means that any other voice of advice or criticism, any expression of demand or reservation becomes irregular. Society becomes like a volcano in which internal pressure builds up to eruption, because of the structural and institutional arrangements of our states. The mounting pressures operating, in conjunction with what we identified earlier, are ones from which internal conflicts ascend.

4. International Context of Internal Conflict

As already indicated, our principal task in this paper is to probe the international implications of internal conflicts as already defined, and to suggest some remedies or how to avert such conflicts. Clearly, for this, the interconnection between internal crisis and the external situations needs to be properly conceptualized. To this we now turn.

Most of what was said earlier about the fluidity and brittle quality of our political system, to which we applied the terms "amoeba type" and "Bwegege", was meant to show the rather unstable and easily manipulated or exposed form of such politics. Terms such as "dependent", "neo-colonial" and "penetrated" have been used by various scholars to put, with varying degrees of intensity, this quality of our politics into sharp relief. (Galeano 1973; Nkrumah 1965; Rosenou 1969)

Internal coherence means a pervious framework where the insularity of the old polities becomes impossible. Thus, the external element easily intrudes into our politics. Our political systems have faulty roofs where the external storms continue to leak long after the storms have subsided. Entry through the legitimate doors continues to take place, but damage is more possible through the leakages.

Indeed, the situation could hardly be otherwise. Our states were put together by an external force, colonialism, and by the time it departed, the external constituency was so strong that formal independence had to accommodate it. Economically, politically and even militarily, our countries show very clear features of the colonial period. Even underlying assumptions in our scholarship seriously betray the colonial ethos and practices. Many of our leading public servants, the celebrated scholars, the influential statesmen, the forces that shape our economies, our armies many of which have seized power - they bear the clear marks of colonialism.

To make a clear separation between the domestic environment and the external circumstance would be most unrealistic in the circumstances. The contemporary world of which our states are a part is a much smaller world, neatly linked by strongly interlocking economic, political and military forces which find our leaky roofs useful to their goals. Imperialism of various types, so keen to control sea routes, to maintain spheres of influence, is quite at ease with this condition, so it will seek to protect and expand the opportunity. (Nweke 1985; Mazrui 1980)

More important, the global constellation of forces, military-political-ideological, is such that this struggle must intensify particularly in the Third World. Today's multipolar world with its rival ideologies is also a dangerously armed world. The relative balance among powerful countries of the North, with regard to the means of destruction, has been aptly characterized as the balance of terror.

One remarkable aspect of this balance of terror: even though it does not preclude continuation or prolongation of ideological struggles and the flexing of military muscles among the powerful and rich countries, it nonetheless almost rules out any open and direct military clash between East and West in the Northern Hemisphere itself. Or at least, experience to date has shown us that.

Such confrontations, either direct or by proxy, take place instead in far-off lands in Africa, Latin America, the Middle East and Asia. Note the puzzle: those areas of the world where evidence of war, largely internal, is the most dramatic and dangerous are precisely those countries which produce not a single weapon they use. Not even a single bullet or a single gun comes from within!

These are areas which find it very easy to procure military aid for use in internal wars. The testing ground of weapons, particularly conventional weapons which can be used for years without any threat to the supplier, is our own continent. The powerful countries, aware of the consensus among themselves in matters of their mutual security, have engineered the Nuclear Non-Proliferation Treaty; but this affects weapons which few really want to use and which few countries in fact need for internal wars. This treaty they have insisted countries of the Third World should sign - giving the false impression that they are really interested in inter-nation peace and security. But no one excels them in their enthusiasm for handing out either cash or military hardware or both - ostensibly to fight against Communism, as in Latin America; against social imperialism, as the Angola case in the 1970s and 1980s demonstrated; or against international capitalism and USA hegemonism, as the arming of Idi Amin was justified in the 1970s. Not one of them has ever suggested any serious international effort to control or regulate the traffic of arms to the Third World, which trigger-happy governments use with abandon to terrorize their own citizens and ruin the economy.

As Pierre has pointed out (A. Pierre 1982) after having noted that the flow of arms to Africa in the late 1970s was 25 times higher, in constant dollar terms, than a decade earlier, it emerges that such weapons were increasingly originating from the superpowers which had eclipsed Britain and France. They had previously been the traditional supplier of such arms.

Pierre has further noted two other things. First, that initiatives by some Latin American countries in 1974 and 1978 to limit the acquisition of arms from the North for offensive purposes in their region had not received any noticeable backing from the superpowers (p. 284). Secondly and most important of all to us in Africa, Pierre asserts:

> In a world in which the major powers are less likely to intervene with their own armed forces to protect their interests, they are more prone to share up friendly states through the provision of arms or to play out their proxies. As the risk of a direct nuclear confrontation between the great powers forces them to shift their competition to presumably

> safer ground, developments in the Third World are of ever greater import .... Arm sales are instruments of diplomacy as well as security. (Emphasis original) (p. 275)

As a consequence, Pierre notes, that in the case of Africa, the trend has been "towards escalating military expenditures on arms, accounting for more of the GNP on defence than even Latin America". And he could see the trend leading to increasing the potential for armed conflict taking the form of civil wars-jockeying for power particularly among ethnic groups, military coups as a means of transferring power and regional clashes between sovereign states resulting from irredentist claims (p. 255).

In sum, we can state the interconnection between the internal situation of which internal conflict is a predominant aspect, and the external environment shown in the immediately preceding paragraphs, in the following way. Because our political systems are internally incoherent and because aspects of their internal form are projections of the external environment, they are easily manipulated from outside. The external environment is itself also anxious to seize opportunities of various sorts. It is sharply in conflict within itself but also extremely scared of itself. This makes mischief and adventure therein less likely - which is not the case in our context. We thus easily become targets of the external environment. The relationship between the two sides, therefore, is such that the external impinges on our internal situation with a force which breaks through the leaky roofs and uses entry for illegitimate purposes. Internal conflicts in this context can be an opening for others to acquire a foothold. Or they could be a result of an illegitimate entry of the outsider in order to break the backbone of a hitherto strongly fortified nationalistic people.

This kind of conceptualization does not permit us to focus solely on the international implications of internal conflicts. Such would be to direct our concern only to one small aspect of the problem. The point is that internal conflicts have international implications precisely because internal conflict is a product of the interaction between the two domains. And it is precisely for this reason that I have preferred to talk of the international context of these conflicts.

5. Illustrations

In order to demonstrate more concretely the interconnections between the external and the internal, let us cite various instances, some historical, others contemporary.

5.1. Mozambique

Recently in The Guardian a report appeared about the former chief of the Rhodesian Secret Service Organization. Surprisingly, Prime Minister R. Mugabe had had the naivité to continue this person as the boss of the successor body in independent Zimbabwe; and indeed he continued in this role until 1982. In the report in question this General revealed that he and his colleagues under Prime Minister Ian Smith had really recruited what is now the MNR in Mozambique in order to divert the Frelimo Government under President Samora Machel away from active support for the Patriotic Front, particularly Mr. Mugabe's ZANU. ZANU was then launching a serious offensive from the Mozambique side and Ian Smith wanted to inconvenience them by "destabilizing" Mozambique from within.

The General was extraordinarily frank to the extent of saying: "We recruited them, we trained them, we paid them". They really had no programme, no mission: they just wanted money.

From this obscure background, Smith did organize a force of indigenous Mozambiqueans, strong enough to inconvenience Mozambique, while at the same time launching an ugly search-and-destroy terror against the Zimbabwean people, inside Rhodesia. This was one of the conditions which forced Mugabe to enter into negotiations with Smith in the late 1970s.

After Zimbabwean independence, there was no longer any facility for MNR support from Zimbabwe; but, used to foreign money, the MNR were anxious to have another backer, and South Africa has come forth in earnest, pursuing exactly the same objectives for itself as did Smith's Rhodesia. It is now common knowledge that South Africa has invested heavily in the MNR and that the MNR has developed, in the process, into a formidable disruptive force against the Frelimo Government.

The economy of the country, already suffering from the after-effects of a long and bitter liberation war against Portugal, has continued to deteriorate. The consequence was the Nkomati Accord, a form of hood-winking which South Africa duped Zimbabwe into, possibly to embarrass Mozambique and weaken its solidarity with the rest of Africa. (Msabaha and Hartman 1985) It is not surprising that the Nkomati Accord was followed by the bombing of targets inside Mozambique by South Africa and the "accidental" air crash which killed President Samora Machel himself. It is true that the conflict or war in Mozambique is internal, between the Government and its opponent but the money the dissidents use, the logistical support and training they receive, the weapons they use and the objectives for which the offensive is launched cannot be said to be wholly or even mainly internal.

However, it is also necessary to point out that the MNR, bad and misguided as it is, was fundamentally created by an input handling of minority groups which had not been part of Frelimo during the struggle against Portugal. Dizzy with success, after the collapse of Portuguese colonialism, Frelimo leaders descended on their apparently ineffectual opponents, some of whom had been close to the colonial state system, with a rare arrogance and exuberance. Many of them were paraded at jubilant victory rallies as traitors to whom promises of pardon were given, forgetting that public humiliation of this kind sells to very few people. In victory, Frelimo leaders thought that those who appeared weak and defeated had no cards. These cards they have now shown to possess, and the situation is indeed serious.

In short, Frelimo leaders widened the cracks which need not have widened in the internal situation, and the storm of foreign intrusion has turned the leaky roofs into flood channels.

5.2. Nigeria

From the Nigeria of the 1960s is to be found additional proof of the interconnection between the domestic and the external.

The country had three distinct ethnic blocks. The Hausas comprised somewhat over half of the total population of Nigeria, but they were found in the Northern Region. The Hausas, therefore, regionally occupied only one third of the official regions of the country. They happened also to be culturally and religiously different, being Moslems while the other two Regions - the West and East - were mainly Christians. Economically, the North, so barren and semi-desert, was the least productive, a condition further exacerbated by neglect by the British Colonial administration.

The East and the West were the more productive areas, much of them being in the tropical forest zones; moreover, even though the East and the West produced the country's wealth, and had high-level manpower to staff the bureaucracies of the state, politically they were marginal. Democracy had accorded to the majority State - and here the North was also neatly organized- a capacity to dominate national representative organs; this, in a parliamentary democracy, enabled them to control government.

The situation had of course been worsened by British indirect rule which permitted the most minimal forms of horizontal integration among those ethnic communities of the country least endowed with educational resources, culturally and religiously more conservative than the rest. Nonetheless, the North could, by sheer weight of numbers, control the destiny of the country. In a situation such as this, sociology will show that a dominant group with these characteristics will want to exercise power in a trigger-happy way because to lose power is to lose the only means available to compete effectively in the deficient areas with those who are superior. And any census will be rigged to maintain numerical superiority over a strong and threatening minority.

In Nigeria of the 1960s, all these were evident. The state, once under the Hausas, had to remain so while this created nervousness among the disadvantaged. In desperation, a group was organized which was characterized by sectarian excesses, particularly by the Ibo Army officers against others, mainly Hausa leaders. In response, Hausa officers and men as well as rural communities directed their vengeance towards the Ibo, particularly the business elements throughout the country. Hundreds of Ibo were murdered within hours, without the slightest feeling that these were fellow members of the same country. No wonder, from 1966-70, the country was engulfed in a serious civil war in which the Ibo state of Biafra was proclaimed. There can be no doubt that within Nigeria, there were cracks in the polity roof. Internally, the system was incoherent because of a combination of factors such as imbalance in economic development in the country, religious distinctiveness and a tradition of being separate. Those in the control of the state demonstrated an incapacity to establish a reassuring balance of hopes and advantages between the different peoples of Nigeria. To the extent that Nigerians failed to reassure their anxious compatriots, failed to manage their own diversities, and ended up shooting at each other in a gruelling civil war, we can talk of an internal conflict. The war between Biafra and Federal Nigeria was definitely a war between Nigerians but with divergent hopes for the future. It was to all appearances internal.

But indirect rule was not created by Nigerians; further, uneven development between the North and the rest of the country had colonial roots which had become internalized and which gave the impression of being a legacy of Nigeria. To this extent, this denotes both externality and internality.

However, of the greatest importance is the fact that East/-West ambitions endangered the lives of millions of Nigerians. Nigeria is an African giant that could be a prize to any non-African state that gains a foothold on it. Britain was the former colonial power and, consistent with the "sphere of influence" mentality among powerful states, Nigeria was considered to lie within its orbit. After all, it was part of the British Commonwealth. Britain was present in Nigeria and wanted to continue there, if not to strengthen its base.

But Nigeria was also an independent country that had developed relations with other countries such as the Soviet Union, which also wanted to strengthen its roots, if not weaken the roots of its rivals such as Britain. Attention was focused on Nigeria, with the USA somewhat far-off, looking on anxiously to see whether Britain might slacken and give it an opportunity to step in. Countries which believe that Third World countries cannot be independent and can only trade imperialism, cannot do otherwise. They have to keep watching any possible power that might jump in.

So it was when Nigeria found itself faced with internal difficulties. Britain rushed in arms aid to assist the Federal Government, in accordance with tradition. However, such aid become more substantial and long-lasting when also the Soviet Union extended military assistance. The official reason was to save the integrity of a sovereign and independent Nigeria. Yet, beneath all these apparently disinterested gestures lay a sordid military and foreign policy calculation on the part of both countries, to ensure that neither supplanted the other by being seen to have tipped the balance in the civil war in favour of the Federal Government. (Ogumbadojo 1976)

In the process the Federal Government, which might have been willing to reach an accommodation with its dissenting region, was turned into a belligerent because of the overconfidence which Anglo-Soviet assistance gave it. Not to be outmaneuvered by both the Soviet Union and Britain, de Gaulle of France came to assist Biafra. Logistical problems, arising from its actual location, plus the fact that no country had yet recognized the independence of Biafra, made French support both subtle and ineffective. But it gave to Biafra a false feeling of security, a feeling that better days might arrive. The end result was that this external intrusion escalated the level of violence, leading to horrors against the Ibo in Biafra. Nigerians began murdering each other on an unprecedented scale, fuelled by sectarian arms "aid" motivated by national interest.

Thus, the Nigerian civil war was a case where externalities and internalities were combined in near mutual harmony.

5.3. Uganda

The case of Uganda is more well known to us; in an earlier work I have myself gone into our tragedies and our irresponsibilities in some detail. (Mujaju 1987/88) There can be no doubt that our leaders over the past 25 years have failed us; and their failures are, in a great measure, also attributable to us as society.

Ours is a small country, with sharp religious, political and above all ethnic cleavages but at the same time with a large educated middle class ever ready to dwarf the achievements of every leader. Indeed, Uganda is a tragic case that has turned every available opportunity into a cost. We have truly become the Beirut of East Africa. We may note the uneven development between a militarily powerful Northern Region (by virtue of its dominance in the colonial and post-colonial army) but an economically near-impoverished one, and an economically more affluent South, an equally educationally advanced area; the conferring of political power on the North, the weakening of political parties as organs of free popular expression, with too many Kings and royal families in too small a country, coexisting with people with strong republican sympathies. All this has led Uganda to turn itself into a death chamber where successive regimes and their rivals hatch plots for conquest. Indeed it would seem that sometimes this country is gripped by a lynching hysteria.

The arms with which we fight each other are all imported, an externality. The equipment that successive secret service agencies have used to invade the privacy of Uganda's citizens are not made here. The techniques of torture which we have heard so much about are not indigenous to our country. These and others are evidence of strong externalities.

On the other hand, the ineptitude with which regimes handle opponents, frequently turning simple incidents and irritations into crises; their frequent inability to realize that this is the 20th century, when many people demand the right to be different without endangering national interest; their inability to separate regime interests from national interests: all these are internalities. However, there is no doubt that these two reinforce each other, hence the concept of an interaction between them.

5.4. Other African Examples

The further list of cases of internal conflicts which show the inter-connection between internal and external forces is near-endless. Mention could be made of the 1960 Congo crisis when internal complications, themselves a legacy of Belgian colonial rule, plunged the new republic into serious crisis. This necessitated the invited intervention of UN troops which Western countries, led by the USA, used to serve their interests. (Cruise O'Brien 1963) The trouble erupted again in 1964 when, at US instigation, former Katanga successionist premier, Moise Tshombe, was invited by President Kasavubu to head the Congolese Government as Premier - whereupon his internal opponent rebelled against him and set up a regime in Eastern Congo (Stanleyville). OAU efforts to settle the dispute between the two sides, and the arrest of European hostages there by the rebels as a card against Tshombe's advancing troops of white mercenaries, were undermined by massive US arms supplies to Tshombe and the air-lifting of Belgian paratroopers to rescue the hostages. Tshombe, who had earlier shown interest in working with OAU mediation efforts supported by the rebels, felt so secure with these arms that he became uncooperative with OAU peace initiatives. (Carvenka 1977)

The case of Ethiopia is also well known. Ever since 1962, the province of Eritrea has been at war with mainstream Ethiopia, with the hand of external forces clearly in evidence. (Mujaju 1985) Likewise clear is the case of Sudan, where the Arab North, dominantly in control, has been at odds with the Black African (largely Christian) South which started a war of liberation soon after Sudan's independence in 1956. External assistance has come in handy. Although there was a lull in the war between 1971 and the late 1970s, the pendulum has now swung back to armed struggle led by Sudanese leaders hailing from the South, although breaking away from the North is not their stated goal.

In Angola, three liberation armies which had fought against Portugal turned their guns against each other soon after Independence in late 1975. Although the MPLA won the Civil War in 1976, UNITA continues the struggle, backed by South African and US assistance, while Cuba and the Soviet Union continue to be Luanda's main backers. And so the list continues.

6. Implications of Internal Conflict

In the light of the preceding discussions it is not useful to focus on the international implications of internal conflicts. There is a two-way traffic in terms of implications. Internal conflicts definitely have international implications. They excite intervention of anxious powers seeking to control. Internal conflicts exacerbate the fluid internal situation and bring into doubt the future course of our countries. Who will hold sway, which leader or party or army will acquire supremacy, become real issues. For powers anxious to exercise influence and desire to step in and help the preferred party, internal conflict is a bonus.

The real danger of internal conflict for international peace is that it may trigger off competition among powerful states and escalate armament traffic from rival countries towards Third World countries. The illustrations cited above are proof enough of this danger. Internal conflict therefore acts to heighten international tension.

International conflicts are also dangerous because of the refugee crisis, which they worsen. One danger is the human crisis represented by refugee conditions. Statelessness means turning of nationals into homeless people. This further leads to international complications when this flood of rootless people, anxious to find income and stable environments, are pressured into becoming extensions of the underground security networks of rival imperialist countries. In addition to being an abuse of human rights, this is dangerous to the security of their home countries as well as to everybody else. This flood of potential mercenaries at the service of the powerful means constant jeopardy to our states.

Turning specifically to regional implications of international conflict, we note first yet another dimension of the refugee crisis. Whenever a political crisis erupts in an African country, displaced presidents and their political and security aides flee to neighbouring countries. Since no regime is never without some supporters, the domestic constituency of the fleeing leaders, even when the exile leaders mount no offensive from their foreign sanctuary, is always a problem to the new regime; there will always be the suspicion that efforts for restoration are afoot. And so the new regime will look with suspicion at the neighbouring state where its former political luminaries reside.

What makes things worse, however, is that political exiles always want to make a come-back and - either with the express consent of the hosts or without it - some effort at a come-back is always attempted, or at least so it is believed. Nor is this so surprising because refugee conditions are ones of extreme degradation, and no-one should expect his victims either to enjoy them or to be permanently resigned to them. Thus it has been baffling to note the behaviour of post-Amin politicians in Uganda, many of whom had been in exile in the 1970s: their actions made another exile inevitable. This cannot but sour neighbour relations. The new regime, noting internal difficulties in its neighbour's courtyard, may try to foment trouble for the hosts of their rivals - or may simply be suspected of doing so.

The recent (Nov./Dec. 1987) border difficulties between Uganda and Kenya, which brought the two countries to the brink of war and caused so much disruption to the people of the two countries, arose mainly because each side claimed that the other was either harbouring or abating elements intent to subvert the former, following the seizure of power in Uganda by the National Resistance Army.

During the Amin regime from 1971 to 1978, relations between Tanzania and Uganda became tense, largely because former President Obote had been given asylum in Tanzania and was known to be preparing military moves from there. Eventually, Amin did attack Tanzania in 1978, an attack which gave Tanzania and Ugandan exiles there the excuse they needed to answer back and deal a death blow to the Amin regime. (Avergan 1983)

Sometimes the domestic weakness of a regime may force it to take adventurous moves against a suspect neighbour, as a final desperate resort in attempting to acquire internal consolidation by identifying an external enemy. The leaders appeal for nationalism in the arranged hour of crisis, hoping to divert attention. A strong body of opinion in Uganda holds that this was indeed the reason why Amin chose to attack Tanzania when he did. His army was in disarray over many domestic quarrels, not least of which was Amin's handling of the army. Through diverting the army to a foreign war, it is said, he hoped to regain his initiative at home.

The case of Southern African has been cited. South Africa, knowing of Angola's internal difficulties, decided to back UNITA as a way of increasing internal pressure on Angola to disable it from assisting Namibia towards independence. At one time Mobutu's Zaire tried to present a Northern front in a war of destabilization against Angola, and in this effort may well have had some understanding with Savimbi's UNITA which had collaborated with Mobutu's brother-in-law, H. Roberto (Legum 1976; Macoum 1976). Again this was because Mobutu was aware of Angola's continuing difficulties at home.

But Zaire forgot that it too had cracks within its system, and MPLA leaders did not take long to drive this lesson home. In the late 1970s they decided to back Mobutu's opponents in Shaba Province, so as to inconvenience Zaire from the inside. Zaire and Angola were forced to recognize the need for mutual accommodation and a kind of non-aggression pact was signed by then.

The case of the Sudan and Ethiopia is equally instructive. We have already referred to the civil war between Eritrea and other minority nationalities on the one hand and mainstream Ethiopia on the other. Many refugees flee Ethiopia into the Sudan, and Ethiopia has always suspected the Sudan of being too helpful to the opposition. In the process Ethiopia has sought to develop close bonds with Southern Sudanese who are arrayed against the Sudanese Government. It may be of interest to note that Ethiopia, a Christian power in the Horn of Africa, has an additional point of contact with Southern Sudanese who have been fighting against the hegemony of the Moslem-dominated Northern Sudan. In turn Northern Sudan has some religious basis for supporting the Eritrean cause, since Eritrea is predominantly Moslem.

Of course, with the new leadership in Southern Sudan, the Sudanese People Liberation Army, espousing a pan-Sudan cause and trying to transcend the traditional Southern Sudanese ethnic boundary, this array of alliances may change, as current contacts between the two governments tend to suggest. However, the foregoing has been the legacy or a long time.

Finally, we should note that this regional bickering over internal complications does, in the end, have global implications: each conflicting state, in line with historical ties and such others as its security dictates, has a capacity to invoke those ties for its defence, which only deepens the crisis. Thus Angola continues to rely on Cuban forces and Soviet assistance; Zaire continues in the US-Belgian-French camp whose assistance it has utilized whenever it has had internal difficulties. Ethiopia can hardly do much without Soviet support; and the Sudan has gravitated from US/Saudi Arabian support during the final days of Numeri's regime, to Libyan support. There can be no doubt that these internal difficulties are adding to Africa's regional troubles. In the end they neutralize the full exercise of non-aligned status, which is the preferred policy of all African states.

The implications are internal as well. Internal conflicts expose our political system to great pressure, and let others take advantage of our weaknesses. They expose our national independence to great hazards. If we are neo-colonial countries already, internal conflicts can only worsen our condition, since they weaken our resource base to effect meaningful independence. Since internal conflicts are either sponsored or at least financed or subsidized by powerful states and forces outside our environments, this condition of dependence may well be intensified, and real national freedom to choose an independence course may be impaired.

In economic terms, internal conflict worsens the crisis identified in the introduction to this article. The import of more weapons - purchased either with cash procured from sales of commodities in conditions of unfavourable trade, or with aid from powerful sources - diverts useful money into useless things. The productive sectors of our countries are thereby starved of foreign exchange, in favour of internal military adventures. Moreover, internal conflict disturbs the environment for true and constructive efforts, diverting the energies of the people into suicidal, self-defeating preoccupations.

To the extent that internal conflict exposes our states to external manipulation and undermines our independence while worsening our economic situation as already suggested, it clearly disrupts our political stability and development. Heightened tension among groups and communities in our states, intrusion of extraneous interests among the same, the disruption of economic activity and the diversion of valuable economic resources for steady and long-term development - this cannot be a basis for establishing political stability. No country demonstrates the validity of these assertions than Uganda in its 25 years of independence.

7. Conclusion

The underlying contention in this chapter has been that, given the nature of our contemporary state in Africa, internal conflict poses grave risks to our states. It impairs any development efforts and undermines our ability to stand as viable entities. It exposes our affairs to grave external manipulation. Its effects, both global and internal, are far-reaching and depressing. Our discussion about the interconnection between internal and external situations and the illustrations cited should have shown how true our fears are and how justified is our concern.

We cannot conclude without a word about how these internal conflicts may be averted or their effects minimized. In doing so, let us recall that conflicts or disagreements are natural and to be expected. Difference is a fact of life: and disagreements and conflicts arise because of this underlying natural phenomenon. We cannot confront internal conflict by pretending that unanimity and sameness will be achieved or consensus dictated.

We have to start from the point that diversity is natural and legitimate; recognize that it can nevertheless be dangerous, and acquire the skill of managing it so that it can become a useful and constructive resource. Recognizing the legitimacy of diversity, and cultivating a spirit of tolerance for the other side will be one useful step on the road toward domesticate diversity.

Exploring what unites our groups and our parties, what is common among our tribes and our religions - this will certainly move us further in the right direction. Inflation of our differences is most dangerous.

Above all, since internal conflict is related to the goings-on in the external environment, we should view it as weakening our countries in a conflict-ridden world, one in which we fight each other either on behalf of others or in their economic and military interests. To be truly nationalistic and to strive for the interest of our people and countries will be a great asset, because in the process we shall learn to treat each other at home in a manner that maximizes our unity and strengthens our defences against external intrusion and manipulation. When these safeguards are taken, there should be chances of controlling internal conflict. This means talking about the need for a change of attitudes on the part of partialities and leaders to each other, and to acquire tolerance and understanding for the other side. Nor is this in itself enough. There have to be structural arrangements to reduce chances for abuse of trust and office, through constraining power.

Thus, it is necessary to reduce the extraordinarily free hand and unlimited latitude which a great deal of thinking in Africa- the law as well as constitutions - confers to our governments and our armies. We need checks on executive power; we need to insulate individuals and institutions against encroachments by the state. Autonomy of institutions and interest groups (trade unions, the professions, the civil service and the judiciary, etc.) is critical. A measure of self-government through devolution of power at the local level - this too is critical. Such constitutional and institutional constraints to absolutism will facilitate the search for the politics of consensus and banish the politics of dictation, and this then represents the cornerstone of a proper management of diversity. This author is profoundly convinced that the priority issue in our politics today in Africa is to create a sense of national solidarity which can establish a horizontal bond among strata or classes. Without this, every other thing posing as progressive is, in our conditions, seriously at risk.

Within the African continent, there is need to strengthen the institutions for conflict resolution. The African framework for conflict resolution, as it has evolved within the OAU, needs to be strengthened by an increasing acceptance of the idea that African statesmen can help settle conflicts internal to our states. All too frequently, African leaders have been less inclined to accept this, pursuing the principle enshrined in the UN and OAU charter protecting the domestic jurisdiction of states. African leaders will have to recognize that domestic disputes are not at all that "domestic" after all; that, as shown in this chapter, they stand at an intersection point between the internal and external. Therefore, they must be viewed quite early as being both, at least potentially, and leaders must be properly disposed to mediation efforts from within the continent.

In the long run, the OAU may have to move in the direction of a stronger "international" secretariat which, being more permanent and belonging to no particular state, could evolve a cumulative diplomatic competence to do what the OAU Chairman has, over the years, tried to do less ably. There can be no doubt that far too many of our heads of state lack the experience, sometimes even the stature and disposition, to perform a mediation role in the continent. Many simply do not have the time, as they are burdened by recurrent crises at home, while others with a military background may lack the persuasive disposition to handle diplomatic tasks. They do not exercise it in their own countries; they cannot so easily cultivate it abroad. A stronger OAU Secretariat is the most logical solution here. While all this may be too difficult for many leaders to recognize immediately, the disruptive effects of internal conflicts may, sooner or later, make this the only obvious choice.

Finally, we must note that at the global level a serious problem exists with respect to fuelling internal conflicts. Mass propaganda by foreign broadcasts, frequently launching slander campaigns against one side of an internal conflict, is a major feature of contemporary international life. Worst of all is the arming of rival groups with neither the UN nor any other international body expressing concern about the traffic of arms. Not even Amnesty International puts arms high on its agenda as an incentive for human rights abuses. In this connection special attention must be given to instruments of torture. The United Nations, in particular, has had to broaden its concern beyond anxiety about a Third World War, which has been the main focus in disarmament and strategic discussions, to include internal conflict and the arms traffic which is its enabling platform. A mechanism for regulating the flow of arms to the Third World is an absolute must, because no meaningful attempt can now be made to lower the level of international tension as long as internal conflict continues unabated - not in our global circumstances today.

Finally, we must recognize that the phenomenon of internal conflict is a complex one. None of the measures proposed for amelioration can operate magically. A combination of these measures rather than their separate or individual application should produce results, however. It is a problem over which internal political management, institution-building and constitutional engineering within individual states must receive the supplement of OAU and UN assistance, with all levels recognizing that they have a common long-term stake.

References

Aron, R.: On War. New York: Doubleday, 1959.

Avergan, T. et al.: War in Uganda. Dar es Salaam: T.P.H., 1983.

Ake, C.: A Theory of Political Integration. Homewood, Ill.: Dorsey Press, 1967.

Bassiouni, M.C.: International Terrorism and Political Crimes. Springfield, Ill.: Charles C. Thomas, 1975.

Bienen, H.: Tanzania: Party Transformation and Economic Development. Princeton: Princeton University Press, 1970.

Blishcheriko, Z.: Terrorism and International Law. Moscow: Progress Publishers, 1984.

Buchan, A.: War in Modern Society. New York: Harper-Row, 1968.

Carvenka, Z.: The Unfulfilled Quest for Unity. New York: Africana, 1977.

Cruise O'Brien, C.: To Katanga and Back. A UN Case History. New York: Simon & Schuster, 1963.

Decalo, S.: Coups and Army Rule in Africa. Studies in Military Style. London: Yale University Press, 1976.

Eastern African Social Science Journal, vol. II, no. 2, 1986. (Articles by Campbell, Mujaju and Rehmato.)

Galeano, E.: Open Veins of Latin America. New York: Monthly Review Press, 1973.

Gertzel, C.: The Politics of Independent Kenya. Nairobi: E.A.P.H., 1970.

Gingyera-Pinycwa, A.G.: Milton Obote and his Times. New York: NOK, 1978.

Gromyko, A. (ed.): African Countries' Foreign Policy. Moscow: Progress Publishers, 1981.

Hartman J. & Msabaha, I.: "Tanzania after the Nkomati Accord", in Mawazo, vol. 6, no. 1, 1985.

Ibingira, G.: The Forging of an African Nation. New York: Viking, UPH, 1973.

Jørgensen, J.: Uganda: A Modern History. London: Croom Helm, 1981.

Kiapi, A.: Civil Service Laws in East Africa. Kampala: E.A.L.B., 1974.

Kornhauser, W.: Politics of Mass Society. London: Routledge & Paul, 1960.

Legum, C.: "International Development in Nigeria, 1966-1970", in Tandon (ed.): Horizons of African Diplomacy. Kampala: East African Literature Bureau, 1974.

Legum, C.: "The Soviet Union, China and the West, in Southern Africa", in Foreign Affairs, vol. 54, no. 4, 1976.

Littwin, L.: "The Cuban Missile Crisis of 1962", in W.G. Andrews: The Politics of International Crisis, Van Nostran, 1970.

Macoum, J.: "Lessons of Angola", in Foreign Affairs, vol. 54, no. 3, 1976.

Mazrui, A.: The African Condition. London: Heinemann, 1980

Mujaju, A.B.: The UPC as a Party of Government in Uganda", in Canadian Journal of African Studies, vol. 10, no. 3, 1976.

Mujaju, A.B.: "External Intervention and Domestic Instability in Uganda, 1964-71", in Journal of Eastern African Research and Development, vol. 8, 1978.

Mujaju, A.B.: "Reflections on Africa's Interests in Eritrea", in Mawazo, vol. 6, no. 2, 1985, pp. 30-41.

Mujaju, A.B.: Consensus and the Party System in Uganda. Kampala: Orbitas Publishers, 1986.

Mujaju, A.B.: "Regional Cooperation and the Southern African Crisis", in Eastern African Social Science Journal, vol. 2, no. 2, 1986.

Mujaju, A.B.: "The Conquest Syndrome and Constitutional Development in Uganda", in Uganda Journal, vol. 42, 1987/88.

Nkrumah, K.: Neocolonialism. London: Nelson, 1965.

Nweke, A.G.: African Security in the Nuclear Age. Enugu, Nigeria: Fourth Dimension, 1985.

Ocaya-Lakidi: "From Local Government to More Local Administration, 1949-72", in Uzoige, G.N. (ed.): Uganda: Dilemma of Nationhood. New York: NOK, 1982, pp. 299-312.

Ogumbadojo, O.: "Nigeria and the Great Powers: The Impact of Civil War on Nigerian Foreign Policy", in African Affairs, vol. 75, no. 298, 1976, pp. 14-32.

Pierre, A.J.: The Global Politics of Arms Sale. Princeton: Princeton University Press, 1982.

Riker, W.H.: The Theory of Political Coalition. New Haven: Yale University Press, 1962.

Rosenou, J.: International Politics and Foreign Policy. New York: The Free Press, 1969.

Rustow, D.A.: World of Nations. Washington: Brookings Institution, 1967.

Semakula, K.: A History of Buganda. London: Longman, 1971.

Semakula, K.: Amin and the Tragedy of Uganda. London: Weltforum Verlag, 1979.

Shivji, I.: "Working Class Struggles and Organization in Tanzania", in Mawazo, vol. 5, no. 21, 1983, pp. 3-24.

Walter, E.V.: Terror and Resistance. A Study of Political Violence. New York: Oxford University Press, 1969.

Wallerstein, I.: "The Decline of the Party in One Party State", in Lapalombara (ed.): Political Parties and Political Development. Princeton: Princeton University Press, 1966.

Wallerstein, I.: Africa and the Modern World. Trenton, NJ: Africa World Press, 1986.

Wandira, A.: "Opening Address", in Nsibambi, A. & Wangusa (eds.): Regional Cooperation for African Development. Kampala: PWPA, 1987.

Wilson, R.W.: "Moral Development and Political Change", in World Politics, vol. 36, no. 1, 1983.

Wriggin, H.: The Rulers Imperative. New York: Columbia University Press, 1969.

Oliver Furley

Britain from Uganda to Museveni: Blind Eye Diplomacy

1. Introduction

The period 1971 to 1987 has seen some extraordinary changes of fortune in Uganda's history. It has seen almost as many changes in Britain's policy towards successive Ugandan regimes. The relationship has blown hot or cold, according to pressures from various factors. It is sometimes difficult to avoid the conclusion that British policy has been guided purely by pragmatism.

In this study, however, an attempt is made to analyze some of these factors relevant to British attitudes, in the government, the press, industry and the general public. Basically, Britain wished her former possessions in the Empire to succeed, and to become models of successfully reconstructed states, with sound democratic institutions and viable economies. Along with this went a distinct preference for those states which clung to a broadly Western alignment, especially in Africa where there was competition with Eastern bloc countries for winning over new friends. There was also some concern for the growing Arab influence south of the Sahara, especially from Col. Gaddafi in Libya. If Britain's former possessions could remain members of the Commonwealth, so much the better: this was a tie based on history and traditions which also promoted some mutual scientific, technical and cultural benefits: it might include political and military benefits as well. Secondly, the continuation of trade links was a major consideration. Whether it was called neo-colonialism or part of dependency theory is not part of this discussion: but undoubtedly British exporters were keen to preserve and develop the trading relationship with Uganda, while Uganda on her part, with much of her infrastructure built and equipped with British materials and goods, did not necessarily seek to diminish such links. A third basic factor which applied especially to Uganda was the general fund of goodwill in Britain towards what had been regarded as a model protectorate and the "Pearl of Africa". In some other former possessions, where the decolonization process had been violent and stormy, the British press and the public were ready to believe that independence had brought troubles and upheavals. Not so regarding Uganda, where the process had been comparatively smooth, and the political crises of Obote's first presidency did not have the impact in Britain that might otherwise be expected. There was a timelag when it came to public absorption of catastrophes or crises in Uganda, and this partly explains the slow reaction in Britain to subsequent events. Hence even quite late in the Amin period, the appearance of articles in the British press headlined "What has Happened to the Pearl of Africa?"

Another factor guiding British policy was the notion that the legitimacy of any particular regime in her former possessions- whether democratically elected, or installed by a coup or by war - was not a question for Britain to judge. Thus Britain has recognized many de facto governments in Africa, usually with the minimum of delay once it was ascertained that the new regime was established. The idea was to maintain a permanent relationship whenever possible, since breaking off relations would damage the people and the country as a whole (as well, of course, as damaging all the British aid schemes and British trade).

2. Enter Amin

At the time of Amin's military coup in January 1971, Britain had reason to welcome a change from the government of Milton Obote. His "Move to the Left" included plans to nationalize British banks and firms in Uganda, and also might induce many Asian traders with British passports to sell up and seek refuge in Britain. It looked as if Obote was turning to Socialist and Communist support instead of to the West. Furthermore, the Heath government was getting a great deal of criticism for selling arms to South Africa, and foremost among Heath's African critics was Milton Obote. At the coming conference of Commonwealth leaders in Singapore, it was a certainty that Obote would be a sharp thorn in the flesh of Britain. While Obote was at the conference, the coup took place, and there have been many suggestions that it took place with the connivance not only of Israel but of Britain also.[1] Britain was the first country to recognize Amin's government, and the British press spoke favourably of the apparently almost bloodless coup, at first. Amin's obvious lack of education, his love of showmanship, his self-awarded decorations and his claim to be "conqueror of the British

Empire" caused the British public to see him in an amiable light as a clown and figure of fun: hence the long-running series about him in Punch, and the many cartoons in British newspapers.

Britain, standing at a distance, had none of the reservations which Nyerere of Tanzania, for example, had about Amin usurping a duly-elected government by force. Amin was clearly the de facto ruler, and Britain was therefore prepared to support him for the sake of continuity in aid and trade. Throughout 1971, Britain remained Uganda's chief trading partner. Two factors caused Britain reluctantly to realize that the situation in Uganda was not and could not be "back to normal". First, the news filtered through of Amin's wholesale murder of Acholi and Langi army officers and men, in several well-known episodes.[2] The realization soon dawned that underneath Amin's clowning there was a ruthless tyrant, capable of genocide. The murders soon spread to the civilian population as well. Amin had no cash to buy arms in Britain or Israel, so he then executed a volte-face by securing help from Libya's Ghadaffi instead. The expulsion of the Israelis quickly followed, in March 1972. Uganda under Arab influence made the British pause to reflect. The second main factor soon followed: in August Amin announced that he had had a dream in which God instructed him to expel the 50,000 Asians in Uganda, within 90 days. Of these, some 30,000 had British passports, so Britain was now faced, on what appeared to be the whim of a madman, with the prospect of an influx of this number into Britain. In actual fact also Asians who held Ugandan citizenship were expelled as well. The British High Commissioner tried to process the papers of the would-be immigrants in the normal way, but it soon became clear that this would never clear the queue by the November deadline, and deaths might ensue. Reluctantly, Britain had to set up camps for Ugandan Asian refugees in Britain, and process them there.[3] In their flight from Uganda, the Asians suffered from severe looting and pillage by Amin's soldiers. Although the expulsion was popular among many Ugandans, and indeed earned praise from some other African leaders, Britain was on the receiving end, unconsulted and shocked; and the results of Amin's arbitrary rule could be seen at first hand by the public. The government halted all aid to Uganda, including a £10 million loan to support the cotton export industry, and both Britain and Israel imposed an economic embargo on Uganda. Amin recalled his High Commissioner from London. In January 1973 Amin threatened to expel all Britons from the country; British tea estates and many firms were taken over, and it was clear that the 84 wholly British-owned firms in

Uganda were in danger. Assets of British firms worth some £30 million were seized. Guerrilla activity against Amin had begun, in which Museveni's Front for National Salvation (FROKASA) was prominent, and Amin accused Britain and Israel of supporting it and supplying arms to it.[4]

The honeymoon period for Amin's relations with Britain was clearly over, and the British were further shocked by press reports of the murders of the Ugandan Chief Justice, Benedicto Biwanuka, the Vice-Chancellor of Makerere University, Frank Kalimozo, and the public executions of captured guerrillas. Britain recalled its High Commissioner, M.K. Slater, and announced he would be replaced for the time being, representation being left only at the acting High Commissioner level. The British community in Uganda, battered by Amin's increasingly hostile verbal attacks on them, took this cue and left the country in large numbers - at least 6,000 of the 7,000 there had left by March 1974.[5]

Other countries quickly stepped in to fill the gaps left by Britain. The United States became Uganda's chief trading partner; Libya supplied financial aid and banking; while in 1974 and 1975 the Communist countries, anxious to gain a foothold in East Africa, supplied training for several hundred Ugandan army and air force recruits in the USSR and Eastern Europe, as well as Soviet Mig fighters, ground-to-air missiles, and armoured personnel carriers. British trade did continue and some Britons still stayed on in Uganda, but relations between the two countries remained strained. Two events made them worse: in June 1975 Amin threatened to execute a British subject, Dennis Hills, a lecturer and author. Amin clearly relished the situation where he could browbeat the British Foreign Office. Britain sent a delegation to plead Hills' case, in General Sir Chandos Blair and Major Grahene, but this approach proved ineffective. Amin then sent his ludicrous telegram to the Queen, half jocular and friendly - "I personally will never forget you as my former C in C" - and half threatening, demanding that unless the Foreign Secretary, James Callaghan, came to Uganda himself within the next ten days, the sentence of death by firing squad on Hills would be carried out.[6] In this humiliating situation, Callaghan had to fly out, and secured Hills' pardon. The following year when the Israelis rescued the hijacked airliner passengers at Entebbe, one of them, Dora Bloch, who held dual British-Israeli citizenship, was in hospital in Kampala; but no such rescue operation could save her, and she was killed by Amin's men in an act of revenge for the

Entebbe raid. Subsequently Britain broke off relations with Uganda completely, for the first time (28 July 1976).

Then followed the final period in Britain's relations with the Amin regime, when British officialdom became more and more critical of Amin as yet more crimes and atrocities were revealed; nevertheless British firms incurred widespread criticism for continuing to supply the regime, the government being likewise criticized for allowing it. The murder of Archbishop Luwum caused a great outcry in the British press, and in Parliament it was made plain that Amin could not be a visitor to Britain for the Commonwealth Conference in June 1977. In a debate in the House of Lords, the Minister of State for Foreign and Commonwealth Affairs, Lord Goronwy-Roberts, fended off questions that Uganda be suspended from the Commonwealth, and pointed to the dilemma that Britain had to consider "how best to sustain and help the people of Uganda as a whole".[7] Britain wished to issue moral condemnation of Amin, not to penalize Uganda as a country by suspension or exclusion from organizations which could help in the future. The Foreign Minister, David Owen, criticized the decision of the UN Human Rights Commission to reject Britain's proposal that the Commission should investigate human rights in Uganda, particularly the death of Archbishop Luwum. At this time exiled Ugandans formed the Uganda Group for Human Rights in London. The remaining 500 or so Britons in Uganda were advised to leave.

It was the United States, not Britain, who cut off trade with Uganda, after Amin harassed and threatened US citizens in Uganda, in July 1978. That autumn the London-based group, Amnesty International, published its report, Human Rights Violations in Uganda, which was endorsed by the Ugandan Human Rights Committee in Britain, with the plea that "we urge this and other governments to cut off all trade with General Amin because this can create the conditions in which Ugandans themselves can remove the regime"[8] - a crucial point apparently ignored by the British government. Moral condemnation was not enough - the British press in 1977-79 was full of accounts of atrocities - but various types of trade were allowed to continue, along with the activities of British banks.

The most notorious form this took was the so-called "whisky run", regular flights of a Boeing 707 or a C-130 cargo plane from Stansted airfield in England to Entebbe. With US pilots, these twice-weekly flights were loaded with luxury goods from British suppliers. In June 1977 Judith Hart, Minister of Overseas Development, had ordered that the supply be stopped for all goods for Uganda which could be described as potentially of a military nature - Landrovers, radios, spare parts, etc. But other goods could still be flown out - apparently as this would help the people of Uganda rather than Amin's military activities. In fact, this supply line bolstered Amin's regime by keeping up the morale of his Army, as Henry Kyemba has pointed out:

> Few people appreciate the importance to Amin of the so-called "whisky run" ... These flights, each said to carry goods to the value of $70,000, keep Amin supplied with the equipment and commodities necessary to maintain his regime. None of the goods reach the ordinary people of Uganda. The imports, which go directly to the Army shops, are intended for one thing only - to keep Amin's thugs happy. ... As long as the "whisky runs" continue, Britain's denunciation of Amin seems, at the very least, hollow.[9]

The flow of cameras, TV sets, clothes, shoes, car accessories, cassettes, cigarettes and of course whisky and other spirits went on. In February 1979, when Tanzanian forces were at the Ugandan border and invasion was imminent, Britain's lavish exports of Scotch whisky were attacked in the House of Lords, but Baroness Stedman, for the government, replied that "we need to keep trade lines open for other things". The previous year, British exports to Uganda had totalled £19.4 million, of which £300,000 in alcoholic beverages.[10] Early the following month - March 1979- the whisky run was finally stopped, when the Tanzanian invasion was under way.

This did not constitute the full story of British support for Amin, however. When the Tanzanians reached Kampala, documents in the State Research Centre revealed that several British firms had been supplying radios and other equipment vital to the very epicentre of Amin's tyranny, the secret police and other henchmen of the regime. In a highly critical article, the New Scientist revealed that radio-telephone equipment was first supplied in 1975, even though Amin's murders and massacres were then already well known in Britain. Landrovers with radio detection devices were sent, "to detect television license dodgers", according to Prime Minister James Callaghan. The Liberal leader David Steel demanded a Department of Trade enquiry, but this was not done. After Amin fell out with one British firm, Pye Telecommunications of Cambridge stepped in in 1977, with radio-telephone systems which they said they understood were sold to the police and the electricity board, but in fact were used by the State

Research Centre. Various equipment was supplied by them right up to 1979, and Pye have endeavoured to justify their exports by explaining that they traded through a third party, a Nairobi-based firm, and in such cases they were "not always aware of the end-user application". Neither were the Board of Trade fussy in the matter, for the firm was not constrained by export controls.[11] Other British firms, such as Security Systems International Ltd., supplied equipment to Amin's forces - night vision cameras, telephone tapping devices, etc.

3. Righting the Wrongs: Instant Recognition

As Tanzanian forces completed the occupation of Uganda and drove out Amin's forces, the British press was filled with revelations of the horrors of the Amin regime. The public had indeed not been short of such information before, but they now were left in no doubt that Ugandans had suffered appallingly. The British government, which must have been aware that its record in opposing Amin was feeble, was now doubly anxious to appear supportive to a peaceful settlement that would give Ugandans a new chance. Thus when the Uganda National Liberation Front (UNLF) chose Yusufu Lule as the new President of Uganda, Britain gave immediate diplomatic recognition and sent out Richard Posnett to be in charge of the High Commission. With the help of a soldier he broke the locks on the doors which had been closed since 1976.

No doubt the government felt reassured by the fact that Lule declared himself a "non-political" leader, an ex-academic who had in fact been a minister under the British for seven years before Independence. Lule could be expected to turn very much to Britain for support, and this was to be freely given: experts in overseas aid were soon organized. Uganda's Minister of Finance visited Britain for talks, and as a result Britain and other Commonwealth countries sent an eight-man team of economic experts to Uganda, led by Prof. Dudley Seers of Sussex University, to carry out an appraisal of the Ugandan economy.[12] Regular air services between Britain and Uganda recommenced at the same time, with cargo flights.

However, Lule was soon ousted because of political infighting, in favour of a lawyer, Godfrey Binaisa. This posed a problem for Britain as it was uncertain whether Binaisa was merely a "front man" to prepare for the return of Milton Obote, still waiting in the wings in Tanzania. Britain's attitude towards his return and possible resumption of power was bound to be ambivalent, as Whitehall had greeted his previous downfall with some glee. The British government avoided the issue of recognizing Binaisa's government by the argument that it was "not clear whether the need arises for recognition".[13] Meanwhile Britain gave training to members of Uganda's new Police Force, in what was intended to be a pivotal role. Nearly 30 senior officers came to Britain for a crash course, with the object of returning to administer similar courses. Britain also provided police vehicles and uniforms: "the British view is that help in rebuilding the Ugandan police force is far more valuable than the usual areas into which aid is poured in third world countries", it was stated.[14] Certainly Britain was ultra-cautious about aid at this juncture: Binaisa said Uganda needed £50 to £100 million, but all that he had received so far was £3 million, two thirds of it from Britain.[15] He also invited the British trading group, Mitchell Cotts, to return and revive Uganda's tea industry. With its subsidiary, the Uganda Company, this was one of the firms seized by Amin in 1973, with assets worth £7 million. Other British firms sent representatives to discuss the resumption of their former industries and businesses.[16]

A set-back came with the murder of a British professor at Makerere, by one of the many gangs who sought to discredit Binaisa's regime. A spokesman for the British High Commission in Uganda said that under no circumstances would it recommend anyone to come to Kampala to live, in view of the widespread random violence. The six British technical assistants which Uganda had requested in the health service were advised not to go; and although Dudley Seer's Commonwealth economists' team and the IMF recognized the need for a massive aid programme, aid donors hung back in view of the violence and apparent anarchy in the country. Britain supplied £4 million of aid mainly for the cotton crop, but Binaisa complained that aid donors so far had given Uganda "mere chicken-feed". In reply the British said that despite Uganda's great needs, few specific proposals for aid had come through, and better planning was needed.[17] Binaisa's suggestion for a Commonwealth peace-keeping force now that half the Tanzanian troops were pulling out of Uganda was not met with enthusiasm in London - or anywhere else.

When Binaisa, like Lule before him, was ousted as President, Britain halted the £4 million aid programme, and waited to see if the Military Commission, now in power, could bring any stability. British ministers and aides were reported as "still reeling from the exposure of the involvement of British companies, some of them highly reputable and world famous, in the corruption of the Binaisa Government".[18] More to the point, Britain was apprehensive now about the imminent return to Uganda of Milton Obote. Binaisa had already planned elections for the country, and these would soon take place; it was a possibility that Obote would win and be returned to power with his party, the Uganda People's Congress (UPC). Certainly, the first signs were that Obote had no great liking for Britain. In a speech in May he blamed Britain and Israel for supporting Amin; and when he held his first public rally in Kampala, he invited only Eastern bloc diplomats, plus the Chinese and North Koreans, in what was seen as a deliberate snub to the West.[19] In the hasty preparations for the elections, however, Uganda asked Britain for £750,000 to help finance them, and made heavy demands on other Commonwealth countries. According to Western diplomats in Kampala, the British Foreign Office was in a dilemma over this. It would like to see elections take place: there was a belief that Obote would lose, and that if the election took place fairly, the Democratic Party (DP) under Paul Ssemogerere would win - but who could tell whether the Military Commission, with strong Obote supporters in it, including the chairman, Paul Muwanga, would allow this?[20] Muwanga went on a visit to Cuba, and there were rumours of a Cuban presence for the election. Britain's right-wing Daily Telegraph took fright:

> It now seems clear that if the West does not take some action to ensure a fair Ugandan election, yet another portion of former British Africa will be lost to the influences of the Eastern bloc. Kenya will stand alone as last bastion of Western influence.[21]

The quotation neatly encapsulates some of the regular stances taken by the British press: the residual proprietary attitude towards former colonies; and the instinctive reaction to transfer cold war East-West rivalries to the African continent, however inappropriate.

Britain did in fact contribute one third of the cost of the elections, and sent the ballot boxes and ballot papers; she also sent officials in the nine-nation Commonwealth team, who were asked by Uganda to observe the elections and deliver a judgement of whether they were free and fair. The elections, held in December 1980, were judged by the Commonwealth team to have been valid; but the team actually considered the task hopeless and left before the final results had been declared. Obote and the UPC were declared to have won, but the DP considered themselves cheated of victory, and few believed that the elections had been free and fair; on the contrary, they were seen as blatantly rigged. Certainly the British press were sceptical, and clearly did not relish the return to power of Obote: the Observer headlined "Obote's Hollow Victory",[22] while the new Uganda government began its first day in office with a fierce attack on the Western press for its reporting of the elections.[23] Nevertheless, Britain and the other countries of the Commonwealth observer team established diplomatic relations with the new government, following the principle of recognition of a de facto government even if its legitimacy was in doubt.

4. The "New" Obote

There followed a four-year period in which Britain, at first wary of giving much support to Obote, gradually came to regard him as a changed man from his socialist days, and gave various forms of aid and training, until at last the anarchic and oppressive character of the regime came to be realized. This realization came far too late in many critics' eyes, and even when Whitehall knew the full extent of Uganda's appalling human rights record, the "time-lag" referred to earlier was evident, and change of policy was finally forced on Britain by events.

Prime Minister Mrs. Thatcher and Foreign Secretary Lord Carrington sent a message of good wishes to Dr. Obote on his installation as President, and learned that he now wished to court the West in his search for aid. This came with a public pledge to relegate socialist ideology in favour of a mixed economy; very soon it was followed with an appeal to Britain for help in training the newly-formed Uganda Army. Mr. Richard Luce, Parliamentary Under-Secretary at the Foreign Office, visited Obote in Uganda; and in talks which were described as cordial, the request was repeated for military assistance to train the newly-recruited army.[24] A highly significant appointment was made at this time by Obote, in his new High Commissioner in London: Shafiq Arain was the only Ugandan Asian in Obote's cabinet, and he played an important part in developing good relations between the two countries.

Britain was active in various aid programmes, sending a British team to reconstruct Kampala's water supply with a £5 million project met by the European Development Fund, encouraging the European Communities to aid Uganda, and sponsoring, with the World Bank, a meeting of aid donors in Paris.[25] Amid mounting reports of violence and anarchy as the Ugandan Army constantly ran amok, Britain persevered with a programme to help re-build and train Uganda's police force. Sixty-three Landrovers were sent, £800,000 was granted to rebuild police barracks, and Ugandan officers received training in Britain. It is noteworthy that Canada also sent a team of Royal Canadian Mounted Police to help train the Ugandan police - but they soon left, whether from disillusion with the general state of lawlessness, or for other reasons. The wry comment in Kampala was that "the Mounties always get his plane".[26]

They were not the only ones who left. Binaisa, like Lule before him, fled to London, and in the course of the year several British journalists were deported for reporting on the violence and rapaciousness of the undisciplined and uncontrolled army. The British press was full of atrocity stories, yet it was now that the government responded to Uganda's request for a Commonwealth military training team to try to remedy the situation. A British Army major and a sergeant were sent, to report back to the Commonwealth Secretariat, in November 1981. This was at a time when the National Resistance Movement, headed by Lule in London but commanded by Yoweri Museveni in the field, was already making headway and receiving much popular support, especially in the south-west of Uganda. By contrast to the Uganda Army, the guerrillas of this National Resistance Army (NRA) seemed well disciplined and careful to respect the lives and property of civilians. The Observer suggested: "Britain and other Commonwealth countries would certainly hesitate to send troops to train an Army set to crush a popular rebellion sparked by its own brutality."[27]

On the other hand, Obote was winning international approval for his efforts on the economic front. The economic package of the previous year, drawn up in consultation with the IMF, was yielding results. In a gesture of confidence on this score, Britain and West Germany wiped out Uganda's debts, the EC increased its aid, and the IMF granted c. £90 million in aid. In military matters, Tanzania was of course still providing massive military support through her troops still in Uganda, and they helped train the army, as did Kenya and Sudan, according to Peter Otai, Minister of Defence. The United States also offered eight places for military training, which were accepted.[28]

It is therefore not too surprising that the Commonwealth countries at this stage took the view that an effort should be made. The alternatives were to do nothing, or to back a guerrilla movement. A 36-man Commonwealth military training team was sent, with a British commander, Colonel Clavering. They were to be based at the barracks in Jinja, 50 miles from Kampala. Second in command was Major Wilfred Kanu of Sierra Leone, and the rest of the team came from Britain, Canada, Australia, Jamaica, Guyana, Kenya and Tanzania. This was not the only British involvement in military training for Obote's forces: through this period there was also a thread traceable of the involvement of private British firms. For much security work, Obote used a paramilitary unit called the Special Force, trained by a three-man team from Falcon Star, a private British concern composed partly of ex-SAS men. Meanwhile the Commonwealth team held its first passing out parade in June 1982, when 16 officers and 72 NCOs completed their training and became instructors themselves. This was the idea: to train these who would train the rest. But of course, with the increasing size of the army, recruited in random fashion with little or no regulation, this was only a drop in the ocean, and it is doubtful if it made any difference to the discipline or behaviour of the soldiers. In April, Amnesty International issued a report on Uganda which spoke of "widespread tortures and killings" by the army. The Times, in a leader headed "Uganda's Deepening Anarchy", referred to this and to some reports that said life was now more dangerous to the average Ugandan than it had been under General Amin. It was held that repression in those days had usually been confined to circles known to be hostile to the regime, whereas now the violence was largely anarchic and criminal rather than political. "If so, the task of the Commonwealth training mission - disciplining the army - is all the more pressing and urgent", said the Times. Obote was not a leader capable of unifying the nation, it said, "yet it is not at all certain that anyone else could do it better". Therefore British aid and training should continue.[29] The British case indeed frequently rested on the argument that no-one else could do it better. Lule, waiting in London as leader of the NRM, contested this in a forceful letter to the Times, pointing out that resistance to the Obote regime was based on the fact that the 1980 election had been rigged, and the army was composed of Langi and Acholi men from the North who oppressed the rest of Ugandans. "Imposing discipline on such an army will merely serve to make it a more efficient instrument of Obote's repression and entrench still further his dictatorship." It was not for Britain to judge whether anyone else could do better.[30]

It is doubtful if any increase in efficiency was achieved, however. A local observer remarked: "Battalion commanders don't know where units are, who's in charge of companies, how many are in a unit. The army is not paid, not fed, sets up roadblocks as a matter of course just to extract money, raids and loots villages. In such a state of anarchy, anything could happen."[31] The Commonwealth team extended its mission several times at six-monthly intervals; but when Malcolm Rifkind, the new Minister of State for African Affairs, visited Uganda in July 1983, the world was becoming aware of the army's scorched earth policy in the notorious Luwero Triangle, not far north of Kampala. Rifkind joined the Canadian and Australian High Commissioners in voicing concern about violations of human rights in the area.[32] At the end of the year came the violent expulsion of tens of thousands of people of Rwandese origin living in western Uganda, and the unexplained massacre of some 30 Ugandans, many of them children, at Muduuma near Kampala. The Archbishop of Cantebury, Dr. Runcie, visiting Uganda for the installation of the new archbishop, certainly had cause to add to his prepared text in the Cathedral the words, "We must reverse the springs of violence which have beset this country ... In these dark years you have suffered the violation of every human right."[33]

Significantly, the Commonwealth states pulled out their men in the military training team soon afterwards, in March 1984, in the face of the deteriorating situation. Britain, however, who by now was supplying half the team, did not pull out but went on alone. The British policy of support for Obote continued, and a new aid package of £9 million was announced. This was after Mr. Timothy Raison, Overseas Development Minister, had visited Uganda and was evidently satisfied that the Muduuma massacre had been carried out by gangs with a "political" aim of discrediting Obote's government.[34] There was also the fear that if Britain did not take over the military training, North Koreans, already in Uganda training troops, would fill the gap.[35] There was indeed some truth in the notion that some of the acts of violence were to discredit the regime; the author was in Kampala at the time the British military training contract was announced, and several houses of the British High Commission were burgled at once, in what seemed a planned political gesture. The extraordinary fact is that while Whitehall continued to support Obote's admittedly fairly successful efforts to revive the economy, it turned a blind eye to other aspects of his regime, particularly his apparent total inability to control the army.

The turning-point for this regime was the massacre at Namugongo. In May 1984 guerrillas - probably the NRA who were now very strong - attacked the ground satellite station at nearby

Mpoma. The Uganda Army arrived quickly, and alleged that some of the guerrillas were hiding in the Namugongo Anglican Theological College and Seminary. The army followed its usual practice of destruction, killing and beating all those it could find in the college and surrounding area; estimates of those killed ranged from 75 to 300. This news could not be suppressed, and there was widespread international condemnation of such methods. In particular, the US Assistant Secretary for Human Rights, Elliott Abrams, described the situation in Uganda as "horrendous". He claimed that between 100,000 and 200,000 people had died in the Luwero Triangle since Obote had taken office, and declared that the army's policy of terror recalled the regime of Idi Amin. Mr. Allen Davis, the US Ambassador in Kampala, said the human rights situation under Amin had actually been better than the present one. Uganda thereupon cancelled the training scheme for Ugandan officers in the United States. West Germany, Denmark and the Netherlands also condemned the killings.

Significantly, Britain did not agree with the US version, and the government held back its criticism. If Britain withdrew its presence and support in protest, it was well known that Soviet and North Korean advisers were there in plenty, ready to step into any vacuum left by Western influence. Even Cuban media experts had been called in, "to help improve Uganda's image". If by any chance Kenya should fall to a military coup and turn to the Eastern bloc, Uganda would take over as the pivot of Western strategy in East Africa, with the Sudan and Somalia being the only other pro-western countries in the region. As one observer noted: "The international community is lending support to Uganda because of its strategic significance, but it is ignoring a state of internal chaos that amounts to disaster for most of its citizens. This policy is misguided and unproductive. Rehabilitation cannot go hand in hand with repression."[36]

Strategic considerations certainly weighed with the British government, but another factor was Britain's apparent disbelief in the claims that Abrams made. The Foreign Office announced in August that it was seeking an urgent assessment of the situation following the US report, but it was cautious: "We are aware of the reports but we have no evidence to substantiate them." The Times was also unconvinced, and said of the US Ambassador's remark that the situation had been worse under Amin, "That must be untrue ... all that can be said is that Obote is better than Amin, but that though this distinction is worth making, its relevance decreases with every passing day and every passing massacre."[37] Whitehall regarded the estimate of 100,000 dead as month that the agreement with Uganda was signed to formalize arrangements for the 12-man military training team. British industry had no intention of pulling out either. At this time the first British trade mission to Uganda since Amin's time announced it was flying out in November, and the London Chamber of Commerce said they had received no advice from the High Commission or the Foreign Office to make them change their plans. The firms represented covered a wide range, including Sir Alfred McAlpine, Kenwood, GEC Street Lighting Ltd., Mott, Hay and Anderson, transport consultants, and VAC from Unilever. Other areas represented included fire-fighting equipment, lighting for buses and trains, mining and quarrying equipment, educational equipment, etc.[39] Britain at first considered the best way of responding was actually to accelerate the military training programme, and to reinforce the effort by sending a team of police officers, "as part of the plan to try to allocate more security work to the police rather than the army, particularly at roadblocks".[39]

Meanwhile the dispute about Abrams claim developed. The British head of the Uganda government relief programme for refugees, Bill Kirkham, said US reports of 100-200,000 civilians killed by the army "have no foundation and are simply outrageous". The British High Commissioner, Colin McLean, more cautiously said it was not possible to substantiate the US statement. Shafiq Arain in Britain claimed the British investigation had found no evidence to support Abrams. Charles Harrison, the Times correspondent, sensibly pointed out that in fact nobody knew how many had died under Amin nor how many had died since 1979, so it was impossible to prove any such accusations.[40] It was also impossible to obtain accurate news about the situation, since resident foreign journalists were banned from Uganda; but Obote was sufficiently stung to invite in correspondents from Reuters, Associated Press, the New York Times and the Daily Telegraph to address them in Kampala. Kenya and Tanzania declared their support for Obote's continued struggle against Museveni's guerrilla NRA, and interestingly the DP, Uganda's one opposition party, supported the continued British military training programme. There was a rising tide of protest in Britain, however, by both Africans and Britons. Lule and Binaisa fully supported the Abrams claim; Hugh Dinwiddy wrote in the Times: "It is, unfortunately, a terrible fact that countless numbers of Ugandans are currently in total agreement" with the view that things had been better under Amin. Dr. Harrell-Bond, working among Ugandan refugees in southern Sudan, said she had evidence that more than 120,000 deaths had been caused among refugees from one area of Uganda alone in the past five years.[41]

By September, the British government was ready to switch its view on the matter. Malcolm Rifkind, Minister of State at the Foreign Office, said he did not want to play "the numbers game", but said "our view of conditions in Uganda does not differ significantly from that of the Americans." This was quite a switch, and he was responding to strong criticism from the Cambridge group of Amnesty International, which had accused the Foreign Office of being "craven" and "pussy-footing" in its response to Abrams claims. Yet although it was a switch in opinion, it was not a switch in policy. At the same time as International Alert, a new human rights organization was being founded in London to warn the world of imminent mass killings, with warnings that the situation in Uganda was getting worse. Obote asked John Stanley, Britain's Minister of State for the Armed Forces, to visit Uganda to discuss an extension of the military training team's stay. Stanley in fact agreed to renew the contract for a second year, and increased the team from 13 to 20.[42]

From then onwards, Britain continued to support Obote, amid mounting criticism which caused the British government to question and warn Obote, but not to desist from their policy. Richard Dowden, the Times correspondent, headed a strong article "Uganda: Britain's Blind Eye to Terror". There he quoted an observer in the Luwero Triangle, who reckoned that half the population were unaccounted for, and "if things are quieter there, it is the quietness of the grave: There is no-one left for the army to kill". Dowden commented, "The image presented by the Uganda government and underwritten by Britain is looking less and less like the picture presented by people on the ground. It is time the rest of the world was allowed to find out what is going on."[43] In fact, the world was informed to a considerable extent by the publication in that month, June 1985, of Amnesty International's report, Uganda Six Years After Amin. The inclusion of Amin's name in the title is significant: and the report was a horrifying account of the army's reign of terror, with murder, torture, rape and pillage over the last four and a half years. Much of the evidence was authenticated by two British doctors working with victims of torture. The British government could not ignore the implications of this report, and Malcolm Rifkind expressed the government's extreme concern, while still not agreeing that things could be worse than in Amin's time. A leader in the Observer protested:

> This is the moment for the British government to put right its dismal record of pusillanimity over human rights abuses in Uganda ... Public opinion in this country has been shocked by the Report, but the Minister of State at the Foreign Office, Malcolm Rifkind, reacted with deplorable suavity and evasiveness. It will not do. Britain is now the only member of the Commonwealth still willing to keep a military training mission in so bloodstained a country. Of course, the North Koreans are also instructing the Ugandan army; it their reputation for brutality gives little hope for improved treatment of innocent civilians.
>
> As the former colonial power, at the heart of the Commonwealth, we have a particular duty. Sir Geoffrey Howe should tell Dr. Obote that it is impossible any longer to turn a blind eye to so much evidence of torture, rape and murder. This message must not be diluted for mere commercial considerations.[44]

One notes here, as so often, references to Britain's role as the "former colonial power"; to its membership of the Commonwealth, perhaps implying moral considerations; and this time, the plea to ignore commercial considerations. British aid that year, with the consequent commercial benefits, was running at £7 million. Some days later Rifkind did indeed take a harder line, spurred on by representations from Amnesty International: he threatened to cut off the aid programme unless Obote took steps to curb the killings and torture by the army and the National Security Agency, and to bring those responsible to justice.[45]

Ironically, when this threat was finally issued, Obote was about to be toppled by a mutiny in the Uganda Army, faced as it was by the imminent attack on Kampala of Museveni's NRA. The army split into two, with the Acholi, led by General Tito Okello and Brigadier Bazilio Okello, claiming that they had borne the brunt of the increasingly successful attacks by the NRA. Obote had to flee the country, leaving the Okellos in charge of a new military government. Amid widespread looting and violence especially in Kampala, the British High Commissioner warned the estimated one thousand Britons in the country to stay put and "keep their heads down". The thirteen-man British military training team at Jinja did just that, and stayed on waiting to see if they would be needed by the new regime. During the long period of negotiations between the military government and Museveni's NRA, the British team lay dormant, while the British government waited to see if the two sides could be reconciled in a peace treaty, or if Museveni would take over entirely. If he did, the British position, with its record of support to two previous regimes, would need serious review, and new approaches would have to be made cautiously.

5. Conclusions

As we have seen, Britain had in the past been very quick and indeed over-anxious to give diplomatic recognition to successive regimes in strife-torn Uganda. The urge to continue to support the people and the country, no matter what the changes of fortune in government, was strong. Further, it was backed by the historical tradition that Uganda was a former protectorate of Britain's, indeed one which was held in special regard, as the "Pearl of Africa". Britain was no longer the head member of the Commonwealth, but it was a leading member, and the urge to give aid and support to the weaker members of that organization was another factor. When reports came through of the evils of Amin's regime or of Obote's, we have seen with what reluctance successive British governments dropped that support, delaying to the point of incurring strong international criticism, as well as criticism from Ugandans. Even the presence in Britain of Ugandan political branches of guerrilla movements, and of exiled Ugandan political leaders, did not weaken the British government's resolve to maintain its policy. Finally the British press grew vociferous against government support first for Amin and then for Obote; in the latter case this had an effect, along with the publication of the Amnesty International report.

On the commercial side, British firms took a severe dusting from Amin, involving the take-over of many firms with no compensation awarded. Yet there were firms who continued supplying Amin, especially his army and secret service, with vital equipment and with morale-boosting luxuries. This went on until practically the end of Amin's rule. Obote asked British and Asian firms to return; and encouraged by his measures of economic reconstruction, some of them did so. These firms, however, were not so closely connected with tyranny as those in Amin's time.

Finally, there were the very persistent efforts of the British military training team, desperately trying to instil regular methods and discipline into small groups of officers and NCOs who were then to spread this discipline in their own units. This was a worthy effort and not basically wrong but it was a drop in the ocean, given the huge size of Amin's army and the UNLA, and given the fact that so many troops were irregulars who came and went as they pleased. Yusufu Lule's remark that the spread of a little efficiency in the UNLA simply made them better killers and oppressors has a sting in it also.

The feelings of the British press at this juncture, after the Okellos coup, is well expressed in a Guardian leader:

> The coup should also, but probably will not, be an object lesson for Whitehall and Westminster, which have so often hopelessly misread events in the former British colony. (sic) The pragmatic rule at the Foreign Office is to recognize a regime which appears to have established itself in power, regardless of its credentials. We have a military training mission in Uganda which has obviously failed to counter the much more numerous and more gung-ho North Korean instructors at work there. They have been teaching the Ugandans a distinctly different approach to discipline, as they have also done in Zimbabwe with decidedly mixed results, despite the presence of British advisers there also. Other Commonwealth countries like Australia had the wit to withdraw from a hopeless task; Britain should now ask itself whether it is wise to be involved in Uganda in this way, and a little circumspection in dealing with the new military regime would also do no harm. We may hope in the meantime that it manages to bring sorely needed relief to the undeservedly suffering people in one of the most beautiful places on earth, the erstwhile pearl of Africa, which ought to be one of the benighted continent's most prosperous states.[46]

Britain did indeed treat the Okello's regime with circumspection. Now the establishment of a smoother rapport with the succeeding government of Yoweri Museveni is taking longer to achieve. Perhaps this slower pace is just as well, for as this paper has tried to show, there are many fences to be mended in the relationship between the two countries.

Notes

1. "With British firms and the British Government much concerned about the Nakivubo Pronouncements there is some evidence to suggest that a number of Britishers knew more about what was afoot than Obote did." (Low, D.A.: "Uganda: the Dislocated State". Paper presented at the conference on "Crisis of Development in Uganda", Roskilde, Denmark, 25-28 December 1985.) See also

Avirgan, T. & M. Honey: War in Uganda. Dar es Salam: Tanzania Publishing House, 1982, pp. 9-10; and Martin, D.: General Amin. London: Faber and Faber, 1974, pp. 158-63.

2. The major killings began in July 1971 at the very time that Amin was visiting Britain seeking arms and cash. See Kyemba, H.: State of Blood: The Inside Story of Idi Amin. London: Corgi Books, 1977, p. 46.

3. The author urged this solution on the British Minister, Geoffrey Rippon, when he visited Kampala. He replied that if they did that, Britain would be charged with setting up "concentration camps", but it is a measure of the crisis that in fact they had to do so.

4. The Times, 7.2.73 and 9.2.73.

5. Ibid., 25.3.74.

6. Ibid., 25.6.75.

7. Ibid., 24.2.77.

8. The Guardian, 20.10.78.

9. Kyemba, op.cit., p. 253.

10. Daily Telegraph, 6.2.79.

11. New Scientist, 10 May 1979.

12. The Guardian, 12.5.79.

13. Ibid., 23.6.79.

14. Daily Telegraph, 10.9.79.

15. Ibid., 1.9.79.

16. The Guardian, 14.879 and the Observer, 19.8.79.

17. The Observer, 13.1.80, and the Times, 24.1.80.

18. Daily Telegraph, 29.5.80.

19. Ibid., 9.6.80.

20. Ibid., 22.8.80.

21. Ibid., 7.10.80.

22. The Observer, 14.12.80

23. Daily Telegraph, 17.12.80.

24. The Times, 2.2.81.

25. Nabudere, D.: "The crisis in Uganda". Paper presented at the conference on "Crisis of Development in Uganda", Roskilde, Denmark, 25-28 December 1985.

26. Pazman, J.: "Is Uganda Moving out of Tyranny into Chaos?", in The Listener, 23 April 1981.

27. The Observer, 15.11.81.

28. The Times, 24.2.82.

29. Ibid., 8.7.82.

30. Ibid., 12.7.82.

31. The Sunday Times, 5.6.83.

32. The Times, 15.7.83.

33. Daily Telegraph, 30.1.84.

34. Ibid., 1.2.84.

35. Africa Confidential, 26.2.86.

36. "Uganda: 'Pearl of Africa' Loses its Lustre", by a correspondent, in The World Today, May 1984.

37. The Times, 9.8.84 and 11.8.84.

38. Daily Telegraph, 11.8.87.

39. Ibid., 20.8.87.

40. Ibid., 18.8.84 and the Times, 20.8.84.

41. The Times, 20.8.84 and 25.8.84.

42. The Times, 13, 15 and 23.4.85.

43. Ibid., 3.5.85.

44. The Observer, 23.6.85.

45. The Times, 26.6.85.

46. The Guardian, 29.7.85.4

Appendix 1

General Rapporteur, Oliver Furley

Towards a Stable Peace in Uganda: Conclusions and Recommendations Adopted by the Final Plenary Session

1. The Process of Establishing Peace

The search for peace and stability was deemed to be one of the most important goals to be pursued. It was noted that without peace no progress, development or political stability will be possible. However, the peace that Uganda ultimately deserves has to be established on principles of social justice and equality (positive peace) and not injustice and inequities (negative peace). Inequities and unjust peace are inherently temporary and unlikely to endure. The architects of peace in Uganda are therefore encouraged to bear this in mind. It is **recommended**:

1.1. That the problems of internal conflict in Uganda can never be truly settled by a military solution. Uganda's problems are essentially political, social and economic; and military solutions are considered deceptive and temporary. A situation of half victors/half vanquished will not last. We have to consider how to build a nation out of a diversity of cultures, nationalities, regions, etc.

1.2. That a ceasefire and general amnesty, effectively administered for all, are essential preliminaries. We welcome and appreciate the government's Amnesty Statute, and would stress particularly the importance of making arrangements at Reception Points safe and secure for those entering them. We suggest that the International Red Cross could be involved in the reception process, following one of their traditional roles.

We further urge that the Amnesty Statute be given as wide publicity as possible, to reach people in remote areas and across borders, that people may come out of the bush with safety. We urge that the Geneva Conventions be adhered to in particular regarding captured combatants, and make it clear that we are here referring to both sides.

1.3. That there must follow full recognition that civilians from the Northern and Eastern region cannot be looked at in isolation from the general movement towards democratic life in Uganda, and efforts to resist the success of this movement by forces from within and outside Uganda must end. The efforts of the peace mission were appreciated and a further mission should be encouraged. We endorse the recommendations put before us by the peace mission and we accept this position. A ceasefire must be linked with a peace package incorporating a political and economic programme for the north and east, and indeed for the whole country, which has to be sold to the entire country through all forms of communication media. We urge the government to avoid language which might be construed as inflammatory when addressing this conflict, and recommend fact-finding missions to identify grievances of the people and suggest remedies.

We urge NGOs and international institutions to bring pressure to bear, especially through the media, to create a climate of peace. Discredited elements of previous regimes can be isolated from the ordinary people of these regions only through a political process in which the people themselves are allowed to choose their own leaders. The people of these regions must be given the freedom to exercise their rights as citizens and the full expression of their cultures as Ugandan nationalities.

1.4. That full recognition be given by the NRM government concerning mistakes of omission or commission, in the search for a genuine political solution to civil strife. Thus, while the government is fully justified in using the military to defend itself when attacked, the success of its defence lies in its capabilities to defend the people from violence of whatever kind.

1.5. That such a cessation of violence would require the commitment to peace of all parties concerned.

2. Culture, Education, Language

It was widely recognized at the Conference that Uganda was a land of many cultures and traditions. These should be nurtured and protected. Ethnic identities should not be de-emphasized as in Obote's time, when cultural differences were not discussed but were bottled up. It is **recommended**:

2.1. That schools should teach African cultures and traditions to build up pride in national unity. We need to enshrine our cultures in the education system, and the first task is to train the teachers to understand new needs and goals. African traditions should be established as a subject taught in primary schools in the first 3 years.

2.2. That all Africa suffers from internal conflicts partly because of an educational crisis. The only vehicle for expressing democracy is through the values of our cultures, and language especially.

2.3. That the adequate resources be provided to take the necessary steps to establish and spread a national language, through the means of a Language Commission. Kiswahili was a possibility, but this was not agreed to be put forward as a single suggestion. Every Ugandan should be given the chance to be taught in his or her mother tongue for an appropriate period. Linguistic communication, especially regarding the rural poor, should be planned in order that rural development projects such as health care could be more effective.

2.4. That education on gender disparities, traditional and changing gender roles be included in the system, with a greater appreciation of women's role and contribution. Women need education regarding their rights which in some cases they may not know, and watch-dog institutions should be established to safe-guard these rights. Equally, the men and indeed the military should be educated on gender issues; and this must be a continuing process, similarly regarding education in human rights.

2.5. That in all these efforts, direct assistance and encouragement be given to indigenous organizations as well as through governmental and international organizations concerned with women.

3. Economic Reconstruction and Development

It was recognized that internal conflict in Uganda had political, social and economic foundations, regarding the economic regional imbalance, and imbalance between social groups that has persisted and remains a cause of grievance. The primary aim of economic strategy should be to redress the imbalance and explore all ways of achieving a reconstructed economy on a broader basis, which, because the economy has deteriorated so badly, must emphasize <u>accelerated</u> growth. It is **recommended**:

3.1. That investment patterns and resources allocation are still biased towards a narrow range of traditional export crops, e.g. cotton, coffee, tobacco and tea. The production of food and export crops be given equal attention. The issue of marketing should be addressed and marketing monopolies freed. The Government should develop a realistic pricing policy for all products

3.2. That the programme of economic rehabilitation should include the rehabilitation of the social stock of health, education, water supply system and a more democratic form of electrification of the rural areas.

3.3. That priority be given to the rehabilitation of a transport infrastructure. The rebuilding of roads and rail services should serve the needs of the poorest, and more expensive forms of transport such as air travel should be minimized. The Government should devise an appropriate technological package for the development of Uganda.

3.4. That the State should have a more subtle approach to foreign trade. In the absence of certain resources in rural border towns, a distinction should be made between the exchanges made by poor peasants across the borders and the commercial activities of large capitalists who export the wealth of society.

3.5. That the conflict has been linked to the economic foundations of society, so in order to break the monopoly form of the ex-colonial economy there should be more democratic planning. Economic planning must involve a peace package for international consideration.

3.6. That there should be a clarification as to the kind of industrialization that can be based on the realities of the Ugandan economy.

3.7. That there should be more public awareness of the role of the International Monetary Fund, the World Bank and other international financial institutions.

3.8. That Uganda should negotiate agreements with her debtors so as to pay no more than 10% of her export earnings for debt servicing.

3.9. That information on the economy and on international agreements be made more readily available; information should be democratized; real participation in reconstruction can be achieved only when information on financial activities is made available to Ugandans including scholars. More research needs to be supported on the preconditions for achieving a national integrated economy. Research is a necessary component of peace and reconstruction, and documentation and publication of findings are extremely important. The knowledge and scholarly competence of Makerere University should be utilized and developed, and given appropriate resources for all types of relevant research into causes of internal conflicts and conflict resolution.

3.10. That the present land policies of the state represent a great potential for conflict; in some regions this conflict already exists.

3.11. That there should be a clear programme to redress the growing landlessness of some peasants, with an effective system of land management which can guarantee security of tenure for tillers and pastoralists. The system of keeping land records in the Land Office should be improved by, for example, microfilming and safeguarding such records.

3.12. That there should be an immediate programme to provide for proper and effective improvement of the quality of life of the pastoral peoples, without destruction of their livelihood.

3.13. That cattle-rustling is an important source of conflict and is linked to capital accumulation even by members of the state apparatus; democratic and financial measures must be taken to solve this problem.

3.14. That a clear national plan be formulated for the use and regeneration of all natural resources, such as forests, lakes, land and mineral wealth.

3.15. That the present expenditure on military and administration is out of proportion to the needs of economic development. This trend should be reversed, with the process of national reconciliation.

4. Political and Constitutional Reconstruction

The Conference felt strongly that full democratic processes, at the central and local levels, and in all areas of community activities, must be established. First there must be a reconciliation of all the social forces in Uganda. The Conference welcomed the opportunity freely to discuss the principles on which Ugandans can live together as a nation-state as well as the institutions necessary for so doing. Meanwhile it must be recognized that fighting is still raging in the Northern and Eastern regions. No formula can be arrived at for establishing a truly national government unless these regions are part of the process. It is **recommended**:

4.1. That in all democratic processes, group rights should be incorporated, as in some areas sparse populations would result in weaker voting power.

4.2. That the principles of a constitution must be clearly agreed upon, especially those enshrined in a Bill of Rights. It should be republican, with the executive presidency subject to stipulated checks and balances.

4.3. That an expression of federalism, though mooted by some, would not be appropriate at this moment; but devolution of powers to local governments is a principle we can agree on, with a degree of autonomy to elected political institutions at a local level. Some at the Conference did not agree that this could include regional self-determination.

4.4. That the centre of government must be democratically based, and the key issue is to enshrine people's belief that local rights will be safeguarded. The Supreme Court must be able to rule over issues where the central state oversteps its powers.

4.5. That especially strong representation is needed for particular minority groups to protect their interests.

4.6. That the importance of grassroots democracy needs to be stressed, where previous democratic power has been denied to the peasants.

The role of the Resistance Committees is appreciated, while these must be organs of the people, not agents of the state. Their structure, organization and effectiveness should be continuously appraised. There should be a clear commitment to establish Resistance Committees in those areas of the country without them at present.

4.7. That multi-party politics must be respected.

4.8. That control of resources, especially land, by local authorities or the nationalities be constitutionally specified.

4.9. That entry into the army and civil service be through such public and well-known methods as examinations and appointment by commissions. Entry into the security agencies should be through the processes of public recruitment, and myths surrounding these agencies must stop.

4.10. That the army be a national institution, not allied to a party or regime, or to selfish interests. Control of the armed forces by the government is crucial, and the creation of a citizens' army should be considered.

4.11. That all citizens should be exposed to military training. The size of the army should be reduced to a small professional one. Local security should be augmented by a people's militia and there should be some form of national service, entailing life and participation in villages and areas different from one's own home area.

5. The Establishment and Preservation of Human Rights and the Rule of Law

The rights of peoples, groups and individuals was a theme to which the Conference constantly returned. Uganda has supported the UN Declaration of Human Rights and the African Charter of Human Rights and Rights of the Peoples, and should be active in their implementation. Consensus was reached that human rights and people's rights should never again be relegated to the periphery of the national agenda. Peace and stability in Uganda cannot endure without an environment that respects human rights. A Bill of Rights has already been mentioned, and the priority given by the NRM to human rights was appreciated.

In spite of guarantees to human rights in the 1967 Constitution, violations of these rights are still rampant at all levels of society:

(a) the right of every individual as a citizen;

(b) the right of people to family life;

(c) the right of people to property and inheritance;

(d) the right of people to movement, association, assembly, expression and cultural life;

(e) the right of people to full intellectual development;

(f) the right of people to hold political opinions, religious beliefs, etc. It is **recommended**:

5.1. That these rights must now not only be restated as the cardinal principles for establishing a legitimate government in Uganda, but the people must be encouraged to develop the capacity and ability to ensure that the government upholds these rights and principles through well-established and clearly known processes and institutions to keep the government accountable. The government should ensure the rule of law and release all detainees not found guilty on any point of law.

5.2. That indigenous and international NGOs have a humanitarian role to play in areas where human rights have been violated and social deprivation has taken place. The Red Cross, the churches etc. have done good work, and the government is recommended to encourage them strongly.

5.3. That one important source of conflict remains social deprivation. A clear example is housing, where the absence of a rent control board has led to arbitrary decisions of landlords and houseowners. There are also inequalities in the provision of health and educational opportunities throughout the nation.

Index

INTERNATIONAL ALERT

has four main objectives:

- to help bring peace to countries at war within themselves;
- to seek and propose constitutional provisions which protect and respect ethnic, religious, linguistic or other minorities;
- to promote the human rights and development of groups and individuals within national borders and internationally;
- to alert opinion to danger areas of actual and potential conflict, mass killings and genocide.

By promoting cooperation between academics, politicians and other organizations concerned with conflict resolution and minority rights, INTERNATIONAL ALERT seeks to combine the knowledge of scholars and the experience of activists with the reality of those affected by violence and oppression in their own communities.

By emphasizing and strengthening the links between development and traditional human rights, INTERNATIONAL ALERT seeks to extend the work of non-governmental organizations in the process of peace and social change.

By pooling resources, ideas and information INTERNATIONAL ALERT seeks to stimulate and focus public awareness on the existence and the risk of massive human rights violation by governments or other groups. Respect for human rights must be as universal as the rights themselves.

INTERNATIONAL ALERT
29 Craven Street
London WC2N 5NT

Tel: (01) 839 3267
Telex: 94017974 INTA G